AFRICA

BBC

AFRICA

EYE TO EYE WITH THE UNKNOWN

MICHAEL BRIGHT

FOREWORD BY DAVID ATTENBOROUGH

Quercus

CONTENTS

FOREWORD

A new major series on Africa? When I heard that this was to be the next target for the BBC's Natural History Unit, I asked myself if it really would be possible to make such a thing. African wildlife is surely the best known, the most intensively filmed, of any in the world. Big television series need new, un-filmed stories. Where could we find them?

And then I realised that, in fact, film-makers over the years have largely focused on the great spectacular mammals that roam the open savannahs of Kenya and Tanzania. But what about the vast rainforests of West Africa? I remember trying to film there 60 years ago. As we walked into its shade, my cameraman companion took out his light meter and observed gloomily that the only way to get enough light for filming was to cut down the trees. Admittedly, film emulsions and then electronic cameras eventually solved that problem. But at night in the forests of the Congo, the ground is illuminated by tracts of phosphorescent fungi producing a ghostly greenish light that local people call 'chimpanzee fire'. Who could have dreamed that eventually we would have cameras that allow us to record it – and create one of the most haunting sequences in the whole television series?

We seldom see natural history films about the Sahara. Not surprisingly: it is, after all, a desert and the largest in the world, and there is not much there but sand and rock. Caravans of camels cross it and those we have seen on our screens. But what else is there to film? In fact, there are extraordinary dramas, if you know where to look and – perhaps more importantly – when.

At midday, the heat is so crushingly oppressive that even tiny lizards and spiders have to retreat underground. Those that cannot find refuge are scorched to death. And then, at the precise moment when the sun is at its most lethal, ants, wearing what look like silver spacesuits, emerge from their holes. Their metallic-looking covering reflects the brutal rays of the sun. But even so, the ants have to work fast. They gather up the dead and near-dead bodies of other insects that have succumbed to heatstroke and frantically tug them back into their holes for consumption – before the sun kills them, too.

The land that lies just south of the mouth of the Zambezi on Africa's east coast is also largely neglected by visitors. Parts of it are still almost unknown to outsiders. So much so, that

a large tract of rainforest there has hardly registered with many European naturalists. They only became aware of its existence when it was revealed by satellite surveys. So now – unofficially at least – it is known among those trying to document it as Google Forest.

The more we looked, the more we realised how many parts of Africa are still largely un-filmed. What about African monkeys that clamber around in the snow-covered cedar trees – as they do in the Atlas Mountains; hippos that swim in the sea at one of the very few places where the Congo rainforest still reaches the coast; or the immense cavern that lies beneath the Kalahari, which is so big it could accommodate three jumbo jet aircraft, nose to tail, and is filled with so much cool fresh water that still no one knows how deep it is? Even those animals that we might think we know all about prove to have parts of their lives that no one has filmed before – giraffes that fight by slewing their necks with such force that an old experienced bull can knock his opponents off their feet; and rhinoceroses that, far from being ill-tempered solitary animals as they are usually seen, assemble at night for a hidden rendezvous where nuzzling males gently court the females.

As research for the series continued, so the stories began to accumulate and the team realised that we were indeed on to something really new and exciting. In classical times, the people who lived in the cities of Greece and Rome had a proverb about the immense continent that lay to the south across the Mediterranean Sea. 'There is always something new coming out of Africa,' they said. Well, in spite of all the explorations that have taken place in the 2,000 years between that time and this, their saying is still true. And the following pages prove it.

DAVID ATTENBOROUGH

CHAPTER ONE

KALAHARI

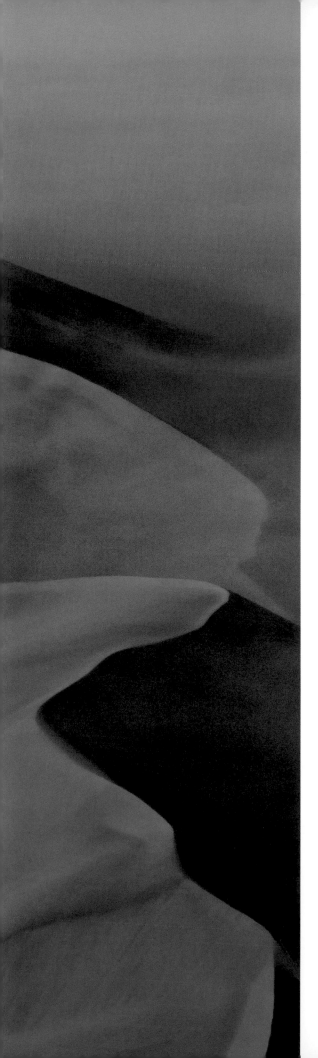

The Kalahari and Namib dominate southern Africa. It's big sky country. Stand in one of the dried lake beds at its centre and you see the curve of the horizon all around you. Stretching from the Congolian forests in the north to the Gariep River in South Africa, this vast semidesert and sandy savannah covers much of Botswana and Namibia, and tracts of South Africa, as well as small parts of Angola and Zambia. There's space in abundance, spectacular for visitors, but a severe test both for the local hunter-gatherer San people, one of the oldest surviving cultures in the world, and for wildlife, with little cover for predators to stalk or for prey to hide.

Sand dunes in Namibia

The Kalahari is a very old and stable part of the Earth's lithosphere, set in the centre of a continental mass rather than at the more vulnerable edge, and as such contains some of the world's oldest rocks. It has survived intact for 2.3 billion years, while much of the rest of Africa has collided or ripped itself asunder in rolling cycles of merging and rifting continents. It means the wildlife of the Kalahari has not been subjected to catastrophic geological change. Climate, however, is quite another thing.

The climate has fluctuated between periods of dry and wet, and even today the annual and daily fluctuations in temperature, 47°C (117°F) at midday in summer and frosts on winter nights, make this a tough place to live. Wildlife here has had to be resilient and able to adapt to these changes.

The word 'kalahari' has been ascribed to several sources. It could have been derived from *Kgala* meaning 'the great thirst' or *Kgalagadi*, meaning 'a waterless place', both from Tswana, the official language and *lingua franca* of Botswana. Either way, they're apt descriptions: the Kalahari has the largest uninterrupted expanse of sand on the planet (the Sahara has pockets of dunes that make up its sand seas or ergs, which cover no more than 20% of its surface) and much of it is dry for most of the year. In the southwest, rain is especially scarce. In the desert, or 'thirst-land' as some call it, life depends on erratic rain and a few water-holes, including boreholes drilled by European settlers.

KINGS OF THE KALAHARI

In the golden light, before searing heat and blinding sun swamp the vibrant colours of dawn, the pride hangs out at the dwindling water-hole. The lions – Kalahari lions – have been out all night, when the temperature was more conducive to travelling and hunting, a comfortable 10°C (50°F), but their target was outside the Kgalagadi Transfrontier Park in which they normally live. Game is few and far between in the Kalahari, and stalking is difficult due to the open nature of the desert. Domestic animals are far easier to catch, but the pride has suffered: a young female was shot. The rest escaped, their bellies full with donkey meat. Now they prepare for the stifling day.

Two black-maned males take the most desirable spot beneath a scruffy shepherd's tree. The rest of the pride is slightly smaller and lighter-coloured than other African lions. A handful of females, still with juvenile spots on their legs and bellies, sprawl in what shade they can find. Some lie on their back, paws in the air and loins exposed to lose heat by evaporation. Others sit and

▼ Water is a scarce commodity for the lions of the Kalahari. These four lionesses drink eagerly but their eyes and ears are always alert to any signs of danger.

pant, one particularly hot and flustered individual wheezing 190 to the minute. The temperature will soon reach a daytime high of about 45°C (113°F).

The pride has an unusually large number of juvenile males; they're the more vulnerable gender and expendable, so it's surprising that there are any here at all. Nursing mothers must travel great distances to find food to replenish their milk supply and frequently they're separated from their young cubs for several days. Many cubs, both male and female, survive predation, but die from starvation. And, later in life, sub-adult males are evicted from their pride and must survive alone or in coalitions with other males; again, many starve.

Yet, despite the harsh conditions, all the lions in this pride are surprisingly fit. They have to be. In one night they might cover 60 km (37 miles). With food sources so thinly spread, they have to patrol a home range six times larger than that of lions elsewhere in Africa, although prides in the east of the Kalahari,

where more rain falls, have smaller ranges than those in the west. One pride in the Kgalagadi Transfrontier Park wanders over an area thought to be close to 4,532 sq km (1,750 sq miles), and with prey density so low, lions often leave the safety of the park, 18–20 times a year on average, to hunt.

But, they can't go for long without water. If standing water is unavailable they'll lick dew from grass or from their own fur, but after a night's hunting and feasting they need more than that; they need to drink at a water-hole, and this one is the only standing water for miles around. Water-holes are the lifeblood of the Kalahari, fed from cracks in the ground where water bubbles up, salvation squeezed from the stone; but they're popular sites and demand is high.

A swirl of dust and loud trumpeting announces new arrivals. The lions are on their feet immediately, looking intently in the direction from which the sound is coming. The two males run out confidently to confront the threat, but this is bigger than both of them: two bull elephants, and they're thirsty. One runs towards the pride, shakes its head, flaps its ears and trumpets, and that's all it needs to do. The lions turn tail and run. Then, in another cloud of dust and a confusion of stripes, zebras appear. They had been waiting their turn at

▼ In a cloud of dust and a confusion of stripes, zebras appear. They had been waiting their turn at the water-hole, but were reluctant to come and drink with lions about.

the water-hole, but were reluctant to come and drink with lions about. They approach the elephants, nodding their heads and kicking out nervously at their neighbours. An elephant raises its trunk to squirt water into its mouth, and the movement is enough to spook them. They fall back, but one by one they move in again, each waiting for another to make the first move.

The Kalahari bulls tower over the zebras, their tusks thicker than a man's leg and a metre (3 feet) long, but the zebras don't give up and one lowers its head to drink. It's what the others have been waiting for, and they crowd around, jockeying for space at the water's edge snatching what water they can. The elephants reluctantly share the water-hole with their highly strung companions, drink their fill – about 200 litres (53 US gallons) – and slowly move away, just two of many thousands of elephants that take part in the largest and longest pachyderm migration on the African continent.

Here in the Kalahari, elephants were once on the edge of extinction, but conservation efforts have been so successful that 150,000 elephants are now living free, and they walk the most incredible distances. A young bull, fitted with a radio collar, was found to have a home range of 24,828 sq km (9,586 sq miles),

an area larger than the size of Wales or West Virginia, compared to 3,000 sq km (1,158 sq miles) for elephants in most of the rest of Africa.

The only populations with comparable movements are the desert elephants of Namibia, Angola and Mali, and some of these are the real giants of Africa. The largest so far recorded was a bull shot by hunters in Angola in 1974. It stood 4.17 m (13.7 feet) at the shoulder. They're the same species as the savannah elephants of East and southern Africa, but they appear to have larger feet and longer legs. This is actually an optical illusion: their bodies are smaller, because they eat less than elephants elsewhere, so their legs look longer. Nonetheless, they're well adapted to the desert. They drink every three or four days, rather than every day, and they're very adept at finding water, even in the worst of droughts. They excavate holes in the dry riverbed, into which water seeps up from below, and this becomes a water source for many other desert animals, as well as the elephants.

With such large home ranges, finding others of their own kind, especially for bulls in search of receptive cows, is something of a problem, one the elephant gets around with extremely loud and very low-frequency 'rumbles'. They can peak at 117 decibels (the equivalent of standing in front of the bass player's amplifier at a very loud rock concert), but most of the energy is at frequencies well below the lower threshold of human hearing. These long-distance calls are emitted mainly at dawn and dusk, when the air is relatively still and they can be picked up more than 10 km (6 miles) away. Females on heat rumble to attract solitary bulls from far and wide, and bulls have a 'musth-rumble' that warns other males to stay away. Elephant herds rumble to each other just to keep in touch, and they also have a 'bee rumble'.

Elephants are afraid of bees. The native bees of southern Africa are noticeably aggressive, compared to their European cousins, and even elephants have soft and vulnerable parts – the belly, behind the ears, around the eyes and inside the trunk. If an elephant even hears a bee it shakes its head and gives the bee rumble, the first-known elephant call to be associated with a threat. Within 10 seconds, the herd will move off.

NOVICE HUNTER

The smaller plant-eaters have much bigger threats to deal with – lions, leopards, cheetahs and wild dogs, along with brown hyenas, black-backed jackals and other hunter-scavengers – although the meat-eaters themselves don't have it easy either. Finding prey that is so spread out and stalking with very little cover means that an ambush predator, such as a leopard, is at a distinct disadvantage compared to its forest cousins.

▶ Top speed for a desert elephant on hard ground is 24 km/h (15 mph). At about 16 km/h (10 mph) they change from 'fast walking' to a kind of 'bounce running', nicknamed 'Groucho-running' after the movie actor Groucho Marx, with limbs bent slightly to move their bodies more smoothly.

◄ The leopard is Africa's sleuth – often no more than a shadow that haunts the desert, savannah and forest.

▼ The warthog is a wild pig and a fast mover. It has to be, because Africa's major predators – lions, leopards and hyenas – are never far behind and would relish a mouthful of wild pork.

A young male leopard has just left his mother and brother and is padding silently through the long, dry grass and brown, shrivelled bushes on the lookout for something to catch. Still to make his first kill, a youngster like this has a lot to learn in such an uncompromising environment. He squints and blinks slowly in that big cat kind of way and his ears turn occasionally to try to pick up the faintest rustle. He freezes. Just ahead is a large male warthog. The warthog stops eating, and raises a great spade-shaped head with two pairs of formidable tusks curved upwards on either side of its jaws. It sniffs the air, almost daring the leopard to attack. The two stare at each other, but the leopard hesitates. He backs down, turns, almost nonchalantly, and moves away, one eye on the warthog in case it should charge. He's worked out one thing at least – which prey to choose and which to avoid.

The hot sun plays on his back. There's no wind, just the incessant sun. Leopards generally hunt between sunset and sunrise, when darkness affords a cloak of invisibility and the air is cool, but this youngster needs to find a meal, and he must do so without his mother's help.

A movement in the grass betrays a steenbok, a small antelope with big ears and long legs. It's browsing on low-lying plants. It rarely drinks, for it can get all the water it needs from its food. Suddenly, there's a cry of alarm. Another animal has spotted the novice hunter, and the steenbok drops to the ground. It waits, all its senses on red alert, and then it picks up the smell of the leopard. Its first tactic is to lie low. The young leopard adopts a stalking mode, but with the steenbok hidden from view, he creeps gradually closer to the last place he

saw his target. He edges forward gingerly, then … snap, he stands on a dry twig and whoosh … the steenbok explodes into life. It races away, following a zigzag path. It stops momentarily and looks back for its pursuer, but the leopard is not there. He gave up the moment he was spotted. He stands, looking vacantly in the direction the steenbok took.

Like a wayward teenager, the young leopard seems to lack any sense of urgency. He lies on the ground, yawns and rolls onto his back, and waves his paws in the air, but eventually hunger gets the better of him and he's off again in search of food. Before long, his nostrils pick up the tell-tale signs of a carcass, and young leopards are not too proud to turn their hand to a touch of scavenging.

He walks nervously towards the source of the smell. It could be the kill of a lion pride and he's no match for half a dozen angry lionesses. Instead, he finds a dead antelope hanging over the branch of a tree, stashed there by his mother. He tries to steal it, but his mother has chosen her spot well.

He climbs into the tree and edges towards the carcass, but the branches can't hold his weight and he crashes to the ground. He tries again, careful this time to climb the main trunk. He grabs the antelope's neck, but loses his footing and hangs there by his mouth, his paws flailing about in mid-air. He swings around, this way and that, but his feet just can't seem to find a branch. Finally he lets go and falls again to the ground. He really does still have a lot to learn.

BULLY BOY

Leopards are the ultimate opportunists, the most adaptable of the big cats. While gemsbok, springbok or even a small steenbok would make a hearty meal, leopards must often be satisfied with porcupines (as long as they can circumvent the quills), bat-eared foxes, hares, and even mice, but one character they certainly shouldn't tangle with is the honey-badger or ratel, lauded by some observers as the most fearless animal on Earth … and they're not far wrong. What it lacks in size, it more than makes up for in ferocity.

The badger emerges from its burrow and struts out across the desert, its gait seeming to say 'don't mess with me', but it's not on the lookout for trouble; it's looking for food. It sniffs, digs and sniffs some more, rooting out a rodent or a reptile, even something as big as a rock python or as venomous as a black mamba. But its prey frequently gets away: in fact, it's so careless that nearly half of all it tries to catch escapes. That's why pale chanting goshawks, the occasional spotted eagle owl and even passing jackals often stick to the honey-badger like glue, in the hope of catching an easy meal, of which the badger is the unwitting provider.

While the badger might enthusiastically dig 50 holes and cover 40 km (25 miles) in search of its main meal of the day, it also has, as its common English name suggests, a sweet tooth. It seeks out honey-bee nests, which can be hidden amongst the rocks of an outcrop or in trees, and it seems quite resilient to the ferocious attacks of the inmates while stealing their honey. The badger is an accomplished climber, capable of reaching colonies up high (where it might also invade the nests of its goshawk disciples and devour the chicks). In season, baby jackals are sought out, so jackal parents nip at badgers straying too close to their dens. And, if the opportunity arises, the honey-badger will scavenge at the kills of bigger predators, well able to defend itself should the owners return.

It rarely visits a water-hole, most of its water requirements coming from its food or, when it's available, the tsama melon – manna of the Kalahari. It's said that, in places with an absence of free-standing water, entire ecosystems would collapse if it weren't for this fruit. It's a crucial source of moisture for predators and plant-eaters alike.

The honey-badger is active both day and night, but when the temperature soars it makes for a burrow, one of many it has dug itself or borrowed from some other creature, such as an aardvark. But this time, it's picked the wrong hole. As it snuffles about inside it comes face to face with a leopard, a mother with cubs – the most aggressive type.

Leopards tend to live in valleys, where brush offers some cover for hunting and small trees can be used to keep food safe from scavengers, and they occupy aardvark burrows as dens for their cubs. This female will defend her cubs against

▼ A pack of African wild dogs receives short shrift from a couple of honey-badgers. The dogs should beware. The honey-badgers are quite capable of seeing off these upstarts and even taking on a pride of lions for seconds.

any threat, no matter how aggressive. The badger backs out rapidly and makes a run for it, but the cats are not far behind. The cubs see this little creature, with the distinctive whitish grey mantle from its crown to its tail, as a plaything and begin to taunt it. With an ear-piercing scream, it counter-attacks, drawing blood, so the mother leopard steps in, only to be viciously attacked too. The family backs away and moves off. The honey-badger has won, and returning to the burrow, it claims it for itself.

In fact, predators are so mindful of the honey-badger's fighting spirit that it's been suggested that the punk haircut of cheetah kittens evolved as an imitation of the honey-badger in order to ward off potential predators. As Charles Caleb Colton wrote in 1820, 'imitation is the sincerest form of flattery'. It just goes to show that the honey-badger really is the undisputed bully boy of the Kalahari – the toughest of desert survivors.

KALAHARI CONFIDENCE TRICK

Many animals in the Kalahari are nocturnal in summer, their activity restricted to the cool of the night, and diurnal in winter, when the daytime temperature averages 25°C (77°F). However, winter nights can be surprisingly cold, around 2°C (36°F) and sometimes well below zero in July, quite a contrast for animals more used to hot desert conditions, and none more so than meerkats.

At daybreak, the meerkats emerge from their burrows under the desert. They don't go far, but mill about in their entrances, some sitting with their front facing the early morning sun, their arms outstretched, soaking up its warm rays. There's so little fat on their bones they could quite easily succumb to the cold, so they can't go for long without food. After shivering off the chill of the night, they start to scratch a living from the dust, but should they come across an animal as dangerous as a snake, they'll mob it. Adult meerkats mob long and hard, while younger ones are less intense. It's thought that the older animals are teaching the youngsters by example, a practical class on predator recognition at the meerkat school.

Even so, with their heads down, they're vulnerable to surprise attacks, but they're watched over as they forage. A sentry meerkat stands on tiptoes or climbs into a bush, scanning the sky and the ground for signs of danger. In the top of a nearby acacia is a fork-tailed drongo, a glossy black passerine bird resembling a shrike, that gives an alarm call when danger threatens, providing additional safety cover. The drongo also gives a reassuring 'guard' call, so the meerkats know it's there and they can forage more widely and look up less often.

From its high vantage point, the bird is often first to spot predators approaching. A martial eagle, one of Africa's most powerful raptors, could well swoop in and grab a meerkat before a sentry had time to react, and anything approaching on the ground could well be hidden, so the troop listens out for the drongo and when it sounds the alarm, the meerkats dive for the safety of their

▶ A meerkat sentinel ensures his family is safe from predators. From his high vantage point he can see lions and snakes approaching on the ground and eagles in the sky. His alarm call warns the troop to dive for cover.

OVERLEAF Meerkats line up in front of the morning sun in order to warm themselves up after the cold desert night so that they are fit to go foraging. With little fat on their slender bodies, they must catch and eat food every day.

burrows. Curiously, one of the drongo's calls is an exact copy of the meerkat's own alarm, and there's a very good reason for that. It watches intently as the meerkats forage. One feisty individual is tackling a scorpion, very careful not to be stung. After a bit of a struggle, it grabs the scorpion and bites off the end of its tail. Suddenly, the drongo cries out in alarm. The meerkat drops the scorpion and disappears down the nearest bolt-hole. The drongo flies down, picks up the scorpion, and flies back to its branch in the tree. There was no predator. It was a false alarm, but it was deliberate. In the winter, when there are few insects on the wing (a drongo's normal prey), the birds stop being good neighbours and resort to cheating to get a meal.

What's more, they don't use the same alarm call every time. The meerkats would get used to that, like the boy who cried wolf. The drongos are much more devious. They intersperse the meerkat alarm with the alarm calls of other animals, such as the southern pied babbler, which it also cheats out of a meal: in fact, drongos are in the protection racket. They take care of flocks of babblers by watching out for predators. It enables the babblers, like the meerkats, to spread out and forage over wider areas without having to look up all the time. The drongos occasionally earn their keep by giving real alarm calls and mobbing aerial predators, but more often they live up to their reputation as gangsters. They give false alarm calls, stealing food from right under the bills of the babblers, while they're momentarily distracted, but the babblers appear to put up with it. It's the price they pay for protection. Meanwhile, the meerkats re-emerge to continue foraging, blissfully unaware that they've been very effectively duped.

MIGHTY FLOOD

Winter is not only the coldest part of the year but also the driest; yet this is the season when the Okavango River in Botswana is in spate. Its source is in the Angolan highlands, 1,250 km (777 miles) away, where a deluge of January summer rains sends a great pulse of water into the river system, but it creeps along exceptionally slowly. So gentle is the gradient from Angola into Botswana that it takes a month to travel the first 1,000 km (620 miles), and then a further four months, meandering wildly, to reach the many channels in the outer stretches of the Okavango Delta in winter, between June and August, when the entire delta swells threefold. But, unlike most other rivers, the Okavango doesn't discharge into the sea, for it's not a coastal delta; instead, it flows into the Kalahari, where it spreads out to cover an area the size of Switzerland, the world's largest inland delta. Its name *Okavango* means 'the river that never finds the sea'.

About a third of the delta is flooded marshland all year round, sustained by quick sharp bursts from summer thunderstorms. This land is lush with groves of wild date palm and stands of papyrus, and open water is carpeted with water lilies, but much of the rest of the Okavango is dependent on the seasonal rains

▶ Opening just before sunset and flowering until sunrise, night-blooming water lilies decorate a lagoon in the Okavango Delta. While flies and bees pollinate day-opening species, rhinoceros beetles visit these nocturnal flowers.

from Angola. Wildlife in these seasonal floodplains has adapted to the rigours of desert life and is gasping for water for half the year, but then comes temporary relief (which can be a mixed blessing for some) for this massive flood inundates everything.

TERMITE ISLANDS

With the water lapping at the door, activity in the termite mound reaches fever pitch. Termites run frantically in all directions. It's a life-and-death race to reach the centre of the mound, but what looks like chaos is, in reality, an organised and very effective flood evacuation programme. Some inevitably don't make it back in time and are drowned, ironically, in the middle of a desert, but the vast majority are safe inside and the water does not breach the colony's walls.

The walls are constructed of sand particles glued together with clay and saliva. The tiny clay particles compress together under the weight of the mound above, forming a super-dense, impermeable membrane. In effect, the termites have made their walls as waterproof as concrete. Even the entrance tunnels are floodproof. They're constructed like U-bends, so that an airlock prevents floodwater from entering the mound.

Inside, the damper conditions at this time of year mean that the soil is moist and easier to work, so with foraging off-limits for the time being, the termites turn to repairing the nest mound on the inside and building extensions on parts that are above the water level. Soil might be brought up from many metres below the ground, and it remains pliable in the 90% humidity inside the nest. With such a warm and humid atmosphere, the mound ought to be a breeding ground for harmful bacteria and fungi, but the termites have a solution for that. Their saliva contains an anti-microbial enzyme with which they cover their bodies and plaster their walls, so their corridors and chambers are effectively sanitised. So, free from diseases and with a constant nest temperature of about 30°C (86°F), day and night, summer and winter, the colony is independent of any changes outside and it can keep working around the clock, building some impressive structures.

Termites may be small, but size for size they construct the world's largest buildings. A single termite mound might stand 2–3 m (7–10 feet) tall, with some up to 10 m (33 feet) high and home to as many termites as we might see people in our larger cities. The mound has built-in, automatic air-conditioning and terraced fungal farms, as well as a royal chamber and nurseries, and a complex system of tunnels that reaches out into the surrounding countryside, but the termites' civil engineering skills do not end there.

◄ During the floods, termite mounds become islands. Silt gathers around the bases and the islands expand and join together. Trees, such as acacia, grow in the fertile soil. Even when the termite mounds are abandoned, the islands with their trees remain, appearing as low mounds during the dry season.

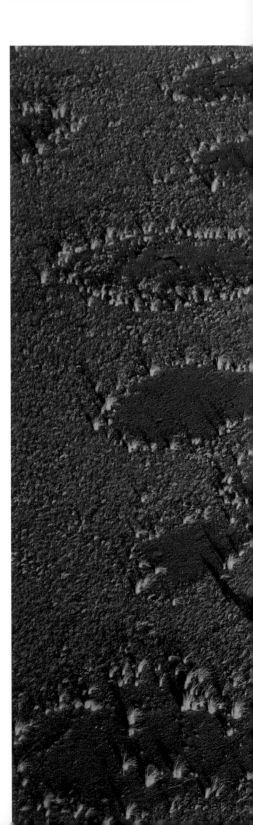

Termites inadvertently affect the hydrology of the Okavango. Their constant activity raises the ground around their mound above the flatness of the Kalahari so that, during the flood, it becomes an island. There are more than 50,000 islands dotted across the Okavango, and termites are thought to have started two thirds of them; and it doesn't end there. Silt deposits build up and the small islands expand, gradually joining with other mounds to form bigger islands. At first they acquire a fringe of low vegetation, and then trees, such as date palms, jackalberries, knobthorns and sycamore figs, take hold, each island with its own flora growing in the rich, fertile soil. Eventually, the termite mounds are deserted and become defunct, but the islands remain, some blocking channels and diverting the flow of water. The Okavango is never the same for two years running. It seems that tiny termites, most little more than 5 mm (0.2 inches) long, have shaped the entire surface of this part of the Kalahari.

FAIRY CIRCLES

Termites were once thought to be responsible for the thousands of circular, barren patches that can be found in a broken belt about 160 km (100 miles) inland that stretches across the Kalahari for 2,400 km (1,500 miles) from Angola to South Africa. From the air, they look like the pock-marks left by huge raindrops, and on the ground scientists studying them have no idea what they are or how they're formed, despite 25 years of research.

Termites have been ruled out, as have ostrich dust baths, mineral radioactivity and toxins left by poisonous plants, such as the milk bush. The circles do not move, for metal stakes hammered into the centre are still in the same place after 22 years, but they do grow, expanding from 2 m (6.6 feet) up to 10 m (33 feet) across. Until new research throws up a fresh theory, scientists are forced to call on the 'fairies' as the best explanation for this quirk of nature.

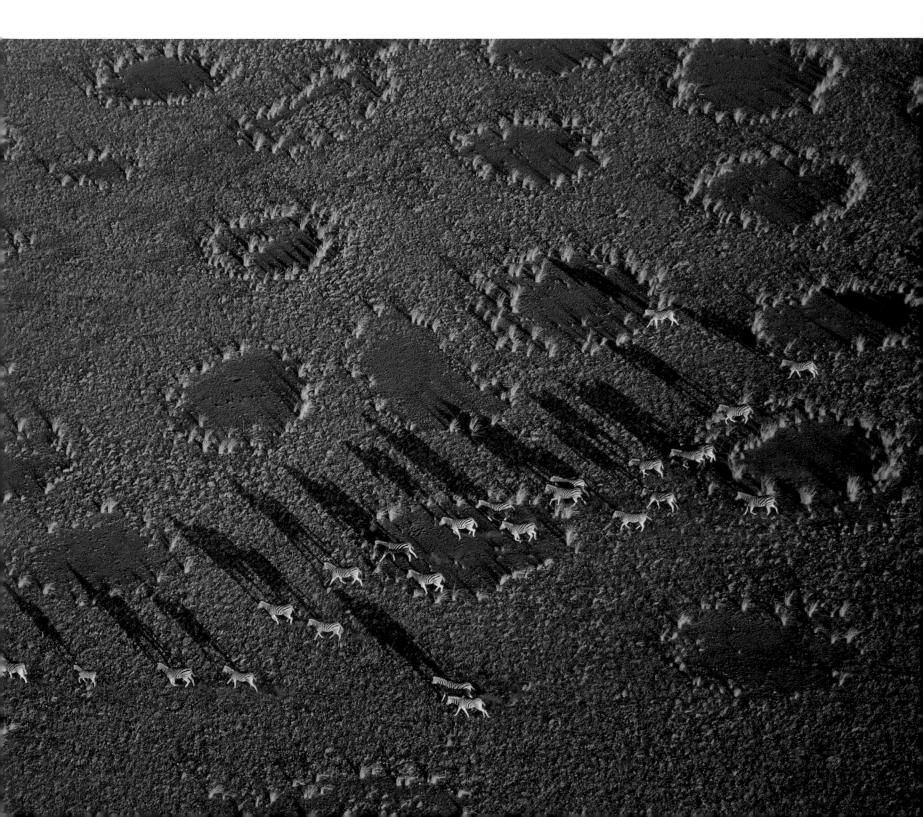

MASS ATTACK

While parts of the Kalahari are flooded, and food and water are readily available, there is a mad rush by many animals to breed. In a stand of large trees, a pair of Africa's most prolific birds – the red-billed quelea – is doing just that. The birds are in a flock of many millions that ranges across the Kalahari and neighbouring lands devouring any wild foods and cultivated crops in its path like a plague of locusts. This pair is one of several thousand that descends on a grove of trees to nest and breed.

The two birds have a nest of woven grass and straw, and the season thus far has been so successful that they are rearing their third clutch. However, it's something of a gamble, for the good times are running out. The flood is beginning to recede, the water evaporating rapidly in the hot sun. It's a race to raise this last family, but there's a more immediate problem down below.

In the soft earth, thousands of armoured ground crickets have hatched and are marching en masse in search of food. They'll eat dry grass and seeds, but it's protein that these crickets really crave. They gather below the quelea nests. They can hear the chicks chirping, and begin the climb to the canopy.

These 5 cm (2-inch) long, fat, flightless crickets are as big as the chicks, but significantly stronger. The exceptionally thick external skeleton on their thorax sports short, blunt spines, giving the appearance of a miniature suit of armour.

Strong, biting jaws and sharp spines on the legs complete their weaponry, making them formidable little beasts. They climb the tree, using their long antennae to 'feel' their way, but it's the sound of the chicks that attracts them to the nest, and it's the chicks that can provide them with vital protein, salt and water.

A cricket reaches the nest, crawls in and clamps its jaws on the soft flesh of a chick, but then a parent returns and, realising the threat, starts to hammer at the cricket's soft and vulnerable abdomen with its bill. At first the cricket fails to let go but the rain of blows is so intense, the cricket itself is in danger. It takes evasive action, seeming suddenly to explode, ejecting green, acrid blood or haemolymph laced with toxins from the cracks in its body. The jet squirts about 6 cm (2.5 inches), causing the startled bird to back off. The cricket tries to escape but falls from the nest. It tumbles to the ground and immediately tries to clean off the blood on its body, but it's too late. Attracted by what they perceive as an injured and vulnerable insect, other crickets swarm around and tear it apart. Given the chance, armoured ground crickets are cannibals, and the best source of protein and salts they need just happens to be other crickets. It's a cricket-eat-cricket world.

GREAT WHITE PLACE

In little more than sixteen weeks, the sun will have caused the water on Okavango's ephemeral floodplains to evaporate and the desert to encroach once more. In some places, rapid evaporation has left a sparkling, salt-laden landscape, and one of the biggest salt pans is to be found many kilometres to the east of the Okavango, in northern Namibia. The Etosha Pan is a vast dried lake bed that is so encrusted with mineral salts that little grows, yet in this harsh and unforgiving place, as is often the case, life can be found.

A lanner falcon is perched atop the dead stump of a tree. From here the bird surveys a lunar landscape tinged in green, the colour left over from the infrequent times that a shallow layer of water covered the land and blue-green algae and brine shrimps thrived, providing food for flamingos. The flamingos have long gone and won't be back until the waters return, but the falcon is here and prospecting for prey.

All around, blocks of compacted clay have split into hexagonal shapes as it dried and cracked. Little river water reaches here these days. The pan was once fed by the Kunene River but thousands of years ago it changed its course, so now the lake itself never fills to more than 10 cm (4 inches) from the very sporadic rains that fall in this region; even so, there *is* water here. Where the crust is thin and the water table close to the surface, rain that fell some distance away gurgles up from below, and animals trek here, travelling hundreds of kilometres from the surrounding dry savannah lands and thorn scrub, just to drink.

A small family of elephants, which journeyed from the mopane forests to the south, stands reluctantly alongside ranks of anxious springboks. Two young males joust at the water's edge, ignored by two gemsboks that walk almost regally through the shallow water.

◄ The thorax of the flightless armoured ground cricket is covered in formidable spines and the insect has a powerful bite, well capable of slicing up a red-billed quelea nestling. It defends itself by squirting blood up to 30 cm (12 inches) from its body or regurgitating its stomach contents. If normal foods are in short supply, these crickets turn to eating each other.

OVERLEAF A bull desert elephant towers over the zebra, wildebeest and springbok at a Namibian water-hole. While not considered a different species to Africa's savannah or bush elephant, it has a slightly smaller body, which makes its legs appear longer and its feet bigger.

Giraffes – the world's tallest animals – are here, as are ostriches, the world's largest living bird and one of the few animals that can subsist on the pan itself. The ostriches generally get enough water from the food they eat, but here they take advantage of this scarce commodity. They take turns at drinking or watching for predators, their heads rising and falling in a comical fashion. They are able to conserve 25% of their water intake by exhaling unsaturated air, where most other animals breathe out saturated air. How they do it is a mystery.

A male ostrich, accompanied by a bevy of young chicks, appears but stops short He helps raise the brood, teaching them how and where to feed and protecting them from danger, and he has led this group across the sun-baked wasteland just to drink, the female bringing up the rear to hurry along any chicks that dawdle. Dust devils swirl around the water-hole and the heat is fierce, but

▼▶ Baby ostriches are vulnerable to predators on the ground. The parent birds guard them closely, often the lighter-coloured female on guard duty during the day and the darker male at night.

with so many animals, there's the danger the little ostriches will be trampled. They all wait at a safe distance, the parents alert to anything untoward.

Water-holes are inevitably a focus for predators, but for now only a small herd of zebra tries to barge in, along with some smaller birds that can squeeze in but fly off quickly if necessary. It's just what the lanner falcon has been waiting for.

A small group of Cape turtle doves, their dark neck stripes clear to see, crowd around and drink at the water's edge on one side of the pond, while helmeted guinea-fowl, their bright blue and red naked heads a stark contrast to their grey-black and spangled-white plumage, gather at the other. A sandgrouse parent wets the feathers on his belly. He'll carry the water, like a saturated sponge, back to his mate, who might be 40 km (25 miles) away, so their chicks will be able to drink.

He's too big for a falcon to tackle, but then a flock of grey-backed finch-larks wheels overhead before dropping down, each bird jostling for its place between the larger animals. They all settle to drink and the falcon sees an opportunity. Flying close to the ground, like a bullet from a gun, it scatters the flock but without making a catch. It tries again … and again, but in this open landscape the smaller birds see it coming and escape every attack. Then, it spots a capped wheatear standing on a rock, but in a flash it's safely away. The falcon returns to its desert perch and waits.

By late afternoon, the ostrich chicks still have not reached the water, but the long shadows of the other animals and the legs of the many visitors merge to produce a confusion of light and dark stripes. The falcon seizes the opportunity. Using the bodies of the large mammals to hide its approach, it swings in and grabs a small flying bird and carries it back to its perch; and not a moment too soon, for a lion pride bursts onto the scene. Every other animal scatters, but the lions are not hunting; at least not for the moment. They just want the place to themselves.

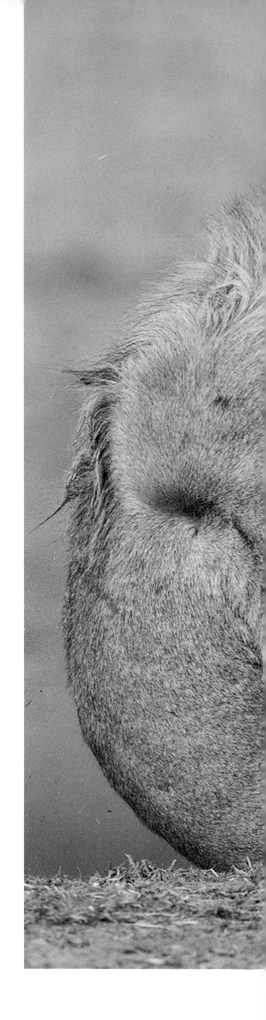

> ▶ **The male lions rise up on their hind legs, claws and teeth ripping at each other's manes, as they charge across the salt pan, each vying for the female's attention.**

In a barrage of growls and roars, three male lions brawl. They may be brothers, but when a female is on heat the gloves come off. They rise up on their hind legs, claws and teeth ripping at each other's manes, as they charge across the salt pan, each vying for the female's attention. The pride's lionesses, meanwhile, chase after a young giraffe, but his long legs and loping stride let him put a safe distance between himself and his pursuers.

By this time, the water-hole is deserted. The ostrich father ushers his chicks to the water, looking around carefully in case the lions return; at last, they get to drink – their very first mouthful of life-giving water. For many, though, it could also be their last: on average only one chick per clutch reaches its first birthday. With darkness falling, the day shift makes way for the animals of the night.

FAMILY REUNION

By sundown, at water-holes across the Kalahari most birds have returned to their roosts and animals are retreating to cover. With other creatures gone, by one very secret water-hole a black rhinoceros and her calf creep out from the scrub. She moves cautiously, the youngster close by her side, their reflections in the water illuminated by a full moon that's pushed above the ragged horizon. There are more of these belligerent and famously grumpy animals in the region than anywhere else in Africa and, apart from mothers with babies, they are generally solitary, but something strange is happening tonight.

More rhinos appear, first one at a time, and then several together, until a dozen or so have gathered at the water-hole. The rhino mother walks deliberately towards another and squeals a greeting. It's one of her older offspring. She snorts back. The water-hole has turned into a family meeting place. In a barrage of grunts from the adults, accompanied by the baby's bleating, her offspring is gently introduced to some of the others in the clan, but with lions and elephants about, the mother is understandably nervous. Her trumpet-like ears twist this way and that, listening out for the slightest hint of danger, and she sniffs the air, her excellent sense of smell making up for her myopic eyesight.

Another rhino appears, but he's a stranger. The others turn as one, grunting loudly. An adult charges, puffing and snorting like a steam engine. With such shortsightedness (they can't see stationary objects more than 45 m [150 feet] away), they tend to attack first and ask questions later.

Nocturnal rhino rendezvous

At a secret location in southern Africa, black rhinoceroses converge on a water-hole in the middle of the night and meet with others of their kind. (1) A youngster is nose-to-nose with another adult who might be a relative, maybe an aunt or a distant cousin. (2) Scientists are at a loss to explain why these nocturnal meetings take place. Maybe it is no more than coming to the water-hole under cover of darkness to grab a drink.

The intruder retreats. It'll have a long, dry walk to the next water-hole. The others return to their socialising, and some head for the water to drink. What goes on at these gatherings is something of a mystery, but by midnight the party breaks up and the rhinos melt back into the bush … until the next reunion.

NATURE'S WHEEL

While parts of the Kalahari have at least some water, at first glance the Namib Desert seems completely waterless, and it appears to have been this way for at least 80 million years, maybe 130 million according to some geologists, making it the oldest desert in the world.

The desert itself is a long and narrow strip of land sandwiched between the Atlantic Ocean and the Great Western (Namibia) Escarpment. In the south, the desert ripples with spectacular dune fields, where some of the world's tallest dunes, many over 300 m (984 feet) high, move up to 100 m (328 feet) a year depending on the strength of the wind. Their sand is coloured all shades from pink to red to burned orange, and the many tracks across their surface betray a fauna that has evolved undisturbed for thousands, if not millions, of years. In fact, directly below the shifting dunes is a fossil dune field, between 40 and 20 million years old, which contains fossils of animals remarkably similar to those we see today. Many of the Namib's residents are found nowhere else on the planet and, by day, they're nowhere to be seen, as most hide from the sun under the sand. There are a few exceptions, including a large and very menacing black wasp!

It's a female pompilid wasp and she flits in short bursts over the face of the dune, her feathery feet dabbling in the sand; and that's her secret. She has sensors on her feet that enable her to find spiders hidden below the sand. If she locates a victim in its silk-lined burrow, she excavates the sand so fast with her front legs that she's just a blur, shifting up to 10 litres (610 cubic inches) of sand in one dig. If the wasp is lucky, she'll avoid the spider's fangs and manage to sting and paralyse it, but not kill it. She'll then deposit a single egg on the spider's body, and bury it again. The hatching wasp larva then feeds on the 'fresh meat'. One spider, however, has a surprising way of escaping this fate worse than death.

When flushed from its burrow, the golden wheel spider runs for a short distance, then flips onto its side, curls in its legs, and rolls like a wheel down the dune face. Depending on the steepness and length of the slope, the spider makes good its escape at up to 5.5 km/h (3.5 mph), which is faster than it could ever move when running. It also blurs its outline and leaves only a faint track, so the wasp has difficulty following or relocating it. In this way, most wheeling spiders live to burrow another day.

Dune spiders are able to occupy burrows in the sand because they can stabilise the sand grains with silk, forming a flexible 'sock'. One species has turned this into a trap. The buck spoor spider turns around and around, weaving

◄ Rhinoceroses are generally solitary creatures that avoid others of their kind. However, on occasions rhinos emerge from the bush when darkness falls and socialise at traditional meeting sites.

a circular 'trapdoor' of silk and sand. It then flips onto its back underneath the lid and waits for its prey to walk by.

Most other small animals, however, without the ability to produce silk, cannot construct burrows. Instead, dune snakes and lizards, for example, 'swim' through the sand during the day, coming to the surface when it gets dark. One creature, the golden mole, lives permanently in the sand, using its acute hearing and an ability to pick up tiny vibrations to hunt down insects such as termites. The Namib Desert can be a surprisingly busy place at night.

LAND OF OPEN SPACES

Early morning in the Namib, which means 'vast open space' in local dialect, is an in-between time, when most nocturnal animals are finding places to hide under the sand, and a few hardy diurnal creatures – mostly beetles – are warming up for the day. There's no surface water and just a few dried riverbeds, but there is a surprise on this particular morning – fog. It's a real 'pea-souper', with visibility down to a few metres. The moist blanket envelops the dunes in an eerie silence, but the fog's real value is that it's life-giving.

Its existence is partly down to the icy cold Benguela Current, flowing northwards from the Antarctic, which brushes the western edge of the desert. Warm, moist air from the Atlantic condenses over the cold waters of the Benguela, and the resulting thick banks of fog roll inland at night for 50–60 km (30–40 miles). During the cold-dry (June to August) and hot-dry (September to February) seasons, they reach the central desert on at least 60 days of the year, and sometimes more. For many of the plants and animals living here, fog is the only, albeit irregular, source of water, and desert wildlife has developed many different ways to collect it: dune grasses drip the moisture towards their roots, the black hairy thick-tailed scorpion runs its pincers over vegetation and drinks the water, black-backed jackals lick stones, and snakes and lizards lick moisture from their skins, but it's the beetles that have fog capture down to a tee.

There are more than 200 species of 'tok-tokkie' or darkling beetles in the Namib, including the only known white species. They rely on the wind to sweep in the dead plant and animal material on which they feed, but when it comes to collecting water, they take to 'fog bathing'. A whole row of these little black beetles stands on the crest of a dune, facing the light wind. Each stretches its back legs so its head points down, but it's the beetle's back that holds its secret. These head-standing beetles have grooves on their wing covers or elytra that help direct water to their mouths.

Another fog bather has an even more efficient system. The elytra on the spindly-legged Namib desert beetle have a pattern of wax-coated hydrophobic troughs and non-greasy hydrophilic bumps. These two features cause the fine fog to coalesce into larger droplets which roll down the beetle's back (held at an angle of about 45°) so the water drips into its mouth. It's so efficient that the

▶ **Facing the light wind, each beetle stretches its back legs so its head points down, but it's the beetle's back that holds its secret: grooves on its wing covers or elytra help direct water to the mouth.**

British research company QinetiQ and researchers from Massachusetts Institute of Technology have mimicked the technique and developed artificial beetle-back membranes to be used to collect drinking water in arid countries.

Another species of beetle constructs a pair of parallel ridges in the sand, each about a metre (3 feet) long, with a trench in between. Water from the fog accumulates on the ridges and runs into the trench, concentrating nearly three times more here than would collect on the desert's flat surfaces. Every so often, the beetle strolls along the trench and drinks its fill.

Acquiring water is one thing, but keeping it is quite another, so most of these beetles have the means to conserve the precious liquid. They secrete waxes that form a waterproof layer over the surface of their bodies. One species of dune beetle loses just 0.11 millilitres (0.0004 fl oz) of water per hour due to evaporation, one of the lowest rates of water loss recorded for any animal. It's just one of the many adaptations that enable these insects to live in the extreme conditions that exist in one of the hottest and driest places on Earth, where the midday air temperature in summer regularly approaches 50°C (122°F) and rainfall is often a distant memory.

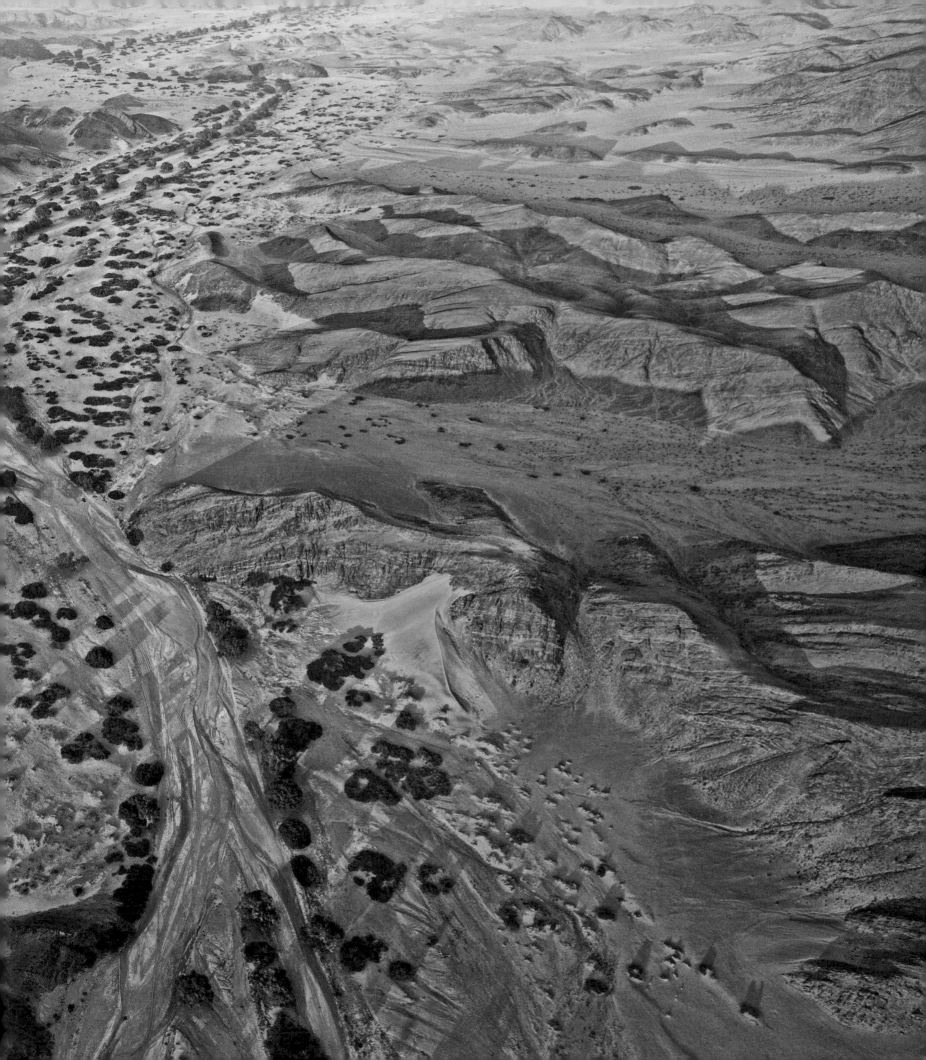

GIRAFFES OF HOANIB

The Hoanib should be a proper river, its source being in the mountains on the western edge of Etosha and draining a catchment area of close to 17,200 sq km (6,640 sq miles), but it isn't, and it hasn't been for several months. While the hot-dry season dominates this part of southwest Africa and despite the odd shower – the so-called 'small rains' of October to December – there's no water flowing in the river at all.

It must once have been a substantial waterway, slicing down through bedrock to create spectacular canyons and steep-sided valleys, but today it flows westwards for just a few days, and sometimes a few hours, each year, and only reaches the sea if the flood is powerful enough to push its water through the 20 km (12-mile) wide Skeleton Coast dune field. For most of the time, the riverbed is almost completely dry, with any water that does intrude becoming trapped in a string of ephemeral ponds. The rest is underground, tapped only by deep-rooted Ana trees, camelthorns and mopanes that line the dry watercourse.

Four ostriches, clearly visible against the pale sand, strut like awkward ballerinas across the steep-sided valley where the river should be. A desert elephant that's feeling the heat pushes his trunk into a pouch – known as a pharyngeal pouch – at the base of his tongue, from which it extracts some water and squirts it over his back and behind his ears. The pouch is his own natural jerry can in which he can store up to a gallon of water for emergency use.

Not far away, unconcerned about his fellow travellers, a young bull giraffe reaches up into an Ana tree and plucks off a twisted, brown seedpod that's still attached to the tree. The seeds are rich in proteins and the pods themselves are full of starch, and the giraffe might well get an extra protein boost from the caterpillars of the brown playboy butterfly, which eat Ana tree seeds from the inside out. The tree, also known as the apple-ring acacia on account of the shape of the pods, is almost 30 m (100 feet) tall, one of a long grove of trees growing beside what should be the riverbank. Its lowest branches are about 3 m (10 feet) from the ground, the direct result of browsing by generations of giraffes.

Giraffes are generally thought of as savannah animals, but this young bull is right here in the middle of a desert, and he's remarkably fit and healthy. He's part of a race that's been isolated from Africa's other giraffes, both by the desert and because another nearby population has been hunted to extinction. The Namibian giraffe is more closely related to the extinct giraffes of Angola, also desert-adapted animals, and like them it depends on the woodlands in and around the region's

PREVIOUS PAGES **Aerial view of the Skeleton Coast, Namib desert, Namibia. A substantial waterway must once have carved this valley, but now water flows in the Hoanib river for as little as several days or hours each year.**

▶ **Although looking quite out of place, the giraffes of northwest Namibia have adapted to desert life. They might walk up to 10 km (6 miles) a day, in search of food. Generally water is obtained from the vegetation they eat.**

ephemeral river courses for year-round foraging and shade. By early afternoon, when the temperature has peaked at 50°C (122°F), feeding and walking take a back seat. It's time to rest, ruminate and extract vital water, for the moisture content of his food is more important than its abundance. Later in the day, he'll continue with his business, looking for a home range he can call his own.

As one of the few large, living things to occupy such an inhospitable place, the giraffe attracts smaller 'friends'. Pale-winged starlings fuss about his body, looking for parasitic goodies, but he shakes his head irritably if they get too close to his ears. They quickly learn to restrict their gleaning to the mane and back, and hover expectantly around the giraffe's tail for ticks and whatever else they can find. They perch and peck for half a minute, then fly off to a branch on the Ana tree, but they're back almost immediately. They play the same role as oxpeckers do in East Africa, harvesting ectoparasites from the giraffe's skin.

The animal backs into a toothbrush tree and scratches his behind, trying to relieve himself of the more bothersome ticks, and the birds scatter to the trees as a pied crow swoops in, landing on the animal's back, a convenient lookout post for insects disturbed in the grass. The crow looks around, dips its head several times towards something it spots approaching, and calls in alarm with its raucous 'karh-karh-karh-karh'.

▼ Bull giraffes fight sometimes to the death for access to a breeding female. Their main weapons in these encounters are their head and horns, which they wield like a medieval spiked mace. Target areas are the neck, legs and rump, and the impact of the blows can be heard from some distance away. A fight can last for half an hour or more.

The giraffe is suddenly alert and turns his head to find another giraffe just a few metres away. It's another bull, but older. Just beyond him is a female. The young male was drawn to this area, as were several other males, by the scent of the female, but he has wandered inadvertently onto the big bull's patch. Normally, they would assess each other's size and strength, and one would back down, but this prime real estate and a potential partner are worth fighting for. The territory holder squares up to the young trespasser and they eye each other, like two prizefighters.

At first, they saunter side by side, pushing gently at first, each testing his opponent; then they clash, the long neck of one slamming into that of the other. The younger animal swings but misses, only to have his opponent's neck crash down on him again and again. They lean into each other, each trying to set the other off balance and gain the advantage, and then they let loose an increasingly violent exchange of blows, each giving as good as he gets, the short, blunt horns on their head smashing into one another's necks and rumps.

The fight stops momentarily. The two bulls walk parallel to each other, pushing and shoving, but not losing body contact. They bow several times, looking for a weak spot, then separate and hesitate, before changing tactics. They lower their necks, the older animal making a glancing blow to the other's legs,

which he pays for with a ferocious strike to his rump. They exchange blow after painful blow. The younger animal presses home the advantage, swinging his neck and slamming it into his opponent's rump time after time, until the old giraffe's leg muscles give way and he collapses. The young bull goes for the knockout punch against the older animal's neck, but the old boy is not done yet.

Lying on the ground, he ducks, so the young pretender misses, and with a monumental effort he brings his head and neck around to slam into the youngster's legs. The young giraffe loses his balance and crashes to the ground, his head hitting the ground and knocking himself out. The older animal rises shakily to his feet and limps away towards the female and into the valley, his valley … at least, for now. The youngster is still on the ground, unable to stand. To be seriously injured in this place guarantees a slow death. The distant roars of desert lions warn that, if he does not get up soon, his life could be brought to an abrupt end.

The older male, however, may have retained this patch of desert, but with scarce and widely scattered food and water, and the constant search for receptive cows, a desert bull must range over hundreds of square kilometres, the largest home ranges of any known population of giraffes. But, for now, his tree-lined valley will provide. It's the end of the hot-dry season, and there's the prospect of rain falling in the mountains on the western edge of Etosha, source of the Hoanib River.

The old giraffe pricks up his ears. It's not the sound of lions, but a distant rumbling. The air is suddenly filled with the fragrance of damp earth mixed with the overwhelming sweetness of herbs and dried shrubs. First a trickle of water appears, soaking quickly into the sand, then gradually more. A brown stain spreads across the valley floor, and then water begins to flow, filling hollows and swamping trees. The giraffes climb to higher ground, but only just in time. Within seconds, a wall of angry brown water crashes around the canyon walls, carrying boulders, trees and bushes that have been torn from the ground. The roar is deafening, the flash flood rolling on down the valley engulfing everything in its path. Then, just as suddenly as it began, the noise ceases, leaving behind the gentle gurgle of a flowing river. Life-giving water has returned to the Hoanib … at least for a few hours.

◄ **First a trickle of water appears, then gradually more … life-giving water has returned to the Hoanib, at least for a few hours.**

CHAPTER TWO
SAVANNAH

The quintessential savannah is located in East Africa. It's the Serengeti and Ngorongoro, Masai Mara and Amboseli, kopjes and water-holes, acacias and grass … rolling seas of grass in the wet season and brown stubble and bushfires in the dry. There are great herds of wildebeest, zebras and gazelles from one horizon to the other, as well as the 'big five' – lions, leopards, elephants, buffalo and rhinoceroses. It's a familiar place, a land of tourist buses and television programmes, of high-speed cheetahs and low-octane lions, but actually this region is much, much more.

Victoria Falls, located on the Zambezi River between the countries of Zambia and Zimbabwe

There's another side to the savannah and East Africa, a darker place of unexpected landscapes and extremes of weather, where survival means adapting to constant change, a place that's far from comfortable, where gargantuan forces are at work. A gash in the Earth's surface, stretching from the Afar Depression in Ethiopia, across East Africa to Mozambique, is gradually widening over time and will split Africa asunder. It's the East African Rift, not one but two parallel rift valleys about 600 km (373 miles) apart.

The Western or Albertine Rift contains the iconic Lake Tanganyika. At 1,470 m (4,823 feet) at its deepest point, it's Africa's deepest lake. The continent's most extensive mountain ranges – the dramatic Virungas and Mitumbas along with the mysterious Rwenzoris – overlook it. They separate the grassy plains of East Africa from the rainforests of the Congo Basin.

There's a darker side of unexpected landscapes and extremes of weather, where survival means adapting to constant change, a place that's far from comfortable, where gargantuan forces are at work.

The Eastern Rift has shallow soda lakes, hot springs and violent geological activity, giving vent to active volcanoes, such as *Ol Doinyo Lengai*, the 'mountain of God' to the Maasai, which pushes up through the bedrock of Tanzania, and *Erta Ale*, 'smoking mountain' to the people of the Afar, which dominates northeast Ethiopia. Sandwiched between the two rifts is Lake Victoria, the world's largest tropical lake, source of the White Nile and home to the greatest diversity of freshwater fish in the world.

And there's something even more special here. The earth movements that are ripping apart East Africa today, together with a fickle climate that, during the past couple of million years has oscillated many times between wet and dry, might well have helped shape our early development. East Africa is the cauldron that boiled hot and simmered cold, to give rise to an ape that came to dominate the entire planet.

A LOST WORLD

It's cold … ice cold. The dark rocks and sparse vegetation glisten with white rime from the freezing fog. A snow-capped peak appears in a shaft of watery sunlight, and then hides once more behind milk-white clouds. Snow begins to

fall and where more snow has accrued than has melted, there's glacial ice – but this is not Greenland or Alaska or even Europe's Alps. We're less than 50 km (30 miles) from the Equator and the steamy tropics, yet there are permanent snowfields and glaciers, and all about us is a black mountain landscape carved and shattered by ice.

A crystal-clear glacial lake surrounded on all sides by sheer rock faces and fed by a silver ribbon of cascading melt water is barely discernible through the mist. The unmistakable shape of a leopard – dark, almost black, its rosettes barely visible – moves effortlessly and silently through a scattering of boulders, each block encrusted with rusty brown moss and black lichens. A cluster of white, papery everlasting flowers peeps out from their tangle of down-covered stems, and in a flash of iridescent green feathers, a sunbird lands gently on a plant more akin to a fictional 'triffid' than anything earthly. The leopard's here one minute and gone the next. Piercing screams of alarm announce that tree hyraxes have spotted it and taken flight, but every other living thing's suddenly mute – alert and listening. In the eerie stillness the calls of distant chimpanzees drift up from the forests below. This is a strange and mystical place, a lost world on the roof of Africa.

The cat is a rarity, the Rwenzori leopard, for these are the Rwenzori Mountains, a chain of high peaks straddling the border between Uganda and the Democratic Republic of Congo. Unlike Kilimanjaro, these mountains are not volcanic, but made from ancient crystalline rocks that were thrust up in the western part of the Great Rift Valley about three million years ago. Their name *Rwenzori* derives from the Bakonjo and Baamba people, from a local word meaning 'the one who brings rain'; and it's more than apt.

Thick clouds and mist obscure the sky and much else besides for most of the year, as the mountains trap water-laden air delivered by prevailing winds and the southeast monsoon. The rainy seasons run from March to May and from September to December, but they seem to last much, much longer. Depending on the altitude, these mountains experience a deluge or blizzard on just about every day of the year, making the Rwenzori undoubtedly the wettest mountains in all of Africa. What's more, it's a place of extremes: at night, temperatures up here rarely rise above zero, but during the day intense solar radiation desiccates and then bakes every living thing. Swedish botanist Olov Hedberg once remarked, 'it's like having summer every day and winter every night'.

It's these unusual conditions close to the Equator that give rise to an unexpected diversity of plant life. The Rwenzori mountain slopes are like a gigantic botanical staircase, each tread a different zone with its own distinctive flora. At the top, about 5,000 m (16,400 feet) above sea level, places like the snow- and ice-covered Stanley Plateau feed the glacial streams below. It's mostly rock, much of it vertical, with little more than lichens and moss, but a few hundred metres further down the mountain bare soils and rocky outcrops are

◄ Sunbirds are Africa's equivalent of hummingbirds. They drink nectar from flowers, but will also take insects and spiders, especially when feeding chicks. Most perch to feed but some species can hover.

decorated with stunted everlasting flowers, grasses, and clumps of East Africa's very own version of lady's mantle.

With such an abundance of rain, melting snow and ice, trails are water and mud; and vast, sponge-like, high-altitude bogs, splattered with orange and yellow bog moss, tussocks of sedge and edged in rushes, are waist-deep in the brown, clinging ooze. The eye-catchers, though, are mainly in the zone below, a strange landscape filled with frost-tolerant succulents – the richest Afro-alpine flora in all of Africa – what Hedberg described as 'Africa's botanical big-game'. They would look more at home in a science fiction movie than at the top of an African mountain.

These strange plants are scattered about in the thin acid soils. Giant tree groundsels resemble elaborate candelabras the size of oak trees, with stout woody stems topped by massive rosettes of cabbage-like leaves. They share the alpine landscape with the tall phallus-like flower-spikes of giant lobelias, which push up from low rosettes of sword-shaped leaves.

On this frosty morning, there is a small reservoir frozen at the base of each of the leaves of the giant lobelias. These ice-cubes insulate the leaf buds and prevent them from freezing, giving rise to the nickname 'gin-and-tonic lobelia'. At one time it was thought that this mucilaginous solution, which is exposed directly to the air, contained antifreeze, but now we know it's laced with pectins – gelling agents – to prevent evaporation.

Reflecting a rare moment of direct morning sunlight is the shimmering metallic green and purple plumage of a red-tufted malachite sunbird, the lobelia's primary pollinator and the highest living sunbird in Africa. The two species have a long history, having evolved up here together, one dependent upon the other. The bird drinks nectar from the flower, and the plant is pollinated for its trouble.

In fact, many of the plants and animals up here have ancient lineages. There are many relict species, like the otter shrew and the Rwenzori turaco, which were once widespread across the central African belt but which have been pushed up into remote and isolated mountain ranges and have evolved into brand-new species and subspecies. This is Africa's Galapagos!

As the hoar frost melts, the protective, layered leaves of the giant groundsel begin to loosen, and tiny hairs help deflect the intense solar radiation that builds throughout the day. The plant was safeguarded from freezing during the night by natural antifreeze in the sap, and the trunk was securely insulated by retaining withered and dead foliage, but this presents the groundsel with a fundamental problem: its leaves do not drop onto the soil below to be recycled, so their nutrients are locked up in the lagging. The plant, however, has a solution: it sprouts rootlets from the side of its stem that infiltrate the insulating layers and extract any nourishment that remains.

Directly below the succulent level another eccentric world is waking. As usual, it's immersed in a thick fog in which the dark shapes of giant heathers

▶ **Reflecting a rare moment of direct morning sunlight is the shimmering metallic green and purple plumage of a red-tufted malachite sunbird, the highest living sunbird in Africa.**

loom out of the gloom, not the low-growing varieties so familiar on European moorlands, but great trees up to 20 m (65 feet) tall. The forest floor is carpeted in wall-to-wall clubmoss and due to the high humidity, the tree heathers are festooned with enormous strands of old man's beard that trail like ragged pennants in the wind. Their boughs and branches are swathed in springy mats of moss so thick that in places it obliterates the sky, so the animals here are hard to see. A group of Rwenzori duikers – the mountain's own subspecies of small forest antelopes – is swallowed up by the sea of vegetation, while a horned chameleon hesitates with one foot in the air and rocks gently before stepping forward uncertainly on a branch that is unusually bare.

It was these extraordinary high-altitude forests and their unique wildlife that became a magnet for European explorers. In 1906, while on the first major expedition into the Rwenzori, Italian doctor and zoologist Filippo de Filippi, from the University of Turin, observed that, 'No forest can be grimmer or stranger than this, the vegetation seems primeval, of some period when forms were uncertain and provisory'.

The Italians, though, were by no means the first Europeans to glimpse these mountains. Seventeen years after his famous encounter with Dr Livingstone, Welsh-born journalist Sir Henry Morton Stanley is credited, in 1888, with being the first modern European to feast his eyes on these mountains. At first he thought he was looking at a silver cloud in the shape of a mountain. 'Following its form downward, I became struck with the deep blue-black colour of its base,' Stanley wrote, 'then I became for the first time conscious that what I gazed upon was not the semblance of a vast mountain, but the solid substance of a real one with its summit covered with snow.'

This persistent cloud cover is probably one reason why previous explorers had failed to gain a glimpse of the Rwenzori Mountains, but there had always been a hint that there was something of geographic significance in this place. Classics scholars identified Rwenzori as the legendary snow-covered *Luna Monte*, which, according to some interpretations of ancient Greek geography, was thought to be the source of the River Nile. In c. 470 BC, the Greek playwright Aeschylus wrote of 'Egypt nurtured by the snows', and Greek philosopher Aristotle offered 'the silver mountain' as the great river's source. Ptolemy, the distinguished geographer of Greek origin but who lived and worked under Roman rule at Alexandria in Egypt, described 'the Mountain of the Moon, whose snows feed the lakes, sources of the Nile'.

It was in about AD 50 that the Greek merchant Diogenes became the first ancient European to set his eyes on the Rwenzori Mountains, having travelled across present-day Tanzania from the coast. Their magical name – the Mountains of the Moon – came from local folk who were struck by their whiteness. Diogenes' description was first recorded in the writings of Marinus of Tyre and then included in Ptolemy's *Geographia*. With the benefit of modern cartography we now know that their waters do, indeed, as Ptolemy had predicted, trickle down through that extraordinary landscape of weird but wonderful plant life and eventually to lakes that feed the River Nile.

ISLANDS IN THE SKY

What the early explorers could not fail to miss were the natural fireworks provided by Nyiragongo and Nyamuragira, two fiercely active volcanoes in the Virunga Mountains to the south of the Rwenzoris in the Democratic Republic of Congo. During historic times, they accounted for 40% of all of Africa's volcanic activity, the most recent occurring in November 2011, when spectacular lava fountains, accompanied by billowing clouds of snow and ash, shot high into the air from the dome-shaped Nyamuragira, its forty-third recorded eruption since 1865.

◄ On a rare clear day during the rainy season, Mt. Stanley in the Rwenzori Mountains appears from behind the clouds. At 5,109 m (16,763 feet) it is the third highest mountain in Africa, after Mt. Kilimanjaro and Mt. Kenya, and named after the journalist and explorer Sir Henry Morton Stanley.

Its neighbour, the conical-shaped Nyiragongo boasts a crater lake that, when full, is the largest of its kind in the world. In 2002 the volcano spewed lava all the way to Lake Kivu, destroying a good part of the town of Boma and leaving 120,000 people homeless. While the lava flows from most volcanoes move relatively slowly, the lava from Nyiragongo is low in silica and very fluid. It can flow down the volcano's steep slopes at up to 100 km/h (60 mph). Fortunately, the current ongoing eruption is confined to the crater

Not far away, several other Virunga volcanoes are less dramatic, but no less important. They're dormant, which is just as well, for on the slopes of Karisimbi, Mikeno and Visoke (Bisoke) live most of the world's population of the critically endangered mountain gorilla. In a region plagued by civil war, where automatic weapons are commonplace, it's a wonder that they're here at all, but dedicated scientists, conservationists and park rangers have somehow protected many of them from the brutality of humanity. Even so, there are thought to be no more than 800 in the whole of Africa today, although in a census in 2010, it was found that there were 100 more gorillas in the Virunga Mountains than in 2003. The population *is* growing, and one of the next generation is awake and itching to get going, if only the rest of his family would do so too.

He shared a night nest with his mother and was up at the crack of dawn. He watched her as she chose which plants to eat and which to avoid, and by late morning she'd had her fill. Midday is time to rest, at least for the others in the group. The little fuzzy-haired mischief-maker has different ideas. He slides down his mother's back, grabs a fistful of the vines that she'd been feeding on earlier and, instead of taking a bite, he topples backwards down the slope, arms and legs flailing in the air, as if to say 'I meant to do that!'. Then he tries to join a rough and tumble with two cousins, but the two boys are too boisterous for such a little thing. He charges back to his mother's arms. For now he's safe, but his world is shrinking.

The gorillas are here because the dense forests are here. Once they covered much of East and West Africa, but when Africa's climate dried, only remnants survived, such as those clinging to the damp hillsides of the Virunga Mountains. It means the gorillas are stranded up here on their islands in the sky. There are few other places to go: only three Virunga national parks located in Rwanda, Uganda and the Democratic Republic of Congo, and the Bwindi Impenetrable National Park, also in Uganda.

They mainly occupy what is known as the *Hagenia* zone, sandwiched between the giant lobelias, groundsels and tree heathers above and the bamboo forests below. It's tropical high forest with 20 m (65 feet) high African redwood, the celebrated *Hagenia* that lends its name to this vegetation zone. There are also East African yellowwoods and red stinkwood, as well as the ancient hog gum tree, a living fossil whose history can be traced back 45 million years in Africa, but which is now found extensively in the New World, where it's known as the hog plum. Rafting Old World monkeys probably carried its seeds there at a

▶ The critically endangered mountain gorilla lives in the Virunga Mountains of Rwanda, one of the few places in Africa where they still survive. There are no more than 800 in the world, but due to heroic conservation efforts numbers are slowly increasing.

time when the continents were closer together. Today, the forests of the Virunga Mountains are populated with their own monkeys, including the charismatic black-and-white colobus monkeys … but to see them at their best and most prolific we must journey south from this lost world on the western fringe of East Africa to the most extensive mountain rainforest on the entire continent.

MONKEYS OF NYUNGWE

First there's one, then ones and twos, followed by threes and fours, until there's a torrent of monkeys streaming across the forest clearing. They use branches like trampolines, bouncing up and down before they lift off and jump the gap, dropping downwards with outstretched arms and legs to grasp the next limb, their long body hairs acting like parachutes to slow their descent. Their tell-tale black coats with white whiskers, beard and long white epaulettes are the hallmark of the Angolan subspecies of black-and-white colobus monkeys. They're at home in the trees, the most arboreal of all African monkeys. Elsewhere, they form troops normally fewer than ten-strong, but this troop is exceptional. There are hundreds, maybe 300–400 in all, possibly the biggest troop of tree-living monkeys in all of Africa.

This is the Nyungwe Forest in southwest Rwanda, about 320 km (200 miles) south of the Rwenzori Mountains, near the border with Burundi and the Democratic Republic of Congo. During the last Ice Age it became a refuge for forest dwellers like the colobus. While many parts of East Africa dried significantly, the mountain forests of Nyungwe remained wet. It was a reliable and stable environment rich in wildlife, and today this place is still a true rainforest, and home to thirteen species of primates, including chimpanzees, but by far the most numerous are the black-and-white colobus monkeys.

Food is abundant, for Angolan colobus eat mainly leaves, especially the tender young leaves at the tops of white stinkwood trees, and they've a complex stomach with 'friendly' bacteria to help them digest plant cellulose. This enormous troop can rise to the challenge and strip a patch of forest bare before moving on.

Some individuals call to each other in a singsong voice, but with a loud croaking roar from a dominant male, the entire troop falls suddenly silent, a sure sign that bad weather is coming. A solitary mother, sitting apart from the others, attends to her baby, but the midday downpour is imminent. She pulls her offspring close to her and shelters under a leafy branch just as the heavens open. The baby is not more than a month old and still has its pure white natal coat, and as it grasps for its mother's fur you cannot help but notice the distinctive feature that it shares with all other colobus monkeys: it has no thumb. It's this peculiarity for a primate that gave rise to the animal's common name *colobus*, meaning 'mutilated one'.

It's rare for these characters to leave the safety of the trees, but by the time the rain has stopped, several monkeys clamber to the ground and root about for

◄ **The baby is not more than a month old, and shares a distinctive feature with all other colobus monkeys: it has no thumb. It's this peculiarity for a primate that gave rise to the animal's common name *colobus*, meaning 'mutilated one'.**

lush herbs beside a stream. The mother and her newborn remain aloft. Little does she or any of her troop know that they live in a very special place, not just for colobus monkeys, but for the history of human exploration. Nyungwe is a watershed. Streams flowing to the west lead eventually into the Congo River and those flowing to the east feed the Nile. In fact, a trickle of water from a muddy hole, a little way upstream from where the colobus forage, feeds the Rukarara River, an indirect tributary of the Kagera River, which in turn flows into Lake Victoria and then the Nile. It was discovered in 2006 by a three-man team – one British and two New Zealanders – who followed and mapped the entire length of the Nile from its source to its most remote headwaters. They claim the spring in Nyungwe to be the farthest source of the Nile, lengthening the river by 107 km (67 miles) to make it 6,718 km (4,174 miles) long, the longest river in the world.

WHALEHEADS OF BANGWEULU

The source of the Nile preoccupied many of Europe's nineteenth-century adventurers, and none more so than Scottish medical missionary and explorer Dr David Livingstone. He was the first European to set eyes on Lake Bangweulu, the place, it's said locally, 'where the water sky meets the real sky'. Here large flocks of wattled cranes congregate on the shore and vast herds of black lechwe stretch across the plain as far as the eye can see.

Wrapped around the lake's northern, eastern and southern shores are the Bangweulu Swamps, a huge wetland area (about the size of Cyprus), which is crisscrossed by river channels constantly changing their course due to blockages by vegetation, such as floating beds of papyrus. Livingstone's last expedition, searching for rivers that might feed the Nile, faltered here, and the great man himself died in the village of Ilala, at the southern edge of the Bangweulu floodplain. His servants buried his heart under a local mpundu (mvula) tree, replaced in 1902 by a stone obelisk, but the rest of his body was shipped to London and placed in Westminster Abbey.

While it was still standing, the tree became a place of pilgrimage for explorers following in Livingstone's wake, including none other than the Irish novelist and poet James Joyce, searching not only for Livingstone's tree but also for idioms to include in *Finnegans Wake*. The tree had an inscription carved into its trunk, which in Africa would make it a 'talking tree'. Joyce included this in the *Wake*: 'Talkingtree and sinningstone stay on either hand' (III.4, 564. 30–31).

Of necessity, Livingstone travelled into the swamps by boat, where he might well have met one of Bangweulu's celebrated inhabitants – a 1.2 m (4 feet) tall waterbird known as the 'whalehead' on account of the size of its head – and more familiarly known as 'shoebill' because of the shape of its enormous bill. It was unknown to Europeans until Livingstone's time, when skins were sent home, so imagine the shock of coming face-to-extraordinary-face with the 'king of the swamp', *Balaeniceps rex*.

Known as the 'shoebill' because of the shape of its enormous bill, the bird's wide nest is built on a small island, and becomes the site of some serious sibling skulduggery.

1

2

Shoebill siblicide

Two shoebill chicks may have hatched in a nest in the Bangweulu Swamps, but only one chick is allowed to live, the other no more than an insurance policy. (1) The mother shields her larger and stronger chick from the sun. (2) She deliberately ignores the smaller one, even depriving it of a life-giving drink of water.

It's an odd-looking bird and no one's sure to which family it should belong. For many years it was classified with the storks, then was thought to more resemble a pelican, but biochemical evidence suggests it should be linked to the herons; after all, it carries its head and neck folded back when flying, just like a heron.

Whatever its lineage, the shoebill favours remote, dense marshes with abundant floating vegetation and undisturbed stands of reeds and papyrus. It's solitary for most the year, but come the breeding season, which starts towards the end of the rains in February, birds pair up. The one-metre (nearly three feet) wide nest is built on a small island, although it could also be perched on a raft of floating vegetation, and it becomes the site of some serious sibling skulduggery.

At first glance only a single chick can be seen, swaying its head this way and that as it waits impatiently for its parents to return with food. But closer inspection reveals a second, much smaller chick hiding in its shadow. As a parent approaches, the larger chick begins to hiccup violently, its way of begging for food. The parent feeds it, but the other chick receives nothing. The second parent arrives and the two adults whine briefly, before one goes back into the reeds. Once again, the larger chick grabs the food and the smaller one is left wanting.

While both parents are absent, the larger chick turns on its sibling and with much pushing and shoving forces it from the nest. The returning parent stares momentarily at its ejected offspring, but steps over it, all its attention firmly on the survivor. The runt was simply an insurance policy. Its fate had been determined from the moment it hatched. Its only chance to live would have been if the larger chick had died.

These birds may live in a habitat that is overflowing with food for much of the year – lungfish, frogs and sometimes small crocodiles – but they are sedentary; they do not migrate even if a drought takes hold and times are tough. They have become so specialised that the smallest change in their immediate environment could be a disaster. They are marooned forever in their isolated wetland, but they could do worse. On the East African savannahs beyond, where the biggest herds of large mammals in the world are to be found, the land is in constant flux. It presents an even tougher challenge for the natural world.

TALES OF LIZARDS AND LIONS

To the east of the wall of rain-drenched mountains and the low-lying, fetid swamps is the East Africa of the holiday brochures: the vast rolling short grass plains with formidable lion prides and their wildebeest fodder, zebra families that are run down by hyena clans or grabbed while they drink by crocodiles, and cute, punk-haired cheetah cubs and their steely jackal adversaries. It's all so familiar, so idyllic: at least for the ecotourist … yet this is a place in turmoil.

Twice each year, dry seasons give way to wet and then return to dry once more, but this natural cycle of boom and bust is broken when widespread floods and devastating droughts punish the land thanks to fluctuations in weather

▶ **The agama lizard stands firm in the morning sun, absorbing the warmth like a living gargoyle, ready to defend his favoured patch against all comers.**

Lizards and lions

A rocky kopje on the Serengeti Plains is a convenient lookout post for a lion pride to watch for the influx of wildebeest, zebra and gazelles during the 'great migration'. (1) The herds bring flies, which in turn pester lions. (2) For the local agama lizards it is a heaven-sent opportunity to catch a meal.

1   2

systems that have their origins half a world away. Clouds of locusts, swarms of armyworms, and huge flocks of red-billed quelea flow easily from one place to the next, devouring precious natural resources. Forests encroach on grasslands, but are driven back by bushfires, some started by humans and others by acts of God. Survival here, for people and wildlife alike, means adapting to constantly changing circumstances, and there are animals living here prepared to take the most extraordinary risks to make a living. Hidden amongst the rocks of a kopje – an isolated granite hillock – is a lizard with nerves of steel.

The lizard is an agama. His metallic red head and blue trousers indicate he's a male of the East African subspecies of redheaded rock agama. He stands firm in the morning sun, absorbing the warmth like a living gargoyle, ready to defend his favoured patch against all comers. All around him other agamas press their bodies against sheer rock faces, soaking in the sun's rays to reach a comfortable working body temperature that will set them up for the day.

A rival approaches, nodding vigorously, and the territory holder nods back. This is prime agama real estate, but its true value will not be seen until the sun is higher in the sky. Suddenly, the shadow of a large bird sweeps across the rocks and the stand-off is rudely interrupted. Some lizards dart for cover, making spectacular leaps across gaps, before disappearing into cracks and crevices. Others flatten themselves in a vain attempt to hide, and gaudy males lose their colour in an instant to blend in with their grey background. But it's a false alarm: a martial eagle with its eyes firmly fixed on larger prey. So, with the danger passed, one by one they reappear, and apply themselves to the serious task of sunbathing, for they have to be ready for the day's big event.

The agama's kopje home is in reality an island of stability in a sea of waving grass and shifting herds, right in the path of the 'great migration' across the Serengeti: the largest movement of terrestrial herbivores on the planet. The plant-eaters are here because the grass is here. It grows on thin soils over a crust of consolidated volcanic ash, the legacy of intense volcanic activity in the recent past, and now it is food for a staggering 1.3 million wildebeest, 200,000 zebra, and 250,000 Thomson's and Grant's gazelles, along with eland, topi and hartebeest, which are, in turn, food for eager predators such as lions, leopards, cheetahs, spotted hyenas, jackals and African hunting dogs.

The procession streams past the kopje, like water flowing around a rock, and it doesn't come alone: all the animals are trailed by an irritating entourage of biting flies, hundreds of millions of them … and agama lizards like flies. So, the visiting herds bring food on the hoof not only for the larger predators, but for the less obvious ones too. The flies land on the warm rocks and the agamas are quick to catch them. Competition is rife for access to the best fly-landing sites, but some enterprising agamas have discovered a far more productive place.

The male, with colour back in his cheeks, leaves his warm-up site and clambers to the top of the rock. He looks up and there towering over him is a magnificent male lion. The cat's perched on an overhang; his regal head held high and his all-seeing eyes scanning the distant horizon for any signs of trouble. His role is to protect his pride, and he has the muscle to do just that. With one slap of his paw he could flatten the agama, but the little fellow, quite unperturbed by the might of the king of beasts, clambers up his thick mane. The lion ignores him, just another irritation unworthy of lifting a paw, but for the lizard it's a heaven-sent opportunity to capture a meal. The lion has attracted his own swarm of flies and what better place to catch them than right on top of the lion's head!

KASANKA'S AMAZING MIGRATION

Change is not necessarily a bad thing. The agama lizard benefits from the change brought about by nearly two million wildebeest temporarily moving into its tiny corner of the Serengeti. And, if change can be predicted, say, with a changing of the seasons, then there's a good chance it can be turned to an animal's advantage.

◄ **The 'great migration' is the largest movement of terrestrial herbivores on the planet, bringing hundreds of thousands of wildebeest, zebra and gazelles temporarily into this tiny corner of the Serengeti.** ◉

Just such an event occurs annually in an evergreen swamp forest that is no bigger than a couple of football pitches and known locally as *mushito*. It's to be found in one of Africa's smallest and least-visited protected areas, the Kasanka National Park in Zambia.

It's about four o'clock and a couple of hours until sunset. It's hot and steamy, a heaviness dogged by the threat of a thunderstorm. Sinister black clouds, which billow up as distant rumbles roll in, squeeze the late-afternoon sun. Everything – rocks, trees and bushes – is bathed in an eerie terracotta glow. It's almost spooky with an air of foreboding, a suitable stage for one of the forest's principal killers, the crowned eagle. It's perched menacingly on a thick branch, cocking its head, acutely aware of movements in the undergrowth below.

The twisted horns of a male sitatunga, Africa's very private marsh-dwelling antelope, are hidden behind gnarled and twisted vines draped over red mahogany and milkwood. The white patches on its face and stripes on its body help it blend in with the marshland plants. It has a strange hunched appearance, for its back end is higher than its front. It moves away silently and deliberately with hooves specially adapted for living in swamps. The bird watches it go. A fawn would be fair game but not an adult antelope. Besides, there's much easier prey to catch right on the doorstep.

All around, the trees seem to be coming alive, and as the movements increase so does the noise, a squealing and a chattering, a wriggling and a jiggling. Hanging in tight grape-like bunches from branches, boles and even from each other are bats – straw-coloured fruit bats – each the size of a fox cub but with a wingspan of up to 70 cm (28 inches). The brown leathery wings, which have been wrapped tightly around their honey-coloured bodies throughout the day, begin to flex. A pair of orangey-brown eyes opens, and the first bat drops momentarily from its branch and then takes to the air. It's the final chance for the eagle to hunt before the bats move away for the night.

The predator moves in like lightning, using the element of surprise. The crowned eagle is not Africa's biggest bird of prey – that title goes to the martial eagle – but it's possibly the most powerful. Its talons can snap the backbone of a monkey like it was breaking a twig, and its short wings and long, flexible tail enable it to manoeuvre amongst the branches and boughs to snatch prey from the canopy. And, here in Kasanka, this is precisely what it does. Grabbing a roosting fruit bat in its talons, it flies back effortlessly to a branch, the bat dead even before the two of them land, and then it takes the prize back to its nest.

▶ At the peak of the season, eight million bats take to the air. It is thought to be the largest gathering of mammals in the whole of Africa, outdoing even the great wildebeest migration for sheer spectacle.

The rest of the roost panics, and great plumes of bats peel away from the trees. There are so many, it's like a tap has been turned on, and because they roost in layers the ones at the bottom have to wait for those on top to leave before they can get away themselves. The noise is deafening.

At the eagle's nest nearby, a single chick peers from an untidy platform of sticks and twigs, about two metres (more than 6 feet) across, in the fork of a tall tree. It's ready for its next feed, craning its neck to see what its parent has brought, but meal-times tend to be rather monotonous in this forest at this time of year. The parent birds could take all manner of prey, some of it much larger even than themselves, but they've timed chick-rearing to coincide with the enormous seasonal influx of fruit bats. Their youngster is guaranteed a regular diet of bat meat that will nourish its early development. As the parent tears into the bat's body, ripping off pieces of flesh and passing them almost daintily to the chick, millions more bats stir in the forest.

The first individuals arrived at Kasanka on or near the twenty-second of October, as they do every year, and numbers peak in late November. They forage at night, leaving en masse from their swamp forest roost at precisely six o'clock in the evening, and it is the most amazing sight. There are so many bats in the air that, for twenty minutes or sometimes more, they obliterate the evening glow on the western horizon. This natural spectacle rivals even the wildebeest migration on the Serengeti Plains.

The bats swirl around. Their long, tapering wings are not only effective for soaring on long journeys, but also, here in the forest, the deep curve on the underside gives greater lift for less energy on the downstroke than is used by

birds, and on the upstroke the wings fold closer to the body, reducing drag. It means they can turn 180° within less than a wingspan … and in the crowded canopy they need to be that manoeuvrable. Close to eight million bats are in the air together, the greatest movement of wild mammals in the world, and being fruit bats they are here for one thing only … fruit.

They head into the Kasanka 'miombo' woodlands to feed on several species of tree that fruit at roughly the same time. The bats favour water berries, wild loquat and red milkwood berries, each bat consuming about twice its own weight before dawn, which, if they all feed well, could amount to 5,500 tonnes (6,000 tons) of fresh fruit each night.

They see well, even in the dark. If they didn't, they'd collide with the trees. But, their long, fox-like muzzles are packed with smell receptors, so they mainly use an acute sense of smell to locate the ripest fruits. Many of the females are in the later stages of pregnancy or carrying newborn pups. Like the crowned eagle, the bats synchronise their own breeding cycle with this superabundance of food, enabling them to give their youngsters a good start in life too. It's a remarkable and rarely seen synchronicity – fruit trees, fruit bats and crowned eagles – all with their life cycles in step.

The bats return to their roost at about 5am, around half an hour before sunrise, when their bellies are full and their fur stained with fruit juice. They might be accomplished flyers but when it comes to landing that's another thing. They crash into the canopy to come to a stop or grab a branch, frequently disturbing bats that are already there. Unlike other fruit bats, which are fussy about the distance between them and their immediate neighbours, the Kasanka

▲ A martial eagle – Africa's largest eagle – snatches a bat in mid-air. Its close relative the crowned eagle tends to take bats at their roost.

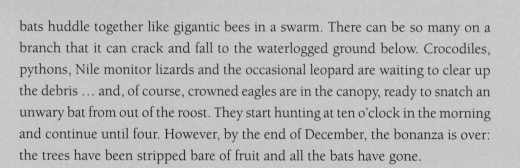

bats huddle together like gigantic bees in a swarm. There can be so many on a branch that it can crack and fall to the waterlogged ground below. Crocodiles, pythons, Nile monitor lizards and the occasional leopard are waiting to clear up the debris … and, of course, crowned eagles are in the canopy, ready to snatch an unwary bat from out of the roost. They start hunting at ten o'clock in the morning and continue until four. However, by the end of December, the bonanza is over: the trees have been stripped bare of fruit and all the bats have gone.

Where all these animals go is still something of a mystery. Many are thought to head into the Congo River basin, others are known to travel 1,000 km (600 miles) or more up and down Africa's central belt; some have even been seen 200 km (120 miles) out to sea. Wherever they go, they are important forest regenerators, accounting for as much as 98% of seed dispersal for forest trees, such as the iroko or African teak, one of Africa's most commercially important hardwoods. Canadian researcher Donald Thomas calls them 'the farmers of the tropics', for every night they scatter seeds in their droppings as much as 65 km (40 miles) from their roost site. However, they'll not be back again at Kasanka until next year, when there's fruit on the trees and crowned eagle chicks in the nest.

WHISTLE DOWN THE WIND
Blissfully unaware of a famous backdrop that includes a snow-topped Mt. Kenya and the rim of the Great Rift Valley, a lone bull giraffe stretches for the juiciest

new leaves near the top of an acacia. It wraps its long and dextrous tongue around a sprig, seemingly immune to the tree's sharp thorns, some of which are 8 cm (3 inches) long. In fact, the giraffe has thick saliva and large papillae on its tongue that protect it and the inside of its mouth from the spines. It chews languidly and looks about haughtily, as only giraffes can, before returning to its chosen branch. Suddenly, it pulls back with unusual haste, shaking its head violently. It's made a mistake. It should have detected the tell-tale smell of the tiny creatures now making its life hell, but it failed to do so and is paying the price: ants with a very painful sting are attacking it.

The ants are in the protection racket. They live in bulbous swellings that join the shafts of several modified thorns, which the tree supplies along with free nectar at leaf bases; and all this in return for security services. While the crowned eagle and its partner took full advantage of changes that Mother Nature provided on a plate, these more pugnacious animals make their own rules and impose change on others.

At the slightest hint of an intruder, like a giraffe that should have known better, the ants stream out from the galls and across the branches ready to fight the monster to the death, but they don't attack every trespasser. They deal with the daily flood of leaf-eating insects, but they leave well alone insects that might pollinate the tree's flowers, and it's the tree that 'tells' them not to. The ants are allowed to protect the buds, but the freshly opened flowers (yet to be pollinated), produce a chemical that keeps the ants away, so any pollinators are not harmed. However, as soon as the flowers have been pollinated, the chemical restraint is removed and the ants can scramble over the flowers once more.

There are several species of acacia ants and the weaker ones prune buds to restrict side growth so that rival ant gangs on nearby trees cannot invade them and take over. The giraffe was confronted by the stronger and more aggressive type and on this day their less powerful neighbours have made a fatal mistake. They've overlooked a twig that's cracked and bent, creating a bridge between two trees. The invaders, ever eager to expand their territory, stream across, overwhelming the opposition in mandible-to-mandible and sting-to-sting fighting, but their hard-won victory is short-lived.

The dry season has outstayed its welcome, so this open woodland on Kenya's Laikipia Plateau is tinder dry. The smallest spark is soon a raging bush fire. The acacia and its ant squad are engulfed by the conflagration, but the tree will

grow again, coppicing readily even after the top has been effectively destroyed. However, every animal capable of running, crawling or flying flees from the fire; that is, almost every creature: lilac-breasted rollers, drongos and bee-eaters are attracted *to* the blaze.

While delivering a barrage of harsh squawks, a roller sweeps down from the top of a dead tree, grabs an escaping grasshopper, and returns to its perch where it batters its prey on the dead wood before swallowing it whole. Blurry flashes of blue against orange flames mean that more rollers are turning this local catastrophe into their good fortune. And, as the draught feeding the flames increases, an almost musical, hissing sound can be heard. It's barely audible over the roar of the flames and the urgent cries of the birds, but it's there nevertheless. These acacias are known as 'whistling thorns', and old spines abandoned by the ants have become miniature flutes. Here, on the eastern escarpment of the Great Rift Valley, the wind really does whistle.

Through the shimmering heat haze comes the unmistakable outline of a family party of savannah elephants, led by the matriarch – the eldest and wisest elephant and leader of the herd.

DRY AND DUSTY LAND

This land was born of fire. In the Eastern Rift, Mt. Kilimanjaro, Africa's highest peak and the world's highest freestanding mountain at 5,895 m (19,341 feet) above sea level, was once a giant stratovolcano that began to form a million years ago. Today, two of its three craters are extinct, but Kibo, the mountain's highest crater, is dormant and could erupt again at any time. The last major explosion was just 200 years ago but, according to a geological survey in 2003, molten magma is little more than 400 m (1,301 feet) below the summit crater and fumeroles on the surface emit sulphurous gases.

In its shadow is the Amboseli National Park, where the animals are easy to spot because long, dry months mean that vegetation is sparse. It can be, however, a place of extremes: the climatic pendulum swings from incessant rain, when the park is turned into a swamp, to years when the rains fail, the land turns to dust, and drought engulfs every living thing. It's these thirsty times that are a challenge for Amboseli's wildlife

Dust devils swirl across the parched ground – not just one at a time, but battalions of them moving steadily across the plain, obscuring everything in their path – and through the shimmering heat haze comes the unmistakable outline of a family party of savannah elephants. Led by the matriarch, they head for places she remembers had the best food and reliable water, but things are different in the drought. The lush sward has been replaced by dirt, and bushes and trees have been reduced to naked branches and twigs. She digs at the dried sod with her feet, but there's barely enough shrivelled grass for her trunk to pick up. Others chew on dried sticks, while a youngster tries to suckle from its mother, but she has no milk. The matriarch – the eldest and wisest elephant and leader of the herd – moves off and most of her extended family moves with her. They pass the desiccated carcass of a wildebeest lying on the trail, but it's so dried out that even the flies have abandoned it.

But the young mother's not with them. Her calf is so weak it can barely move. It drops to its knees, its head and trunk resting on the ground. It tries to stand, but its back legs cave in beneath its emaciated body. The mother nudges it gently, urging it to stand, but it's to no avail. She looks up to see her herd disappearing over the horizon, but she'll not follow. Again, she pushes her hungry and exhausted calf, and in one last monumental effort he pushes up onto his front legs, but his back legs won't follow, and his head sinks slowly to the ground. She tries one more time, but his eyes are closing and the life is leaving him. She stands by him, resting her trunk on his lifeless body; finally, she turns and little by little walks away.

The year was 2009, and Amboseli had had three years without rain. Calves under three months old died from lack of milk, and older calves eight to twelve months old died because of poor milk and no vegetation to start the weaning; but, if youngsters made it to their fifth birthday, they more than likely survived.

▶ **The calf is so weak it can barely move. The mother nudges it gently, urging it to stand, but it's to no avail ... she stands by him, resting her trunk on his lifeless body; finally, she turns and little by little walks away.**

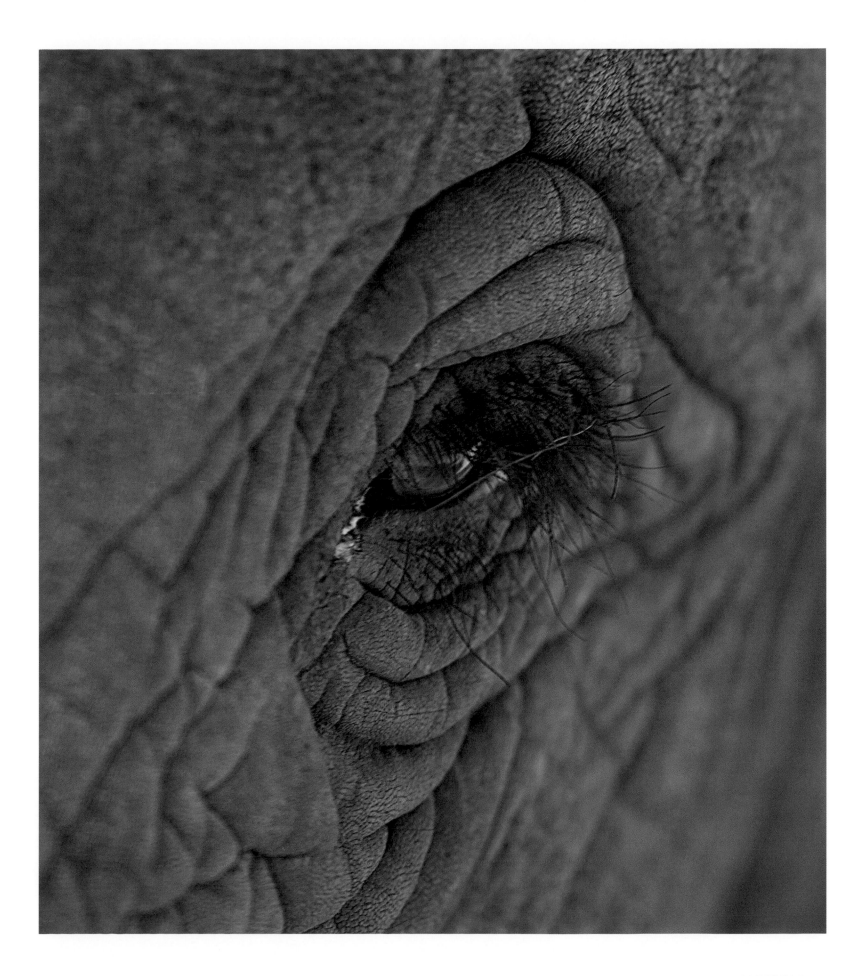

Somehow they found enough food in the dried vegetation to keep them going. Of the adults, it was the older matriarchs that succumbed to the drought. Their teeth were worn and they couldn't process the sticks and twigs. Over 50% of them were gone, including Echo, Grace, Isis, Leticia, Lucia, Odile, Ulla, Qualida, Orlanda, Jill, Joyce, Chloe and Xenia (all named by the researchers who studied them), and their knowledge of the savannah, vital to the wellbeing of the herd, went with them.

Over 15,000 of Amboseli's big game died that year. The resident wildebeest population dropped from 6,000 to fewer than 150, zebra from 7,000 to 1,500 and buffalo from 600 to 185. These were the biggest losses recorded anywhere in recent times.

But, when the rain finally arrived and lots of it, what was left of the herds returned to their ancestral homes. Giant bulls fought for the right to mate, and females who had lost calves in the drought were receptive. There was a baby boom with many calves born and raised successfully, as many as 150 from October 2011 to May 2012 and more to come. Amboseli is now back on track as the elephant capital of the world.

KILLER AT THE LAKE

The drought may have turned parts of East Africa temporarily into a living hell, but an even more unforgiving regime is present in the region every single day, whatever the weather. Imagine a vast lake of hot and burning caustic soda: waters that can strip the flesh off the bone, yet are magnetic to at least two species of birds – lesser and greater flamingos. Somehow, they are able to wade through waters that would be lethal to most other living things.

The Eastern Rift is dotted with lakes such as these. They're shallow, with high mineral content. Lake Magadi, for example, is rich in soda (sodium carbonate), with sediments below the lakebed more than 40 m (130 feet) thick. The salt is exposed and cracked during the dry season, and mined by the Magadi Soda Factory. In such an arid area, the lake is recharged mainly by hot springs, whose waters are at a temperature of about 86°C (187°F), yet even in such an alien environment there is aquatic life: a cichlid fish has evolved that is able to live in the hot, alkaline waters, but only in pools close to the shore where the temperature has dropped to below 45°C (113°F).

One of the smaller lakes is Lake Nakuru. It is strongly alkaline, but like Magadi it's not dead. It has a lush growth of cyanobacteria, also known as blue-green algae, and the more the water evaporates in the sun, the more concentrated it becomes – a magnet for an extraordinary number of flamingos.

◄ (AND OVERLEAF) **Up to one million lesser flamingos gather at Lake Bogoria to feed on the blooms of cyanobacteria (blue-green algae) that grow in its saline waters.**

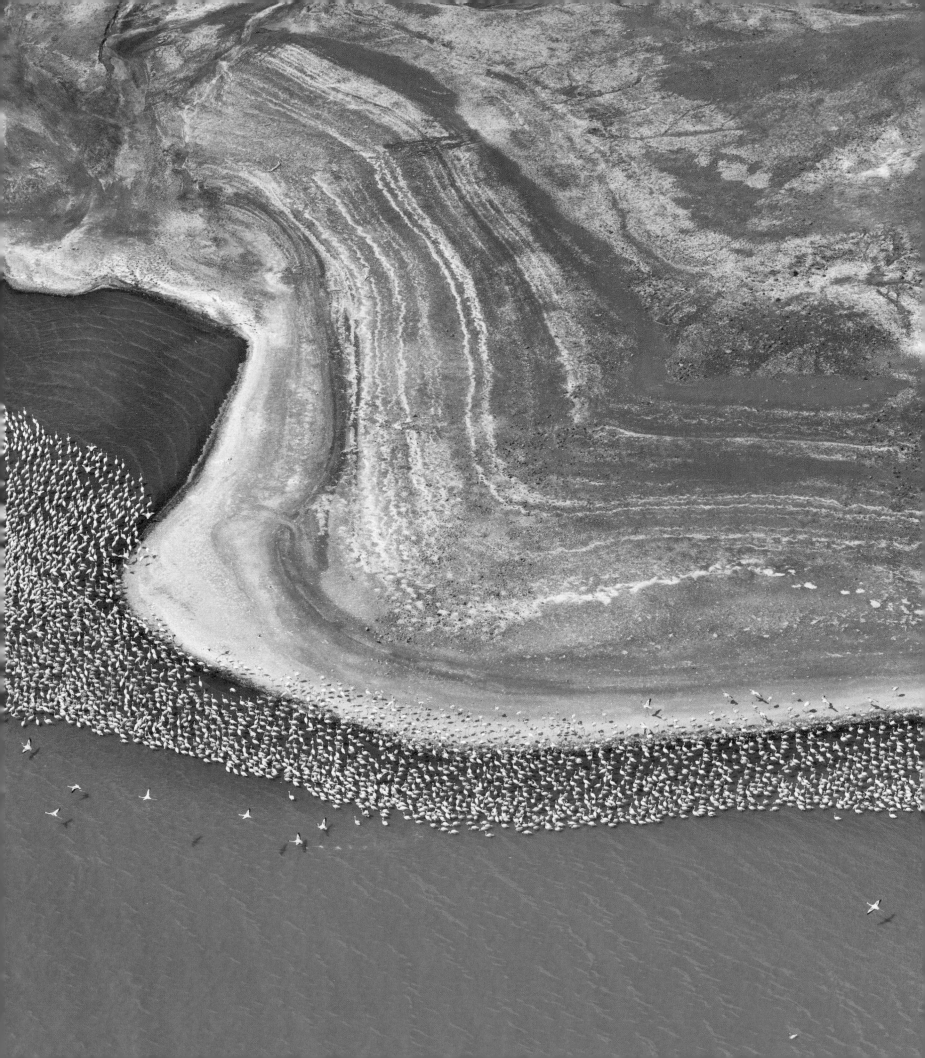

They feed by turning their heads upside down and filtering the water through specially adapted bills, and there are so many birds that they remove more than 250,000 kg (245 tons) of algae from every hectare (2.5 acres) of lake water per year, and *that* means a heck of a lot of filtering. It also means, when full, that the lake can support up to two million lesser and greater flamingos. Their pink colour comes from the photosynthetic pigments in their cyanobacteria diet.

Similarly, Lake Bogoria, north of the Equator, is an irresistible draw, the birds migrating from one lake to the other as water levels fluctuate and microorganisms bloom. Bogoria is shallow; no more than 10 m (33 feet) deep, and at four locations in the lake itself and along the shore are geysers that spout water up to 5 m (16 feet) into the air. The cyanobacteria and occasional swarms of rotifers provide food for the pink tide, but as the flamingos dip their heads, they must watch their backs.

African fish eagles swoop in to catch birds unawares, and steppe eagles and marabou storks will try to steal their catches, but the most eager opportunist here is a lone spotted hyena. This is a formidable beast, a real bruiser. With teeth and jaws capable of severing a wildebeest's leg and grinding it into splinters, the hyena is an accomplished assassin.

The continually moving wall of pink almost overwhelms the hyena's senses as she pads up and down the shore. Birds fly in and out. She looks up, and then looks about, searching for the tell-tale signs of illness, infirmity or weakness. Then, she makes a move. Time and again she rushes, and each time the birds explode into the sky, escaping her terrible jaws, but just once she gets lucky, pinning a bird to the ground and breaking its neck. It hangs loosely in her mouth as she lopes back to her den. She's the alpha female, and head of her clan. It's her responsibility to ensure that her offspring are fed. The speed with which she's reacted to the sudden flood of flamingos has helped to ensure that her children all survive. She's braved the caustic waters (though she'll have sore feet for a few weeks) and taken advantage of whatever is obtainable, whenever it's available. Hyenas are very good at that.

THE CROSSING

Nile crocodiles, unlike hyenas, are prepared to wait. They can wait for the best part of a year, sustained by a meagre diet of fish. What these crocodiles are waiting for – especially the old males of up to 5.5 m (18 feet) long – is red meat. They feel it before they see it. They pick up vibrations from the hoof beats of over a million wildebeest heading their way, and slip into the water, ready and waiting, lying there like floating logs, the perfect ambush.

The wildebeest are following the rains and the promise of fresh, lush grass. However, where there's rain, there are bound to be rivers, and to reach the pastures sometimes they must ford rivers in flood. On the Mara River, which

▶ **As the flamingos dip their heads, they must watch their backs, for this spotted hyena is an accomplished assassin, with teeth and jaws capable of severing a wildebeest's leg and grinding it into splinters.**

flows through the savannah lands of Kenya and Tanzania, the great herds trek to traditional crossing places, often where hippos have created a muddy ramp when entering and leaving the water. It's here that the crocodiles wait.

It's late afternoon by the time an advance party of plains zebra arrive. They know the crocodiles are there. They can see them, but if they cross in tight family groups they have a good chance of making it to the other side without incident. A kick from a zebra stallion could cave in a crocodile's jaw, assigning it to a very long, slow death by starvation. They know when to stay clear. And so the first male zebra makes it safely to the far bank and whinnies loudly to encourage the rest of his family to hurry. Others follow quickly in their wake, until all are across. The crocodiles don't budge; somehow they know easier prey is not far away.

Next to appear are a group of Thomson's gazelles. They hesitate nervously on the riverbank before moving further upstream where a build-up of rocks along a ledge in mid-river has formed a small cataract and the water is turbulent but shallow. They dither at first, but then one leaps into the river. Others follow rapidly behind until the entire herd is in the river. A youngster loses its footing and is swept downstream, no more than a snack for a lucky crocodile.

By evening, when the last few gazelles are safely across, the first of the wildebeest line up at the water's edge. Some lower their heads to drink. Others look out across the dark water, which is sparkling in the light of the setting sun. A log submerges. A ripple spooks them, and they race back up the bank. A few minutes later they return, agitated and impatient to reach the far side. They stand ready, but not one dares to take the first step. Others join them, and then many more. Gradually, the numbers grow until the animals at the back are pushing against those at the front. Something's got to give, and it does. One wildebeest takes the plunge, leaping straight into the river. More logs submerge, and wildebeest pour into the water, but still the crocodiles do not attack. They wait.

The wildebeest don't wait. They literally throw themselves into the river. Animals that can't get to the hippo ramp go over a cliff of crumbling earth. It's more than 12 m (40 feet) high and almost vertical, but that doesn't stop them: they drop, tumble and bounce, and some even somersault to a halt, breaking necks and legs in their headlong rush to cross. The first few wildebeest clamber out on the opposite bank, slipping and sliding on the wet rocks, but the current's

▶ A herd of plains zebra crosses a river during the great migration across the Serengeti. The stallion leads his family party, urging them to hurry across by whinnying when he reaches the far bank. The crocodiles tend to let them cross; a kick in the jaws could mean the end of a crocodile's life.

carrying many to where it is too high and too steep and they can't get out. They jostle and stomp on each other, many drowning in the panicking crowd. It's for this that the crocodiles have been waiting. They don't need to attack the wildebeest; they simply kill themselves. The predators form an orderly queue at each carcass. When it's their turn, they grab a piece and twist their bodies in a so-called 'death roll' to tear away a bite-size chunk, and then, raising their open jaws vertically, they let gravity drop it into their throat.

By morning the river resembles a battlefield. Dead wildebeest litter the shore and bloated corpses are jammed behind rocks and fallen trees. All but a few crocodiles are sated, but as the savannah heats up and the thermals begin to form, vultures fly in from distant nest sites, and along with a gathering of marabou storks and a solitary Nile monitor lizard, they begin to pick the skeletons clean. The vultures time their breeding to coincide with the wildebeest river crossings. It is the way these enterprising birds ensure their offspring thrive in East Africa's turbulent natural world.

THE JADE SEA

The monumental forces at work along the East African Rift influence greatly the pace of evolution. Rifts, faults, catastrophic earthquakes and volcanic eruptions can change the lie of the land, laying waste the delicate balance of life, but Nile crocodiles are born survivors: their ancestors shared the planet with their dinosaur cousins, and even today they can be found hidden away in unexpected places: oases in the Sahara Desert (see page 206) and in Madagascar caves, and in 1917 one wayward individual was seen 16 km (10 miles) offshore at St Lucia Bay, South Africa. Today, one of their strongholds is Lake Turkana on the Kenya-Ethiopia border.

Turkana is the world's largest desert lake, where violent storms are frequent due to the water cooling or warming more slowly than the land. The crocodiles bask on the shore, row upon row, with mouths agape to lose heat. They feed mainly on fish, but should the opportunity arise, they wouldn't turn down a juicy turtle steak.

An isolated population of Nile softshell turtle shares Turkana's waters with the crocodiles. It's a species found in all manner of habitats, from fresh water to salt water, so is able to cope with the saltiness of the lake, and it likes the warmth too. This is just as well for the lake sits in the middle of a searingly hot desert

◄ While following the rains and the promise of fresh, green pastures, the great wildebeest migration must cross the Mara River in Kenya. Many die, not from crocodile or lion attacks, but from being trampled by their herd mates in the scramble to reach the other side.

with an average year-round daily temperature of 30°C (86°F), and highs of up to 60°C (140°F) claimed in the nearby Suguta Valley. Three rivers enter Turkana, but none leaves, the water evaporating from the surface in the intense heat. The presence of the turtles, however, indicates that at some stage in the past, when rainfall in the area was far greater than it is today, Turkana was connected to the Nile river system.

The turtle spends much of the day and night adopting a lie-and-wait feeding strategy, buried in the bottom sand or mud, with just its long, snorkel-like snout sticking out. It can remain there for long periods because it is able to absorb oxygen directly from the water through its skin. Hiding is a defence measure too, for its leathery, pliable carapace offers little protection from crocodiles – and Turkana is home to one of Africa's largest populations of Nile crocodiles, with an estimated 15,000 crocs, some brutes reaching 5.5 m (18 feet) long.

The turtles hang out on the shores of a large island, known as Central Island, also a favoured nesting site for crocodiles. The island is a volcano with 15 craters and cones and three crater lakes that change colour with the seasons. It spewed out molten sulphur and steam as recently as 1974, fumarole activity concentrated on the east side of the central crater, a gentle reminder that Lake Turkana sits squarely in Africa's volcanically active Great Rift Valley.

THOSE THAT FLEE FROM THE SUN

An incandescent fountain explodes across a lake of molten lava, which bubbles and hisses, like a cauldron of burned porridge. Fumaroles, their openings tinged with yellow and rimmed with sulphur stalactites, spew out throat-tightening gases that smell of rotting eggs. Red-hot liquid rock oozes out from hornitos and spatters on lava already solidified. Columns of searingly hot air carry away long strands of crystal-lined Pele's hair (fibrous threads of volcanic glass, spun from molten material by the wind) and they litter the ground like confused spider webs. And all around are the black ropes of old lava flows, the legacy of ancient eruptions. It's almost a throwback to a time when the Earth was young: a primeval landscape in one of the world's most geologically active regions, the Danakil Depression at the northern end of the rift.

The volcano is *Erta Ale*, the most active in Ethiopia. It's not high – just 613 m (2,011 feet) – but it's mighty broad, at 50 km (31 miles) across. At the summit are two large and one small pit craters, containing one of the five permanent lava

The solifuge possesses a pair of huge pincers, lined with teeth, with which she tears up prey before liquefying it and sucking in the resulting broth. She's one of the few animals that can survive in such a hostile place.

lakes that exist on the planet, and possibly the oldest. The local Afar tribesmen call it the 'gateway to Hell', and it's probably as close to Hell as it's possible to get. Everything here is hot … very hot. Even the air temperature is thought to climb to over 60°C (140°F). It's probably the hottest place on Earth.

Yet, there is life even here. A female solifuge – also known as a camel spider, wind scorpion or sun spider – remains motionless in the sun. Although related to spiders, she's not a true spider, and she looks to have ten legs rather than an arachnid's usual eight. The first two, though, are not legs but pedipalps, which function like an insect's antennae. They have an eversible adhesive organ at the tip, enabling her to catch flying insects. She also possesses a pair of huge chelicerae or pincers, lined with teeth, with which she tears up prey before liquefying it and sucking in the resulting broth. Large central eyes complete her hunting kit.

But she's not hunting today. She's guarding her buried clutch of a hundred eggs, and a scorpion is approaching. It's unlikely to be any danger to her unhatched young, but she reacts to anything that moves. She, in turn, moves rapidly, slamming into her adversary and bowling it over. It scuttles away, its tail not between its legs but held aloft, over its back. Quick though she is, the solifuge's speed is often exaggerated. Nevertheless, compared to other invertebrates of a similar size – a leg span of up to 12 cm (5 inches) – she's fast, reaching a top speed of about 16 km/h (10 mph), about half as fast as a human sprinter. And, she's resilient, tolerant of heat and drought. She can be out of the shade and in the sun, where the air temperature is 50°C (122°F), for a whole 24 hours without suffering. She loses very little water when breathing, and obtains most of the moisture she needs from her prey. She's one of the few animals that can survive in such a hostile place.

The base of Erta Ale volcano is 75 m (246 feet) below sea level in the barren Danakil Depression, making it one of the Earth's lowest terrestrial volcanoes, and it sits in a region that's geologically exciting, for it's at the junction of three rift valleys: the northern end of the East African Rift, the Gulf of Aden and the Red Sea. The sea has already invaded the latter two, and now Africa is slowly splitting apart along the East African Rift so it'll do it all over again.

The energy comes from a rising plume of hot, partially molten rock 2,900 km (1,800 miles) below the surface, which is stretching the Earth's crust to breaking point. In 2005, the sudden eruption of a series of fissures 60 km (37 miles) long – the Dabbahu fissure – represented the birth pangs of what might well become a new ocean. Locals told of a violent earthquake, after which ash and rocks were thrown into the air, and of a column of 'smoke' that billowed into the sky, forming a giant mushroom cloud like the aftermath of a nuclear explosion. Cracks appeared in the ground. Some were a metre (over 3 feet) or more wide. Many people were evacuated, but there were no casualties, bar one, a wayward camel that fell into a fissure.

> **Most of the lake's water comes not from rivers and streams, but from hot springs with an extraordinarily high salt content. If any creature should land here, the moisture in its body is sucked out and it is instantly mummified by salt spray.**

LOWEST POINT IN AFRICA

One place that even the solifuge would have difficult surviving is southeast of Erta Ale. Lake Assal is a large crater lake in the Danakil Depression, in Djibouti. The lake's desert shore, where the summer temperature routinely reaches 52°C (126°F) and oven-like winds buffet anything protruding above the surface, is 155 m (510 feet) below sea level, making this the lowest point on the African continent and the third lowest land depression on Earth (after the Dead Sea and Sea of Galilee). Most of the lake's water comes not from rivers and streams, but from hot springs that are fed by the nearby Gulf of Tadjoura, itself an extension of the Gulf of Aden. They have an extraordinarily high salt content. The salinity – nearly 35% at the surface and 40% at a depth of 20 m (65 feet) – is higher than that in the Dead Sea (33.7%). High salinity and high water temperature – about 34°C (93°F) – means that nothing lives here except extremophile, salt-tolerant bacteria. Indeed, if anything else should land here, any moisture in its body is sucked out and it is instantly mummified by salt spray blown by the high winds. All around the shore are pebbles made of salt and if broken open a dead insect can be found inside. Larger lumps are the salt coffins of dead birds.

If it were not for the Danakil Mountains, which separate the Danikil Depression from the Red Sea, the entire low-lying area of the depression, including Lake Assal, would be seabed. All it would take is a major earth movement, and the waters would invade, eventually flooding the entire East African Rift to form a new inlet of the Indian Ocean. By that time, the wildlife in parts of East Africa would have lost its ongoing battle with drought, famine, fire and flood, relinquishing the land to the sea … and Africa would have lost its Horn.

CHAPTER THREE

CONGO

The tropical rainforest is the beating heart of Africa. Sited firmly at the centre of the continent, sandwiched between the searing deserts of the Sahara to the north and the Kalahari to the south, and with the warm Atlantic Ocean bathing its western edge, tropical Africa is clothed in what can only be described as jungle. Giant ancient trees, fetid swamp forests and strangling greenery occur in rainforests so vast they create their own weather. Rain can fall all year round, but intense rains deluge the forests during two wet seasons each year, and as they lie to the north and south of the equator there is always a rainy season somewhere.

The yellow-billed turaco bird

The rain arrives in buckets, with electrical storms so powerful they deliver more lightning strikes here than anywhere else on Earth. Annual rainfall in Africa's tropical rainforest is upwards of 2,000 mm (80 inches) and the average temperature is a sultry 30°C (86°F). All that rain drains from the forest and flows into major rivers like the mighty Congo, a waterway that seems to come second in everything. It's the second longest river in Africa (after the Nile), which drains the second largest rainforest in the world (after the Amazon Basin), and has the second largest flow (after the Amazon River). But it is the world's deepest river, 230 m (750 feet) deep in places. More importantly, it's a vital artery, like all of Africa's major rivers, a highway for the region's people and for its wildlife.

Tropical Africa is also a biodiversity hotspot, with the Congo Basin having one of the highest concentrations of endemic species in the world. Overall, the rainforest and its rivers are home to over half of all Africa's species of plants and animals, including the elusive okapi and pygmy hippopotamus, as well as our nearest living relatives – chimpanzees, bonobos and gorillas – but theirs is a secretive world, almost claustrophobic, where hunters and hunted live cheek-by-jowl, neighbours are rivals in the relentless struggle for space and light, and anyone's triumph comes at someone else's expense.

SWEET TOOTH CHIMPANZEES

On the forest floor, it's dark, even at sunrise. The temperature is already 25°C (77°F) and the relative humidity is close to 80%, yet the day has hardly begun. Chinks of light penetrate the closed canopy of mahogany, black ebony and chocolate trees, just three of at least 300 species to be found in Africa's lush tropical rainforests. Their lower branches are draped in lianas and decorated with epiphytes, and their thick trunks surrounded by a tangle of vegetation.

Huge emergents (the tallest trees, which extend up above the rest of the canopy), such as the African walnut, tower 40 m (130 feet) into the sky, but the dense understorey is not as impenetrable as feature films would have us believe, for many of the larger animals follow well-worn pathways through the forest. Even so, this *is* primeval jungle, Conrad's *Heart of Darkness*, a dank and mysterious twilight world where plants and animals alike fight not only for life, but also for light.

In the gloom, movement in the leaf litter betrays a giant millipede, one of the forest's recycling brigade. It eats decaying leaves, among other things, but with the light spreading, it'll hide away during the day. It curls into a tight spiral and waits for the return of night. A pair of large eyes lock on, the distinct smell of

The mighty Congo is a vital artery, a highway for the region's people and for its wildlife. Over half of Africa's species of plants and animals call the Congo Basin home.

▶ A pygmy hippopotamus nuzzles her calf as they wallow together in the water. Although native to the forests and swamps of West Africa, the pygmy hippo is seldom seen, for it is both reclusive and endangered, with fewer than 3,000 remaining in the wild.

curry the tell-tale sign of a potto. It's another of the night shift and it's on its way to the top of the canopy where it'll spend the day asleep. It stops momentarily, peers down, but experience reminds it that these multi-legged creatures taste bad (in fact, they produce hydrogen cyanide as a defence) and anyway, the ground is not a place where pottos tend to go. It continues its ascent, slowly and deliberately, always gripping the branch with at least two limbs, until it disappears into the foliage. It's time for the creatures of the day.

First up are some of the forest's most industrious insects – sweat bees – stingless bees not much bigger than a grain of rice that are attracted to the salt in human sweat. Like most eusocial insects, their queen is a tyrant, with chemical control over an army of workers, all of them her daughters. She's the only one permitted to breed. The rest are tasked with the endless search for pollen and nectar, foragers visiting up to 2,000 flowers each day.

The nest is hidden in a hollow behind the bark of a tree. Inside, the bees manufacture honey and store it in tiny wax pots which stand alongside thousands of carefully nurtured egg capsules. The capsules are joined together with struts like a molecular model in a science laboratory. Each capsule contains an egg, provisioned with pollen and nectar for when the larva hatches out. After pupation, the adult bee emerges from the capsule and starts to contribute to the

▼ The nocturnal potto is also known as the 'softly-softly' for the way it creeps about in the canopy. Three vertebrae in its neck have sharp points just under the skin that can be used in defence, especially if it is grabbed by the neck as cat predators might do.

working of the colony. About 25% of the new bees are potential queens, their destiny dependent on how much honey is placed in their larger than normal brood capsules; but bee larvae are not the only consumers.

Slam! With a tremendous crash, the queen's entire world falls in on her. A huge piece of wood has smashed into her nest – a club, a tool – and holding the implement is not a person, but one of our closest relatives. Chimpanzees like honey, and hanging from a branch a young female hammers at the bark with a short, stout stick, then tears away the loosened bark to get at the delicious honey underneath; but the nest is quite extensive and she can't reach the upper stories.

The teenager – known to be an expert honey-gatherer, a skill she learned from her mother – clambers back down the trunk and finds a longer stick. She breaks off the spindly twigs, and cracks the stave on the edge of a buttress root so she has a long but stout branch to reach the rest of the honey.

This honey-pounding behaviour is unique to chimpanzees living in the Goualougo Triangle in the Republic of Congo. In other parts of Africa, chimps use different techniques and tools, from probes to levers. In Uganda, for example, the Sonso community in the Budongo Forest collects leaves to mop up honey, and in Ivory Coast and Gabon the chimpanzees use fabricated dipping sticks.

More often than not, the bees' nest is high up in the canopy and the chimpanzees must hang from branches at precarious angles to reach it. It can also be difficult to break apart, so an ape could be pounding it for 40 minutes or more before gaining access to the egg-shaped pots of honey inside. Once it has made a big enough hole, the Goualougo chimp uses its fingers to scoop out the sweet, sticky food.

In Gabon's Loango National Park, the chimpanzees have been seen to manufacture a sophisticated tool to extract the honey. First, they remove the bark from evergreen *Garcinia* trees and fray the end by chewing on it. Then, the stick is dipped into the honey pots and the honey licked off. They have three- to five-element tool kits, some tools having multiple uses.

The honey itself is not of great nutritional value, but is simply a mixture of sugars with a few antioxidants and vitamins. The staple diet of these rainforest chimps is fruit, but they have a sweet tooth just like people!

The Goualougo chimpanzees mainly target the nests of stingless bees, but these insects store less than a kilo (2.2 lb) of honey at any one time. African honeybees, on the other hand, produce many kilos, so the chimpanzees sometimes try their luck with these more aggressive insects and the greater prize. The bees, however, defend their nest vigorously. They stream out and swarm around the chimpanzees, trying to drive them away, their barbed stings ripped from their body, as each bee sacrifices its life for the defence of the colony. Alarm pheromones direct the workers to the invaders, but the chimps are not deterred. They're just as ruthless with these potential killers as they are with the less painful sweat bees, and they'll be back. Chimpanzees have an intimate

1

2

3

4

Chimpanzee tool kit

Chimpanzees in the Congo rainforest may use several tools to obtain the honey produced by sweat bees.
(1) A young chimp learns the skill by watching its elders. (2) The older chimpanzee smashes the bark with a

knowledge of the forest. They not only have a mental map of where the best fruiting trees and bee colonies are to be found, but also have an understanding of the best time to visit. Chimps are smart.

When the pillaging is over, the chimpanzees move out, but the nest is usually trashed beyond repair, and this loss of bees means a loss of pollinators in the forest. Every animal here counts, no matter how small.

WEB MASTERS

Size can be a handicap for small creatures in a big creature's world, but for one of the rainforest's tiny inhabitants smallness can have its advantages. This 'lilliputian' is a spider, a female barely one centimetre long (0.4 inches), and she's quite capable of tackling the huge cricket that's tangled in her web. It's many times her size but, as the prey struggles to free itself, she stabs it, injects it with venom and, instead of wrapping it in silk immediately to restrain it, she taps out a Morse code message on the web using her abdomen, and from all directions other spiders come running from their hideaways beneath leaves that have tangled in the web. This female's not alone. She's a social spider.

Their web is enormous, about 20 m (65 feet) across, stretching up into the canopy in a series of horizontal sheets linked with vertical scaffolding, and it's home to upwards of a thousand spiders. With this the colony can catch a greater number and larger items of prey than a spider with its individual web. The

females deal with the prey, which can be anything from a fly to a small bird or even a bat. Juvenile spiders tend to throw silk over their victim from above and from the side, while the adult females throw silk from below. Once it's subdued, they transport it to the tangled centre of the web where they share the food, first injecting venom containing digestive enzymes and then sucking in the resulting soup. Any hard parts are cut loose, and the team is ready to tackle its next victim, as long as it's not a praying mantis. They're recognised as dangerous and the spiders will cut them loose.

The reduced cost of maintaining the web is another advantage of working together. The daily torrent of rain or the movements of large animals could easily destroy an individual web: in fact, individual webs are totally destroyed on nearly half of the days during the rainy seasons. A group of spiders, however, can maintain their web effectively and continually, and they each use less energy: energy investment for each spider in the colony decreases with an increase in colony size. The male spiders undertake the building and repair work, usually under cover of darkness. They ensure the web is fully functional at all hours of the day or night, the biggest and deadliest trap in the jungle.

ANT ATTACK

For sheer numbers there's a tiny creature in Africa's rainforests that's hard to beat. The first sign that it's about is a soft pitter-patter, like the sound of rain, but it's not water that's falling, it's ants – driver ants, the dreaded *siafu* – probably the most feared ants on the planet.

These ants are an advance party that's been foraging in the trees, searching for anything that's living; anything that can be sliced and diced and carried back to their bivouac a kilometre away. They crawled up the trunk from the forest floor, but having swept the tree clean of its resident insects, they find the quickest way down – and that's to drop – so it's raining ants.

They cannot see. They have no eyes. They follow scent trails on the ground and up through the trees. Their entire life is governed by smell. The scouts lay the first trails and the others follow, an army that moves through the forest at about 20 m (65 feet) per hour. When a caterpillar or other juicy creature is found, the aggressive workers – each no longer than 0.5 cm (0.2 inches) – emit an alarm odour that encourages many others to come running and to launch an attack. Soon the target is completely smothered by a squirming mass of black bodies, each worker equipped with razor-sharp mandibles for cutting through flesh like a knife through butter.

Large soldier ants, each 1.5 cm (0.6 inches) long and armed with enormous jaws, line the supply columns to protect the busy workers as they run frantically between the front line and the bivouac. The nest itself is made from the living bodies of ants. Inside are living corridors and chambers, all made of ants.

The innermost sanctuary contains the gigantic queen and her consort.

◀ **The web is enormous, stretching up into the canopy in a series of horizontal sheets linked with vertical scaffolding, and it's home to upwards of a thousand spiders.**

At 5.5 cm (2.2 inches) long, she's the largest ant in the world. She lays 1–2 million eggs every month, the hatching grubs attended by nursery workers who feed them with meat brought back by the rest of the foraging workers.

There are so many of them – over 20 million in a single colony – and they are such efficient killers that they can strip a patch of forest of its small animals – earthworms, insects, spiders, scorpions and sometimes even nestlings and small mammals – in a few days, and then be forced to move on to find new feeding grounds elsewhere.

Moving the bivouac is a major military manoeuvre. First the scouts find a suitable campsite, and then the rest of the army follows. They travel along an avenue lined by soldiers. They even form a living roof across open ground, so the rest of the moving colony is safe. The smaller workers carry eggs and larvae delicately in their jaws, passing rapidly along the makeshift corridor in a continuous stream and depositing them in the nursery at the new nest site. Last to leave the old site is the queen. When she arrives at the new location, the avenue breaks down and the daily massacre resumes, the workers stripping bare another part of the forest.

MONKEY PUZZLE

No less deadly, but quite unexpected, is a gang of substantially larger killers. It's long been known that primates other than humans are meat-eaters: chimpanzees catch colobus monkeys and olive baboons hunt baby gazelles, but another primate has joined their exalted ranks, until recently thought to be an out and out vegetarian.

The trees in this corner of the Dja Reserve in Cameroon are alive with

monkeys. They're everywhere in the canopy, each and every one of them quite literally stuffing its face with fruit. Figs are in season, a favourite of grey-cheeked mangabeys, and their cheek pouches bulge as they indulge their satisfying fad. Resembling small, long-legged furry baboons, they're almost black with a brownish mane around the neck and shoulders, a tufted crest of long hair on the head, and grey, almost white, hair on the cheeks. There are about 20 or 30 of them, mostly females with their young, accompanied by a couple of males, and they're causing quite a stir – grunting and chuckling with the occasional bark – as one is startled by an insect it's disturbed.

In the distance, the faint call from a troop of closely related agile mangabeys brings proceedings to an abrupt halt. Unlike the grey-cheeked troop, which spends most of its time in the trees, the agile group is moving along close to the ground. It has just had a baby boom, so with competition rife, this super-troop of monkeys travels rapidly through the forest grabbing whatever fruit or insects it finds as quickly as it can. Like looters in a shop, they pull away the bark and strip off leaves from trees, dig out termites from their earthen nest, and even dive into streams to see what they can catch. They steal food and squabble, ruthlessness being the key to an individual's success.

The grey-cheeks hear them coming. An adult male gives a loud and distinctive 'whoop-gobble', air sacs in his throat amplifying the sound, a warning to the neighbours that this patch is occupied. Then, the entire troop falls silent, waiting for a reply. These monkeys rarely come to blows. The troop first at a food source usually stands its ground or approaches the intruders, but this time, with

▲ A column of driver ants has workers of various sizes carrying the colony's larvae and pupae from their old nest to the new site. The ants are blind, but follow chemical trails on the ground. The queen is last to make the journey.

a glut of fruit in the forest, they'll keep out of the other's way. The entire grey-cheeked troop leaves silently, heading in the opposite direction.

A pair of black-and-white casqued hornbills fills the silence. They're key seed dispersers in Afrotropical forests, feasting on the fruits of the forest trees and lianas only to carry the seeds in their gut and deposit them some distance from the parent trees. Their droppings even provide the germinating seeds with a helping of fertiliser, but the trees won't grow tall until one of the ageing trunks falls and a hole is punched in the canopy. Then, it's a race for the light.

The grey-cheeked mangabeys shift a fair number of seeds too, and with large incisors they're exceptionally good at cracking hard nuts, but they're about to do something most monkeys are not expected to do. They're moving through the forest like ghosts, their dark fur blending in with the shadows. Barely a leaf is disturbed, which is a baby duiker's undoing: it doesn't hear them coming. Like a scene from a macabre horror story, a mangabey grabs the unfortunate creature and rips it apart. Blood stains its fur as others in the troop gather around excitedly, each hoping for a piece of meat, but there's not enough for all. The troop moves on, breaking the silence, chattering perhaps about the dramatic moment in an otherwise routine fruit- and seed-gathering life in the trees.

JUNGLE DANDY

With the sound of rustling and the occasional grunt, another large group of animals is moving slowly and deliberately across the forest floor of Lopé National Park in central Gabon. Flashes of red and blue amongst the green foliage confirm the identity of mandrills, and they're foraging. They eat mainly fruit, but will consume leaves, bark, mushrooms and even insects, frogs and eggs, and like their baboon cousins on the savannah they'll catch and eat young duikers and other small antelope.

There are about 40 in the troop, mostly females with young, led by a very big male – the world's largest and most distinctive monkey – for he's exceptionally colourful, a case of testosterone overload. His hormones ensure his muzzle has a bright red stripe, the raised ribbing on either side of the snout is a gaudy electric blue, his lips and nostrils are red, his beard is yellow with white tufts, and his rump is multicoloured – red, pink, blue and purple. When he yawns he shows long canines, and each time he gives a two-tone grunt, it's the signal for the troop to move on. He's the notional boss, but he's only there because his females allow him to be, and there's a young upstart ready to take his place.

The young male sees an opportunity and steps forward to contest the leadership. He struts around, trying to intimidate the dominant male, but his colours are just not bright enough to impress. It's not the male who chases him away, but the females. They determine who goes and who stays, but their current chief is past his best. He has sired all the current crop of babies, and it's beginning to show.

◄ **The male black-and-white casqued hornbill has a larger bill and casque than the female. It not only functions as a sexual display, but also as a large radiator to dissipate body heat and keep the bird cool.**

A few weeks on and the challenger reappears, but this time sporting brighter colours, while the colours of the exhausted incumbent are actually fading. Faced with such a gaudy challenge the current leader simply gives up without any fighting, not even so much as an angry spat. Ostensibly, the troop has a new leader, but he still has to convince the females. They're uncomfortable with the newcomer and reluctant to accept him. It'll take several days, maybe weeks, for him to win them over, but he has time on his side.

Towards the end of the day, the troop clambers into the trees. They'll spend the night up there rather than on the ground. They're turning in a little earlier than usual because there's another kind of storm brewing.

BANANA FROG FACE-OFF

In late afternoon, a huge, dark thundercloud threatens the forest in Sierra Leone. The anvil takes on the colour of a nasty bruise, and it looks menacing, even intimidating, but it's not unusual. Rain falls here throughout the year, usually accompanied by the mother of all storms, but there *are* seasons – wet and dry – and this is the start of the wet, when there's considerably more water in the atmosphere than during the rest of the year. For the next few weeks, as regular as clockwork, the heavens open, lightning rips through the air and thunder seems to shake the very ground itself. Violent gusts of wind thrash the tops of the tallest trees, and rain falls in unbroken curtains.

The plants here have evolved to deal with the daily deluge. The leaves on many rainforest trees have drip tips that ensure water is funnelled away from the surface, reducing the risk of mould and fungal infections, but the wet season's first major downpour is more than just a rain storm that's wetting leaves: it's a trigger. The torrential rain prompts a sudden rush to procreate, and one of the noisiest breeders is the banana frog. As the light fades in the early evening, a male frog does what comes naturally: he heads to the highest point he can reach in the forest's understorey, for that's where the female frogs will go looking for a mate.

On reaching the top of his leaf, the frog finds that he's not alone. Other males had the same idea, and they're already singing loudly; this calls for altogether tougher action than a sing-off. He sidles up to and turns his back on a singing male, and then … boof! He kicks him hard with one of his back legs. The other frog doesn't budge, so he kicks him again, and again. His opponent, meanwhile, is not going to take this lying down and kicks him back, and they exchange a barrage of blows until one of them is kicked off the leaf and has to start the laborious climb to the top all over again.

When the females arrive, the frogs with the best singing spots gain most attention, but the males are taking a great risk by being so conspicuous, even in the dark. They could attract something they hadn't bargained for: spiders.

Large hunting spiders are abroad. They're fast and armed with fangs that deliver potent venom. They're quite capable of catching and overpowering small

▶ **Flashes of red and blue amongst the foliage confirm the identity of mandrills, led by a very big male – the world's largest and most distinctive monkey. He's exceptionally colourful, a case of testosterone overload, and he has sired all the current crop of babies.**

frogs, but even if an amorous pair is spared the worst and consummates its liaison, the female frog still has to find a place to deposit her eggs that's safe not only from spiders, but also those marauding driver ants down below.

The female banana frog has an effective solution: she wraps her small clump of white eggs in a long leaf folded lengthwise. They develop inside their protective origami nest, and a week or so later tadpoles are ready to emerge. It's at this point that the placing of the leaf becomes vitally important. If it is overhanging water or above a pond that fills during the wet season, at the next available deluge the tadpoles are washed out and fall into the water below.

LAKE MINIS AND MONSTERS

The rising water level triggers killifish to hatch too. These little fish live in ephemeral ponds and their eggs have been lying dormant in the moist mud since the end of the last wet period. They must hatch, grow and breed before the pond dries up again: in fact, one species – the turquoise killifish – is just 5 cm (2 inches) long and has the second shortest lifespan of any known vertebrate (the shortest being the coral reef pygmy goby that's found on the Great Barrier Reef). Its desiccation-resistant eggs can survive for up to two years in the mud, but the adult fish dies after a maximum of twelve weeks.

Killifish courtship is therefore short and frantic. The males, recognised by their bright colours, are just five weeks old when they reach sexual maturity. They fight violently, sometimes to the death, and the brighter the fish, the more aggressive its attacks. And, while the large, feisty males are locked in combat, 'sneaky' males can slip in and steal away the ghostly tawny-white females without the big boys even noticing.

During the short time they're on this Earth, killifish eat mosquito larvae (amongst other things), making those living in more permanent water important in the natural control of mosquitoes and the diseases they carry. In parts of Gabon, where rivers have been polluted and killifish are absent, malaria is rife.

A disturbance not in the pool, but in the vegetation at the water's edge betrays another wet season mover. It's not an amphibian, but a fish, a climbing perch or gourami. Using its gill plates, fins and tail, it wriggles through the undergrowth from one pond, over the hill and into a large lake. Part of its first gill arch is modified as a 'labyrinth organ', which enables it to take oxygen directly from the air. As long as it remains moist it can survive out of water for enough time to complete its short journey. Like almost everything else around here, it's time for it to breed, and the bigger body of water offers more opportunities.

On the margins of the lake, the trees come right down to the water's edge, and submerged limbs or broken branches that litter the lakebed hide another oddity. The upside-down catfish is aptly named for its curious habit of swimming belly-up and grazing on algae hanging below submerged logs. The little fish is no more than 10 cm (4 inches) long, with three pairs of barbels and a drab, marbled

◄ **The male banana frog will kick a rival off his leaf so he has a better chance of attracting a female.**

Tadpole cache

(1) Rain droplets collect on leaves in the rainy season, the time when the female banana frog deposits her fertilised eggs on a leaf. (2) She folds it carefully and glues it shut with the eggs safely inside. (3) During a heavy downpour, the hatching tadpoles are washed out. (4) They drop into still water, such as a pond, puddle, ditch or even a shallow rut, where they develop first into froglets and then into full-grown frogs.

colour, yet it attracted the attention of the ancient Egyptians, who included it in their wall paintings. And some species not only swim the wrong way up, but their underside is darker than their back, the opposite way round to most other fish, so these fish blend in with the darkness of the pond when seen from above, even though they're upside down.

Just below the lake surface is a shoal of small fish that do not turn on their backs, even though they are interested in what's above them. They're freshwater butterflyfish, each little more than 13 cm (5 inches) long. An upturned mouth and eyes looking upwards indicate that they are surface predators. They're built to snatch insects and other small creatures from the water's surface, so they're quite capable of taking a banana frog tadpole or two should they plop in: but large and ominous dark shapes cutting through the water below them mean that the little fish could become victims themselves.

The shapes scythe this way and that, approaching perilously close to the smaller fish. Suddenly, all around, butterflyfish are leaping from the water. They wave their unusually large pectoral fins like butterfly wings, and appear to glide. In reality, they acquire the necessary forward motion to get airborne by swimming rapidly to the surface. They're so-called 'ballistic jumpers'. The wiggling fins have little effect, although each fish moves through the air for a short distance that's several times its body length to escape the larger predators below.

However, the biggest and most ferocious predatory fish in these parts is unlikely to pay much attention to tadpoles or tiny fish. After sunset, the lake becomes the exclusive domain of the goliath tigerfish, Africa's equivalent of South America's piranha, though it's not related. Enormous, interlocking razor-sharp teeth and a muscular, bullet-shaped body built for bursts of speed are the hallmarks of a voracious predator that possesses a unique prey detection system. Its gas-filled swim bladder acts as a low-frequency sound receiver, able to pick up vibrations in the water and guide the fish directly to its target, even though it can't see it. A single adult can tackle fish as big as itself, and several together have even been known to attack people. With a length of 1.5 m (5 feet) and weight in excess of 50 kg (110 lb), they're a serious danger, especially as they patrol in small groups. There have been several reported human deaths, especially in the Congo River basin, where the goliath tigerfish has earned an almost mystical reputation amongst anglers as the greatest freshwater game fish in the world.

SANDBANK LIVING

Breeding in the wet season is not universal in tropical Africa. African skimmers wait for the dry season. Their insistent 'kip-kip, kip-kip' shatters the peace of a tall, white egret wading in the shallows as the noisy flock of thirty or so of these tern-like birds surrounds it on a sandbank in the middle of Cameroon's Sanaga River. Despite being sandwiched between two blocks of equatorial coastal forest and fed by rain-soaked highlands inland, the river has dropped significantly and

▶ **When they're ready to fish, the birds fly in a line with slow wing beats, beak open with the lower bill just skimming the surface of the river. If it makes contact with a fish, it automatically snaps shut.**

exposed sandy islands are the perfect place for skimmers and other birds to nest. They nest in loose colonies safe from most predators, although monitor lizards and snakes could, if they were so inclined, swim to the island. The skimmers have chicks in the nest, as many as three for some birds, and parents spend their time either protecting the young from the heat and cold or looking for food.

It's dawn and the noisy gaggle contains mostly parents preparing to go fishing again, as they have been doing on and off throughout the night; and they go about it in a very unusual way. The skimmer's bright red-orange lower bill is longer than the upper one, and flattened like a pair of scissors. When they're ready to fish, the birds fly in a line with slow wing beats, beak open with the lower bill just skimming the surface of the river. If it makes contact with a fish, it automatically snaps shut and the bird's head swings down, catching the fish while the skimmer flies on without stopping.

On the sandbanks, chicks imitate their parents. They run along with heads low, and their beaks skimming the ground. They'll even practise skimming across small puddles, stopping to examine anything – a twig, grass stem or pebble – that they happen to snag.

Their parents bring them real food, the last feed occurring before the light from the sun causes the fish to swim deeper and out of range. Then, it's time to

sit out the intense heat of the day. One of the parents wets its breast feathers in order to keep the chicks cool, but disaster waits for any youngsters caught out in the open. Pied crows swoop in.

Intelligent, resourceful and dangerous, crows and their relatives are a threat to young birds the world over. The parent skimmers try to mob the crows and the chicks themselves are camouflaged with their sand-coloured down and black spots, but it's all to little effect. If a crow has a clear target, it's more than likely to make a hit: an unguarded skimmer chick in its open nest scrape is highly vulnerable to predation and the crows won't leave the skimmers alone until they've collected enough food; after all, pied crows have babies to feed too.

ROCK NEST

Deep in a West African forest, more babies stir. The nest is a simple cup of dried mud, reinforced with grass, dried leaves and lined with moss, built on the underside of a rocky overhang beside a stream. There are two nestlings here and they're the pride and joy of a pair of one of Africa's most elusive birds, the white-necked picathartes or rockfowl. The nest has been reused many times, but is spruced up each year before a brood is raised during the wet season.

The parents have black wing and white body feathers, and the bare skin on their heads is bright yellow with two large black spots behind the eyes. They don't fly much, preferring to hop like kangaroos around the forest while scouring for columns of driver ants. They join mixed flocks of birds that follow the ants and feed on the insects and other small creatures flushed from the undergrowth, occasionally feeding on the ants themselves, although chicks are fed mainly frogs and lizards.

The chicks leave the nest after about twenty-five days, when they're still 30% smaller than their parents. Many will enjoy a long lifespan, for once they become adults, 90% of birds survive into old age.

MATERNITY WOOD

That birds are diligent parents may come as no surprise, but in these forests there is a mother, not only of enormous proportions, but also big on parental care. She's almost 5 m (16 feet) long, eats crocodiles whole, and could squeeze the life out of a human. She's a rock python, Africa's largest and most powerful snake.

Every morning she lies in the sun, so her body is warmed to a near-lethal 40°C (104°F), and then she glides back to her nest in a hollow tree trunk and wraps herself around her brood of about fifty eggs. She holds them so tight that an imprint of her scales can be seen on their surface, and she incubates them like this every day for the ninety days it takes before they hatch. Even then, she'll guard them for another couple of weeks to ensure that predators don't grab the 50 cm (20-inch) long hatchlings. After that, they head out into the forest and they're on their own, taking another thirty years to reach the size of their mother.

◄ The African rock python is a non-venomous constrictor. One of the longest recorded specimens was shot in a bougainvillea hedge in Ivory Coast in 1932. It was 9.81 m (over 32 feet) long. However, most found today average little more than 5 m (16 feet) long.

Picathartes residence

This pair of white-necked picathartes or rockfowl has built its nest below an overhanging rock by a stream in the rainforest. (1) One bird carefully places the nest material for on-the-spot repairs. (2) The other bird heads out to find food for the chicks. (3) Shortly after, it returns with their supper. (4) While parents consume mainly insects, especially driver ants, they catch frogs to feed to their chicks.

FOREST HOGS

African rock pythons are not venomous, so the baby snakes are vulnerable. They disperse under cover of darkness, but they remain on the forest floor where they can fall prey to monitor lizards, birds of prey, big cats and forest pigs, and it's the hogs that are out foraging at night. The local heavyweights are a family of red river hogs. They're led by a large boar, and he certainly wouldn't turn up his nose at a defenceless snake, although it's a tree dropping fruit by the bucketful that's attracted them to this part of the forest.

The hogs are resplendent in reddish-brown coats, with white ear tufts and a white stripe along the spine. White face markings contrast with a black nose, and the boar has large tusk-like lumps on either side of his muzzle, making them almost clown-like. They all snuffle through the leaf litter on the forest floor, using their energetic snouts to root for fruit, seeds, berries and mushrooms, as well as slugs and snails, insects, small vertebrates and even carrion. As the hogs push on through the trees, they leave behind another of nature's mysteries.

Where the hogs have disturbed the thin rainforest soil, there are patches of bright green bioluminescence. Microscopic fungi cause it, the result of a chemical reaction between the enzyme luciferase and the chemical luciferin. The pygmy people call it 'chimpanzee fire', but in England and Japan it's known as 'foxfire'. Even Aristotle wrote about it in 382 BC, but why the fungi glow is as big a mystery now as it was then.

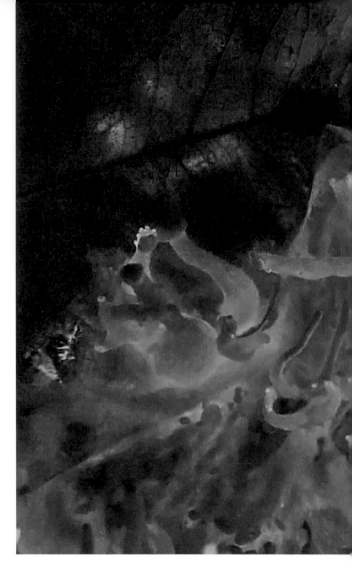

▲ As the hogs push on through the trees, they leave behind another of nature's mysteries. Where they have disturbed the thin rainforest soil, there are patches of bright green bioluminescence. The pygmy people call it 'chimpanzee fire'. ◉

VILLAGE OF ELEPHANTS

In the heavy darkness of night, long, low rumblings permeate the rainforest. They're more felt than heard and difficult to pinpoint, with most of the sound below the threshold of human hearing. Other than that the callers are remarkably quiet; hardly a footfall can be heard, which is quite something when you realise that the largest of them is 2.5 m (8.2 feet) tall at the shoulder and can weigh up to 6 tonnes (13,200 lb). These are the biggest creatures in the forest – forest elephants – which many people recognise as a separate species from savannah elephants.

They're following well-worn tracks that zigzag through the forest, each elephant using its trunk to check for malevolent odours on the path ahead, like a blind person using a stick, only elephants use smell rather than touch or hearing. The small family herd includes a mother with twins, unusual for elephants. The youngsters stay close to her, occasionally reaching up for a mouthful of milk, but she won't stop now for the family has almost reached its destination.

As the moon emerges from behind a cloud, they step out from the forest and into a vast clearing. All around are other elephants, some standing, others drinking or digging. The small group walks towards another family. They were once in the same herd, but it split and each group went its separate ways.

But now, after months apart, they greet each other with much trumpeting, rumbling, ear waving and touching of trunks. Others look up to see what the fuss is about, and then go about their own business.

There are nearly a hundred elephants scattered about the place, for in the dry season they converge here from all points of the compass. It's known locally (and indeed internationally) as *Dzanga Bai*, meaning 'the village of elephants'. The clearing is located in the Dzanga-Ndoki National Park in the southwest corner of the Central African Republic, and even though the rains have slackened, parts of the sandy floor are still flooded with water from the Dzanga stream.

The elephants come here throughout the year for a dietary supplement: they dig minerals from the soil. The large males use their feet and downward-pointing tusks to dig the biggest holes, while the females use their trunks to blast minerals from the swamp bed under any standing water. During the dry season, however, there are many more animals and many more holes, the swelling congregation here for a very different reason.

Several large males stand apart from the others. They raise their trunks from time to time, smelling the air for signs of people, their greatest enemy, and other dangers. For most of the night, some of the bulls have been hanging around an especially large hole made by an especially large elephant. He's the biggest bull to visit the clearing. He has the best mineral site, so the other bulls wait for him to leave before squabbling amongst themselves for the right to dig there.

Fluid oozing from pores on the sides of his head, however, shows that he's in 'musth' and on the lookout for potential mates. This is when he's at his most dangerous. He gives short thrift to any young upstart that challenges his position, chasing them mercilessly, kicking up water and prodding them with his tusks; but entering the clearing is a second large bull. He sports large, straight tusks, a circular notch in one ear and a hole in the other, and this male is less likely to give way. There's going to be a fight.

The two huge animals square up to one another, their trunks extended almost horizontally as they sniff for some kind of recognition. The larger animal places his trunk on top of the smaller one's head, the tips of his tusks directly in front of the other bull's eyes. If this is meant to intimidate, it doesn't work. The smaller elephant raises his head and lays his trunk on his opponent's trunk, and the two gently push. First one takes a step back, and then the other. They part, raise their trunks, and re-engage, but after a short tussle the challenger backs down, exiting as gracefully as a defeated elephant can.

PREVIOUS PAGES **A handful of forest elephants visit the clearing at Dzanga Bai to obtain minerals from the ground to supplement their diet. Bulls dig with their tusks and feet, and females blast muddy puddles using their trunks.**

▶ **A forest elephant goes beachcombing in Gabon's Loango National Park. The tracks of hippopotamuses, buffalo, lowland gorillas and leopards may also be found in the sand.**

At that moment, a bongo emerges from the forest at the southern end of the clearing. It's joined by several more until a dozen or so are milling about, wary of the sparring elephants. Their brown to auburn coats and narrow white, vertical stripes may help camouflage them in the jungle, but in the moonlight these striking antelope stand out starkly against the churned-up mud. The males sport massive, lyre-shaped, swept-back horns with a single twist, while the females' horns are noticeably smaller and more parallel. Their ears twist constantly to ward off flies. The group takes a few paces forward. Like the elephants, the bongos are here for the minerals, and under cover of darkness they make the most of what the elephants have dug up.

At dawn the bongos melt back into the forest while the large bull elephant stands guard over a female coming into heat, rumbling almost imperceptibly, and the other elephants continue their mining; and, with the light arrive new prospectors. Forest buffalo wallow in the yellow clay, red river hogs root about in it, and swarms of milky-white butterflies drop down to drink the mineral-rich water. Bee-eaters hawk for insects, waders probe for anything that squirms, and the big elephant almost chokes on a trunk-full of water. He can't believe his eyes. Racing straight towards him is his challenger again, and he has fire in his eyes.

The two bulls engage, the smaller animal having the advantage of momentum. They push violently, until they all but disappear into a dust cloud made from the dried mud shaken from their bodies. The tension and noise level rise abruptly as the other elephants seem to egg them on. They trumpet, scream and roar, and some family groups with very young offspring run to the safety of the forest lest they be trampled in the fight. Then, the larger bull turns and runs, crashing into and demolishing a dead tree as he goes. The challenger is close behind, stabbing at his rear as he disappears ignominiously into the forest. The king has been deposed; long live the new king!

BESIDE THE SEASIDE

Another elephant, in another place seemingly a world away, shifts his enormous foot to reveal a ghost crab standing right alongside it. The little crustacean scuttles away as the equally enormous trunk sweeps down to pick up seaweed from the strand line. Not far away a hippopotamus wallows in the surf, and a forest buffalo stands nonchalantly close to the water's edge, his back to the sea like some Bank Holiday sunbather.

It's an unusual and, perhaps, unexpected scene, but it's a regular everyday occurrence for rainforest animals at Loango Beach in Gabon; at least, those lucky enough to live at the edge of the Atlantic Ocean. They're lucky for several reasons: on the open beach they'll see predators approaching; there are fewer biting flies and other insects; and sea spray coats any vegetation nearby with a thin layer of salt, a useful addition to their diet.

▶ **A hippopotamus wallows in the surf, an unusual and unexpected sight, but in fact a regular everyday occurence for rainforest animals lucky enough to live at the edge of the Atlantic Ocean.**

In a shallow creek, a troop of rare red-capped mangabeys explores the tangle of mangroves, where they gnaw on the plant's aerial roots for their fix of salt. Their cackles and barks echo through the trees as they keep in contact with each other and signal their position to neighbouring groups. They move with their tails arched over their backs, the white tip held just above the head, and occasionally they flash their conspicuous white eyelids. There are a couple of males, but the rest are females and their young, and they seem to live peacefully together; no squabbling. They usually forage for fruits, young leaves and the odd insect, but they have strong incisor teeth for cracking hard seeds, nuts and thick-skinned fruits, which gives them an advantage over many of the other monkeys with which they share the forest.

On the beach, the lone buffalo is joined by several others of his kind, the small herd almost obscured by a fine mist from the breaking waves. They graze the salt-laden grass above the tide-line, accompanied by a busy entourage of expectant cattle egrets and oxpeckers; but with midday fast approaching, one by one they flop to the ground, some hidden in the low vegetation, their flicking tails the only giveaway, and others sitting, chewing the cud at the edge of the sea. Tropical Africa's coastal rainforest seems a strangely idyllic world … at least for now.

CHAPTER FOUR

CAPE

A maelstrom builds regularly off the southern tip of South Africa. Warm and cold ocean currents fight against opposing winds, often blowing at 180 km/h (112 mph), to produce rogue waves, huge breaking walls of water the size of ten-storey buildings that come, quite literally, out of the blue. Since 1990 more than 20 vessels have been struck by freak waves off the South African 'Wild Coast', and one of these rogues was thought to have overwhelmed the SS *Waratah* – Australia's *Titanic* – that disappeared without trace between Durban and Cape Town in 1909.

Seal Island in False Bay, South Africa

It's a phenomenon that was recognised when Europeans first rounded the Cape of Good Hope, for ancient mariners were more than wary of a treacherous but warm southward-flowing current that brushes southern Africa's east coast. Its name is the *Agulhas Current*, and it was already well known by the mid-1500s when Portuguese trading ships were forced to sail far offshore on their way to the Orient, and close, but not too close, to the African shore on the voyage home. It's narrow and fast, one of the world's most powerful ocean currents and the second fastest, after the Gulf Stream. As it reaches the Cape, it fights icy currents heading north from the Antarctic and swirls into the Indian and South Atlantic oceans in great eddies, influencing profoundly the circulation, salinity and productivity of both.

For Africa itself, the Agulhas brings not death, but life. The weather patterns that it feeds invigorate what otherwise would be a barren landscape. Instead, large swathes of Mozambique and South Africa are lush and fertile, with a profusion of secret, almost magical places, some directly at the coast, others far inland, and in an age when few parts of the world are unexplored, they're only just being discovered.

EPIC RACE FOR LIFE

First a dusty head and then a pair of disproportionately large flippers push up through the sand: a turtle hatchling, no more than 7 cm (3 inches) across and a dirty grey colour, appears on the surface of the dune. Its limbs flail about wildly as it stretches and strains every tiny muscle in trying to free itself from the clinging sand. It had been incubating for two months underground, before breaking out of its leathery egg case and digging its way upwards, the danger of being buried alive never far away. It and its nest mates – over a hundred of them – waited patiently just below the surface for the right moment to make the final push.

A sudden drop in temperature at sunset was the trigger. Now, in the twilight, the baby turtle finally emerges, but the pit from which it has tried to escape collapses. It's near disaster. The turtle tumbles back down, but it's still on top of the heap, so it scrambles over the tangle of heads and flippers of the other hatchlings and heaves itself onto the surface of the sand. The brightness of the sea in front and the darkness of the land behind the nest ensure that this tiny scrap of life heads in the right direction, but there are many obstacles blocking its route, and the youngster has the dubious distinction of being a handy bite-

▶ **Breaking out of its leathery egg case and digging its way upwards, for a baby turtle the danger of being buried alive is never far away. All around it, other babies are making the same headlong rush to the sea ... but not all will make it.** ◉

sized packet of protein, so there are many here taking a close interest in its first journey to the sea … in fact, its first journey anywhere.

Flotsam, washed up and dumped on the shore, becomes an insurmountable barrier, and even ripples in the sand slow down the hatchling's dash across the beach. It must not stop, but keep on going. It has to reach the water's edge in the shortest possible time. Its life depends on it. Its limbs are actually adapted for swimming but it's exceptionally nimble over the sand. On dry, loose sand it moves forward by pushing against the solid wedge of sand particles that forms behind its flippers, and when it reaches the wet sand it advances by digging in with a claw on each flipper so it doesn't slip.

▼ When they emerge from the sand, green sea turtle hatchlings head unerringly towards the sea, but all manner of dangers are waiting for them on the beach. Most make their run at night, when fewer predators are about, but the latecomers must run the gauntlet in daylight and as a consequence the casualty figures rise.

All around it, other baby turtles are making the same headlong rush to the sea. They come from the many hundreds of nests dotted along the beach, but not all will make it. Pied crows swoop down and pick off any hatchlings tangled in tide-line debris, and ghost crabs intercept many of those that do get through, hauling them into their burrows in the sand before tearing them literally limb from limb. It will be a miracle if even a handful reach the ocean, for the first wave of hatchlings bears the brunt of attacks; but the sacrifice of a few hundred ensures that the following thousands have a better chance of making it to the sea.

The hatchling is a baby green sea turtle, born on the island of Mwali (Moheli) in the Comoros Archipelago. She's a female, as are all her nest mates, their sex determined by the temperature of their nest. While the eggs were incubating, the temperature of the sand regularly rose above 29°C (84.2°F), so the entire clutch are females. Below 26°C (78.8°F) and they would have been males. It means that this little female hatchling will be out at sea until her twentieth birthday, when she'll return to this same beach to deposit her first batch of eggs in the sand … that is, if she ever reaches the water's edge. Only 30% make it this far, and the beach is only the first hazard. In the shallows there are more predators waiting and more obstacles to negotiate.

The hatchling swims powerfully, her head down and flippers pulling hard against the water. As she comes up for air she switches to doggy-paddling, raises her head above the surface for a quick breath, and then powers on through the surf, except that at 25 g (less than an ounce) the baby is turned over in the breaking waves and battered against the sand.

On reaching clear water beyond the surf line she surfaces for air again. It's what the kites have been waiting for. They swoop down and scoop hatchlings from the surface, and even those hidden below are not safe. There are sharks offshore ready to intercept them on their way to deeper water. Even fewer will have made it this far, but the little female ploughs on towards the open sea, though her pace is gradually slowing, until it levels off after about twelve hours. All the while, she's been swimming almost non-stop using the remnants of her yolk sac for energy; and she carries over ten times more yolk than she needs in her break for freedom so that she can keep going without feeding for up to fourteen days.

By that time, she'll be swept along in the Mozambique Channel in a series of enormous anti-cyclonic eddies, each up to 300 km (186 miles) across. Where she and all the other survivors go for the next twenty years is a mystery (and only one in a thousand survives to adulthood), but wherever that might be will depend on the strength and direction of the ocean currents, especially those in the Mozambique Channel, birthplace as well of the formidable Agulhas Current.

The equatorial sun to the north powers the system, and it swirls inexorably southwards between Madagascar and the African mainland. Here, it strongly influences the climate of much of Mozambique, one factor that helps maintain an extraordinary and unexpected diversity of fauna and flora unsurpassed in much of the rest of Africa.

▶ **On reaching the water, the hatchling heads for the open sea, searching for upwellings where food is concentrated. It will live in the ocean for up to five years, feeding on zooplankton and small marine creatures, before heading for sea grass meadows along the shore where, while still an immature juvenile, it becomes a herbivore.**

A LOST EDEN

Mozambique may have suffered 15 horrific years of civil war, and the landmines and other debris from the conflict are still in evidence, but this sustained separation from outsiders means that, apart from the large mammals that were killed for bushmeat, the country has kept much of its natural richness, and even today great swathes of it are almost unknown and unexplored. Thus, a team of naturalists led by the Royal Botanic Gardens at Kew in London chanced upon a hidden mountain forest, which was discovered, at least initially, not in the field, but on Google Earth. They were searching Africa for unexplored wildlife hotspots and then trekking to each to see what was there. They hit the jackpot at Mt. Mabu, one of the many inselbergs or isolated granite hills and mountains that dot the Mozambique countryside. It appears on few maps or charts and was kept secret by locals who found refuge here during the civil war, so the area escaped any development and most of the disturbances.

Inselbergs resemble islands in the sea, often rounded like sugar loaves, but Mt. Mabu is different: it's cloaked in virgin forest and soaked in rain delivered care of the warm waters of the Indian Ocean, the largest medium-elevation rainforest in southern Africa, and home to an assemblage of plants and animals that is entirely new to science.

◀▲ In the lush mountain rainforests (left) on Mt. Mabu, delicate butterflies – some entirely new to science – emerge from their chrysalis cases (top right) before heading up the slopes to the mountaintop to dance in an extraordinary 'butterfly ball'.

There's a pygmy chameleon, a new species of tropical mistletoe, and a bush viper whose nearest relatives live more than 1,500 km (930 miles) away in the Congo Basin. It all suggests that the Congo rainforest once reached into northern Mozambique, and that when it receded, it left behind plants and animals that became isolated on these rain-sodden hills and evolved into unique species and sub-species, like the finches on Galapagos. Now, some live on Mt. Mabu and virtually nowhere else in the world.

Four new species of butterfly are on the list, but even more exciting is the way that they behave. Tracking the rivulets and streams, the butterflies rise gradually towards the summit, 1,700 m (5,577 feet) above sea level, dancing up through the rainforest to break out above the tree line, a location for the most extraordinary butterfly ball. Thousands of males fill the sky, engaged in aerial dogfights, each battling to the death for the right to mate. It takes place for just a few weeks each year, and for a few hours each morning. Swifts scythe through the air picking off the distracted insects, and peregrines fly overhead ready to swoop on the smaller birds.

▼ **Thousands of male butterflies fill the sky, engaged in aerial dogfights, each battling to the death for the right to mate. Swifts scythe through the air picking off the distracted insects, and peregrines swoop overhead.** ◉

And what goes up must surely come down: not only the mated females who return to the forest to lay their eggs, but also the rain. The torrential rain gathers in mountain streams and flows from the peaks, cascading down in spectacular waterfalls and winding limestone gorges to the floodplain below. Here the sediment in rivers and lakes nourishes life on a grand scale.

WHERE NOAH LEFT HIS ARK

A strange pattern of bubbles forms on the surface of Lake Urema. It's early morning and there's little wind so the water is flat and calm. A wispy mist drifts gently over the lake as more large bubbles burst, but the bubble blower fails to appear.

Lake Urema is to the southwest of Mt. Mabu, set in the marshes and savannah lands of the Gorongosa National Park, an area twice the size of London at the southern end of Africa's Great Rift Valley. Dominating the park is forest-clad Mt. Gorongosa, which acts like a sponge, regulating the flow of water into the park, itself a meeting place for rivers arriving from three points of the compass.

It's August and the peak of the hot, dry season. The lake has shrunk and the flat, exposed land is covered with grass. Patches of bushes and trees mark where the edge of the lake would have been during the wet season at the beginning of the year, when water levels were higher, but now the water has gone. Knobthorns, flame creepers and fever trees are in flower, and, with much rumbling and the occasional trumpet, a small herd of elephants socialises in a grove of drought-resistant apple-ring acacias on the fringe of the floodplain.

All around are the many species of birds that survived the widespread slaughter of wildlife during the civil war. Now, they reap the benefits of having been almost sole occupants of the lakeside and wetlands for many years. Yellow-billed storks and African darters fly over in untidy groups, while a flight of white-faced ducks streams past, whistling as they fly. A gang of pink-backed pelicans squabble for the best places on a palm tree, while a flock of their great white cousins wheel together before settling on the lake for their first fishing expedition of the day. A kingfisher hovers, drops with a plop, and then rises again with a small silver fish in its bill. A white-backed vulture, like some sinister sentinel, perches motionless on the branch of a dead tree, his eyes firmly locked on to a fish eagle dissecting its prey in the branches of a tall acacia. A marabou stork catches small catfish in a drying pool, while a black-headed heron looks on, waiting for the more aggressive and bad-tempered bird to move off. It's just the everyday activities of predators hunting and fishing at Lake Urema, but below its surface lurk hunters of a very different kind.

Offshore, the bubbles continue, a sure sign of activity below, although the perpetrator is hard to spot. It's an enormous catfish, and its slippery, dark brown skin blends in with the muddy water near the lakebed. More usually nocturnal, it's still hunting at sunrise, not the best time for catfish (or any other fish, come to that) to be out and about. Even giant catfish have enemies.

It's eel-like and over a metre (more than 3 feet) long, with an impressive array of cat-like whiskers or barbels, each lined with rows of external taste buds for finding food in murky water and even in the dark. A group of them blows bubbles to trap fish; a 'bubblenet'. Working together they have more success than fishing alone, but even enormous fish like these could be prey for something bigger. Too large to fall prey to any bird, even one as powerful as a fish eagle, a mature catfish must avoid just one animal in the lake – the Nile crocodile. Row upon row of these monster crocs are hauled out on the shore, and one by one they slide silently into the water. They've not spotted the bubbles, but they *have* seen the pelicans fishing, and where there are pelicans, there are bound to be fish and maybe more besides.

The birds are bunched together, thrusting their voluminous bills into the water together like synchronised swimmers. They also herd shoals of small fish into the shallows then dip in unison and grab what they can; but one bird has trapped a catfish by mistake. It's far too big, and the splashing attracts the wrong kind of attention. Suddenly, the pelicans explode into the air, but the one struggling with the big fish is just not quick enough. A crocodile grabs the bird, pulls it below and drowns it. The enormous reptile glides away from the others to swallow its kill in peace. It'll eat meat, bones, feathers, claws – the lot – for it can digest just about anything and quickly too, and it does it in a unique way.

The crocodile has a four-chambered heart (like we do) but it can revert to a more primitive system when needed. Normally de-oxygenated blood is shunted to the lungs via the pulmonary artery, but when the crocodile has eaten, the animal can divert carbon dioxide-rich blood towards the stomach, where gastric glands use it to boost the production of gastric acid. It's so effective that the crocodile produces ten times more gastric acid than has been recorded in any other animal. It means it'll soon be ready to grab and digest something else. The catfish, meanwhile, lies remarkably still on the bottom mud. With so much activity, it won't blow another bubble until sunset.

Above the surface, the cacophony of panicking birds is broken by the familiar laughing grunt of a hippopotamus: that it's here at all is surprising. It hasn't lived here long, and it didn't walk here on its own. The hippo came by truck, one of a continuous stream of large mammals translocated from other parks, such as the Kruger, to restock Gorongosa.

Gorongosa was once a safari treasure house – wildebeest, Selous' zebra, elephants, lions, hippos, reedbuck, eland, sable and hartebeest, and 14,000 Cape buffalo, the greatest concentration in all of Africa, but during the war the butchers took their toll. Now, thanks to an initiative financed by US philanthropist Greg Carr (of voicemail fame), Gorongosa's wildlife and its former glory are returning, so that the site once affectionately described as 'the place where Noah left his Ark' will again be home to one of Africa's most diverse wildlife communities.

▲ Pied kingfishers are almost always seen near water. The female (on left) is recognised by the broken band of black across her chest. The two birds are engaged in their courtship display.

OVERLEAF Pelicans fish cooperatively on Lake Urema. They corral shoals of small fish in the shallows and then simultaneously dip their enormous bills into the water to trap what they can.

ISLANDS OF SAND

Gorongosa's Lake Urema drains into the Pungue River, one of many great rivers, including Livingstone's mighty Zambezi and Kipling's 'the great grey-green, greasy' Limpopo, which flow languidly into the Mozambique Channel. Danger in these waterways comes not only from crocodiles and hippos, but also from sharks. The bull shark, known locally as the Zambezi shark, is one of the few sharks able to enter rivers and survive in fresh water. In 2009, the largest bull shark ever recorded – a 4 m (13 feet) long female – was found about 30 km (18 miles) up the Breede River in neighbouring South Africa, and records show that over the years people, livestock and even hippos have been attacked some distance from the sea. On one day in January 1970, a bull shark attacked three children swimming near Gijana, 150 km (93 miles) inland on the Limpopo, and in January 1961, a child was attacked on the same river when five bull sharks were spotted upriver between 190 and 240 km (120–150 miles) from the coast.

The source of the Limpopo is the dry heart of southern Africa, and during its great arc to the sea this sluggish waterway collects and washes an extraordinary quantity of sediment into the Indian Ocean. During the rise and fall of sea levels in the last Ice Age, the river mouth discharged thousands of years of accumulated sediments into the sea, the sands and sediments carried by wind and waves to turn the river's ancient delta deposits into the rock and sand islands of the Bazaruto Archipelago, an extension of the mainland peninsula of Cabo São Sebastião.

The archipelago's warm, shallow waters are brimming with undersea life, including the largest and only remaining viable population of dugongs or sea cows in the western part of the Indian Ocean. They thrive on the Bazaruto's sea

ABOVE Detail of starfish, in waters off Bazaruto Archipelago

◀ In the swirling tides, the male anchors himself to a sea grass stem with his tail, and as darkness falls, he expels his babies one by one, each miniature sea horse the spitting image of its parents.

grass meadows, not seaweeds but five species of flowering plants, related to water lilies and pondweeds, which thrive in saltwater. The beds are flushed twice each day by the tides, but if you look very carefully, you'll see not cows but horses – sea horses. The archipelago harbours one of the least-known species of sea horses in the world, the diminutive giraffe sea horse.

Like all sea horses, the male carries the eggs and later the hatched babies, in a pouch on the ventral or front-facing side of his tail. Curiously, he secretes prolactin, the same hormone that stimulates milk production in female mammals, but although he doesn't actually supply milk as such, it will help ensure that all his babies receive the nutrients and the oxygen they need to grow. Each morning, his life-long partner visits for the 'morning greeting' ceremony, during which they blush a change of colour, before going their separate ways to feed. After a couple of weeks it's time for the big event.

In the swirling tides, the male anchors himself to a sea grass stem with his tail, and as darkness falls, he expels his babies one by one, each miniature sea horse the spitting image of its parents. The tide washes them out to sea where, nourished by the ocean currents, they'll grow before returning, like the turtles, to the places they were born. At the entrances to the lagoons, such is the number of hungry mouths waiting for them – including giant whale sharks and squadrons of manta rays – that barely one baby sea horse in two hundred will make that return to Bazaruto.

▶ A giant moray eel emerges from the coral ready to lunge at any unfortunate fish that are passing too close. The eel has a secondary set of jaws, which it uses to pull food down into its throat.

A DANCE OF GIANTS

To the south of Bazaruto, off Mozambique's southern-most coast, the eddies of the Mozambique Channel join with the East Madagascar Current to feed the narrow, swift and warm Agulhas Current. The water and all of floating life immersed in it (including, no doubt, a certain sea turtle hatchling growing a little every minute) is propelled southwestwards at about 6 knots (6.9 mph) to the Wild Coast of South Africa.

En route, all manner of predatory fishes are there with a mind to catch the youngster. Blue-fin jacks and silversides pin their shimmering prey against coral reef walls, barracudas hover in the water column ready to dart forward in a blink of an eye, and giant moray eels lurk amongst the corals ready to seize anything within reach, but the acknowledged king of the bony fishes in these parts is the kingfish or giant trevally. Weighing 80 kg (176 lb) and up to 1.7 m (5.5 feet) long, this fish is a brute with an astonishing turn of speed, but it has a secret: like the bull shark, it tolerates fresh water, so can embark on an unexpected journey, not out in the ocean, but inland.

The kingfish swim slowly and with purpose, scything forwards against the slow-moving current of South Africa's remote Mtentu River. It's one of the few watercourses in these parts that is free from the influence of people – pristine, no pollution or silting up – two good reasons these fish can be here, but *why* they're here is another matter.

Passing a sand bar near the river mouth, the shoal heads upstream through a thickly forested gorge. Further inland, the shady, south-facing, rocky banks are lined with the feathery fronds of the multi-stemmed Pondoland palms. They're 'living fossils', being the remnants of a lineage of palm trees that was once common across southern Africa. The Mtentu River is one of only two places in the world where they still grow. A troop of baboons forages for the miniature coconut fruits, and as the dark shadows of the kingfish pass upstream, a large male barks an alarm, only to settle back down and concentrate on the task at hand.

When these normally solitary ocean hunters reach a wide, deep pool many kilometres from the sea, the shoal turns back on itself and begins a strange but mesmerising dance, during which the fish follow a figure-of-eight path in the river. No one knows why. They appear not to mate or to spawn as salmon do; they just swim in what seems a deliberate, choreographed routine, occasionally turning onto their sides so their silver bellies flash in the sun. To us, the frontier appears well defined, but these kingfish are blurring the boundary between land and sea in one of Africa's enduring mysteries.

▲ The lazy Mtentu River winds its way down to the 'Wild Coast' of Eastern Cape in South Africa. Heading upriver, between the towering rocky cliffs, are shoals of giant kingfish, or trevally, a marine species that makes forays into fresh water.

▶ A shoal of giant kingfish plays out its mysterious underwater ballet, the fish following a figure-of-eight pattern as they embark on their journey from the ocean into the River Mtentu.

BARRIER OF SPEARS

Push a little further inland away from the coast and you reach the mountains – the Drakensberg Mountains, known to the Zulu people as *uKhahlamba* – 'barrier of spears', where the vultures fly so high they are said to see into the future. Here, sheer cliffs of ancient fine-grained volcanic basalt rock and spectacular waterfalls tower over yellowwood forests and riverine bush with small herds of eland and oribi, the occasional blesbok and black wildebeest, and large troops of chacma baboons. At 3,482 m (11,424 feet), *Thabana Ntlenyana*, meaning 'beautiful little mountain', is southern Africa's highest peak, and like so many of Drakensberg's mountains it is snow-capped in winter. It's located in Lesotho, itself the highest country in the world.

Down the aeons, weathering has reduced the height of most of the Drakensberg range, yet they still pose a formidable barrier to weather systems blowing in from the sea. To the east is a relatively green and pleasant land, thanks to the Agulhas Current and the Indian Ocean; to the west, however, beyond the plateau of the Highveld, so few storms penetrate that in some places it's hard to find

◀ Like a great wall, the Drakensberg Range (meaning 'dragon mountains') is the highest in South Africa, and the most southerly in Africa.

▼ (AND OVERLEAF) The 1,000 km (600-mile) long arid region of Namaqualand is transformed in early springtime as millions of flowers bloom at the same time in places where the landscape appears barren for most of the rest of the year.

a single blade of grass on the vast, dry basin that is the Kalahari (see Chapter 1).

It's not a true desert, for on average it receives more than 250 mm (10 inches) of rain annually. However, severe droughts do occur here on a seven-year cycle, so surface water is scarce, rivers cease to flow, and water is at a premium. The Boteti River, which should drain from the Okavango Delta wetlands, has had no water for over a decade, and any rain that does fall drains away rapidly through the 150 m (492 feet) deep Kalahari sand or evaporates in the sun.

THE BLOOMING DESERT

Move further to the west, beyond the Kalahari, and you hit the sea once more, but it's a sea with a difference. On South Africa's west coast the influence on climate is not from the tepid currents of the Indian Ocean, but from the Atlantic and the ice-cold Benguela Current that flows northwards from the Antarctic. Cold currents release considerably less moisture to the air than warm ones so rainclouds are scarce. It is hot and dry here, summer temperatures on the Richtersveld peaking at 50°C (122°F), but there is often a brief respite each morning as fog banks push in from the ocean. The amount of moisture is modest, but together with regular winter rains, it is sufficient for the Namaqualand desert to bloom, albeit briefly, in early spring (August or September), depending on the arrival of the first rains and the temperature of the soil. What was, for most of the year, bare earth is turned into a vibrant yellow, orange and purple carpet of daisies, the richest bulb flora of any arid region on Earth.

Home sweet home

Male monkey beetles occupy the flower heads of Namaqualand daisies. (1) The beetles fight for the right to be sole residents, and do all they can to evict any rivals. (2) The winner not only has the nutritious pollen all to himself, but also is ready to welcome any female who might happen to drop in.

Moisture also wakens the dead … or, at least, the dormant. Look carefully below the stems and down in the soil something stirs – a monkey beetle – freshly emerged from the underground pupa case in which he metamorphosed from a white grub into a vividly colourful beetle. He has just ten days to reproduce, and the bowl of a freshly opened daisy flower is just the place to find a mate. Around here, of all the insect pollinators, the monkey beetle is the most abundant flower visitor, and the daisies depend on them, for they too must be pollinated and set seed in the few days before the hot, dry weather returns. Pale or dark patches of colour at the base of petals or sepals – so-called 'beetle marks' – attract the insects. And this little beetle is not the only male in town. He will have to fight his rivals with his long back legs for the right to a female, and the push-and-shove contest is held right here in the flower, each trying to throw the other to the ground. Win or lose, inevitably, they'll get covered with pollen so when they land on another bloom they'll inadvertently help in its pollination. Their reward is not the flower's more usual reservoir of nectar, but the pollen itself, and they have pollen-cracking 'molars' on their mouthparts for the purpose.

Meanwhile, the flower tracks with the sun, so the surface has its own microclimate. This also benefits the monkey beetle, for he is bathed in warm sunshine throughout the day, but at night – when the area is swamped by onshore mists and the air temperature drops significantly – the petals close around the beetle and he remains safe and sound inside the insulated flowerhead: his very own sleeping bag.

CAPE JESTERS

Down at the coast, a seabird waddles unsteadily but upright out of the surf. At first sight, the bird – a penguin – seems out of place on an African shore, but the African penguin is one of several species that are found not around the Antarctic or on sub-Antarctic islands where penguins are usually portrayed, but surprisingly close to the tropics.

The young female is returning from an exhausting 50 km (30 mile) fishing trip to catch fresh fish for her offspring. Her body is insulated against the cold with a thick layer of feathers, but the air temperature here is a complete contrast to the frigid Benguela waters. She's four years old, and this is her first proper breeding season. Her partner, who will likely remain her mate for life, relinquishes their eggs in a nest hollow, and after much braying, bowing, neck stretching and grooming, she takes over incubation duties. She'll remain here for two or three days at least, trying to keep her eggs cool by day and warm at night.

For a penguin, with those insulating feathers, the searing heat of midday is the worst. She opens her bill and points it to the sky, panting to lose heat. All around her, other birds are following suit, but for one neighbour the sun is just too intense. He abandons his eggs and waddles off to the cool of the sea. When the temperature reaches an unbearable 40°C (104°F) several others follow.

◄ **With temperatures soaring during summer heat waves, some African penguins abandon their nests and eggs and head for the cool of the ocean, missing an entire breeding season. This mother valiantly tries to stay with her chicks.**

Penguins are just not built for such heat, and in especially hot years not a single egg hatches; they're all abandoned to the gulls.

The female sticks it out; her only company a few other penguins sheltering from the sun and a girdle lizard that relishes it. Her partner will be away at sea for up to ten days. The warm winds along the west coast blow mainly from the land to the sea. This generates upwellings that draw up nutrient-rich bottom waters to the surface to fuel a food chain that includes penguins. The male feeds in the cold, fish-rich waters (that's if the purse seine nets have not reached there first – trawlers fish all the way from southern Namibia, around the Cape, to KwaZulu-Natal). Three days later he returns to his nest and rookery on St Croix, one of 27 known penguin breeding sites. Most of these are on remote islands to avoid land predators, but there are three sites on the mainland.

While he was away, the 40-day incubation period came to an end and the first chick broke out of its egg, followed shortly by the other. Walking unsteadily across the slippery rocks, he meets his two offspring for the very first time. For the first couple of weeks the chicks are unable to regulate their body temperature so their parents must brood them constantly, and when they do finally emerge one parent must be alert to the predatory attention of kelp gulls while the other goes fishing. The parent on guard stands with its back to the sun so its feet, flippers, and face are shaded and it pants to increase cooling.

When the time comes to leave the nest, the youngsters will go alone. They'll perfect their hunting skills, diving down 30 m (100 feet) for a couple of minutes at a time at speeds of 20 km/h (12 mph) in pursuit of fish, and they'll be at sea for a year or two, before returning to the beach where they hatched to moult. Four years on they'll have chicks themselves and the whole cycle will move on again; that's if dramatic changes in the environment allow it.

SEA CHANGE

Overfishing has caused a collapse of the sardine population in the Benguela Current. Off the Namibian coast, jellyfish and salps have taken over, and they're especially good at filtering off the zooplankton that fish would normally eat, even consuming the eggs and larvae of any fish that have survived. Jellyfish and salps, however, are no substitute for fish in seabird diets.

In the past, the fish stocks of the Benguela have fluctuated wildly and the seabirds have adapted, but the new threat is more sinister. Other creatures that normally rely on the sardines and anchovies have also been forced to switch to different foods. The local population of Cape fur seals has taken to eating seabirds: the most dramatic incident occurred at Lambert's Bay where the seals invaded Cape gannet breeding colonies and ate hundreds of adult birds. The seals have also laid siege to Malgas Island, to the south. Here the attacks are not on land but in the sea, and they kill about 6,000 fledglings a year, which represents about 80% of the year's new birds.

▶ **The African penguin is one of several species that are found not around the Antarctic where penguins are usually portrayed, but surprisingly close to the tropics.** ◉

Compounding the problem are kelp gulls. They take unattended eggs and chicks. At Malgas, just ten pairs of gulls steal 5–10 gannet eggs each day, which can add up to thousands across the season. Gulls are inveterate opportunists, so it is no surprise to find them raiding the gannet colonies, but a new kid on the block is totally unexpected.

With such a dearth of fish, gannet parents often go to sea at the same time, leaving their chick unguarded: enter the great white pelican. Pelicans roost and nest on Dassen Island, to the south of Malgas, and when the fish disappeared they first took to eating chicken offal waste fed to pigs on a nearby farm, but when that food source dried up, and having acquired a taste for bird parts, they turned to eating gannet chicks. Every day, about 120 pelicans fly in and wander amongst the gannet nests, swallowing the chicks whole. Any bird less than 2 kg (2.2 lb) is fair game, and the pelicans are so sold on nest raiding that they are stealing from nests on their own island, with Cape cormorants, the wily kelp gulls and the hapless African penguins taking the brunt of the pillaging. They're the new neighbours from hell!

WHITE DEATH

Young penguins fledging at Dyer Island off South Africa's southeast coast have more than kelp gulls or pelicans to worry about. Next door, 55,000 more Cape fur seals occupy Geyser Rock and the old bulls, like their cousins at Malgas, have a penchant for penguins and other seabirds. And, if that's not enough, in the channel between the two islands is the world's largest predatory fish – the great white shark. It's a danger hotspot.

The huge dark shadow cruising into the channel indicates a female shark looking for prey. She can't adopt her usual attack pattern of going deep and stalking her chosen target from below and behind because the channel's too shallow. She has to get as close as she can and then rush her victim, but the seals will have none of it. They've spotted her and they mob her, like songbirds mobbing an owl. Overhead, kelp gulls watch her progress. If she makes a kill there'll be plenty of leftovers, for sharks are messy eaters, but the gang following her below the surface is making hunting difficult, if not impossible.

Normally, she'd focus on young seals. Unlike the adults that swim a zigzag course to fool the sharks, the youngsters swim in a foolish and predictable straight line. The sharks know this. The kelp gulls know it too, and both predator and scavenger watch for novices.

But this time something else has attracted her attention. It's no more than a few molecules of a tantalising odour drifting in the current, but it's something well

▶ The formidable jaws and serrated, knife-like teeth of a great white shark make short work of slicing away a mouthful of blubber from a Bryde's whale carcass floating on the sea's surface off the coast of South Africa.

worth a detour. She heads up-current, crisscrossing the odour trail, testing first with one nostril and then the other, moving slowly but steadily towards the area of greater strength and the source of the smell. It leads her to an enormous whale carcass floating on the surface. This is what great whites really like — mountains of energy-rich blubber. Bite-sized fur seal pups are one thing, but a few mouthfuls of whale blubber can keep a shark going without having to feed again for weeks.

Thirty other great white sharks have already discovered the whale — after all, this coast is recognised as the shark capital of the world — but this female outranks them all by her size. She cruises past those already tucking in, arches her back slightly and lowers her pectoral fins, all signs that she's the boss around here. The others defer to her. It's the way of sharks: big is best. After she's had her fill, the others move in but they're extraordinarily restrained — no feeding frenzy, no fights, just an orderly queue, each shark taking its turn to feed.

At one time, it was thought that all these sharks were residents, staying close to the Cape all year, but the mature females, at least, are long-distance travellers. In November, the big female headed out into the Indian Ocean, turning up in February near Exmouth on the coast of Western Australia. The following August she was back in South Africa, a round trip of 20,000 km (12,400 miles) completed in nine months. Why she went is another mystery.

▲ **Dolphins spray the sardines with high-intensity ultrasounds and pick off the debilitated fish, while all around them gannets rain down, plunge-diving into the sea.**

SARDINE FEVER

The sharks and the whales are here at the southern tip of Africa because of the cold Benguela Current. It means the sea is rich in life, and a keystone species is the South African sardine or pilchard. For part of the year, the sardines mill about in the shallow inshore waters of the Cape. This is when Cape gannets and other seabirds nest and rear a family. By the time the gannets fledge, there comes a big change. The sardines move offshore, heading to the Agulhas Bank to the south of the Cape where they spawn. The fish are now less conspicuous from the air, but dolphins know where to look. Huge 'superpods' of common dolphins locate the shoals using their sophisticated echolocation system, and they herd the fish into tight bait balls, but they don't have this oceanic smorgasbord to themselves: many eyes have been watching *them*.

While the dolphins spray the sardines with high-intensity ultrasounds and pick off the debilitated fish, bronze whaler sharks, alert to the mêlée, tear into shoals. All around them, gannets rain down, plunge-diving into the sea, catching fish on their way up rather than on the way down, while Cape cormorants actively pursue fish below the surface … and then the giants arrive. A Bryde's whale, a coastal species of baleen whale that prefers the tropics and warm waters to the polar seas favoured by other giant whales, has been shadowing the dolphin pod.

Feeding frenzy

After a large pod of common dolphins has rounded up a bait ball of South African pilchards (previous page), bronze whaler sharks are first to join the mêlée, with more hungry predators close behind. (1) A huge Bryde's whale powers up from the deep and lunges through the bait ball, gathering up whatever it can. (2) With the feast begun, dusky and spinner sharks, bluefish, tuna, king mackerel, kingfish, fur seals, penguins, gannets,

▶ **Large swathes of Mozambique and South Africa are lush and fertile, with a profusion of secret, almost magical places, some directly at the coast, others far inland, and in an age when few parts of the world are unexplored, they're only just being discovered.**

It powers up from the deep and lunges through the bait ball, gathering up whatever it can before swimming around in a wide arc ready to make another run before the rest of the fish are taken. It lives here all year, and although it does not embark on lengthy migrations like other whales, it must be prepared to travel, for some of the sardines are on the move again.

In May, a tongue of cold Atlantic water pushes up southern Africa's east coast between the Agulhas Current and the mainland. As long as the water temperature is below 21°C (70°F) the sardines follow. Monstrous shoals form, some up to 7 km long (4.4 miles), 2 km (1.2 miles) wide and 30 m (100 feet) deep. Again, dolphins are key: they lead the attack. There are an estimated 18,000 common dolphins in the area, which raid in pods 100 strong. They round up the sardines into manageable bait balls about 20 m (66 feet) in diameter. These tight shoals only last for ten minutes or less, but in that time bronze whaler, dusky and spinner sharks will have joined the feast, as well as bluefish, tuna, king mackerel, kingfish, fur seals, penguins, gannets, cormorants and the ubiquitous kelp gulls. It's a feeding frenzy that's repeated time and again as the whole procession moves northwards, the biggest concentration of predators on the planet.

And as the dark amorphous shoals, resembling huge writhing sea monsters, move close to the shore, fishermen – professional and amateur – also try their luck. They surround the shoals with their nets and haul the fish back onto the beach. Sometimes the predators push the fish right up to the beach, triggering 'sardine fever'. Braving the sharks – including the notorious bull shark – people race into the shallows using their hats, t-shirts, pants – anything in which they can make a catch. There are so many of these short-lived but fast-growing fish, that in terms of biomass it is thought the sardine run rivals East Africa's wildebeest migration – what locals have begun to call 'the greatest shoal on Earth'.

▶ Table Mountain with a tablecloth of orographic clouds.

CHAPTER FIVE

SAHARA

The hot, dry regions of Africa are at the mercy of the interminable sun, extreme temperatures being a greater killer than lack of water. Many plants and animals that live here can survive long periods with little or no water but every living creature, no matter how hardy, has a 'thermal death point', and for many creatures this is reached almost daily in the hot, dry deserts of the Sahara and the Horn of Africa.

Sand dunes, Libya

One of the highest air temperatures ever measured was recorded in North Africa on 13th September 1922. On that momentous day, when foehn winds were blowing away from the Sahara towards the Mediterranean, the mercury is said to have risen to 58°C (136°F) at El Azizia in northwest Libya. The claim is disputed. The weather station was erected on black Tarmac, which absorbed heat and radiated it back to the instruments, and the station operator was inexperienced. Even so, the temperature here, and in the desert regions of North Africa, peaks at an undisputed 50°C (122°F) in summer, yet in winter it can drop to zero and below, especially at night.

The daily swing from hot to cold and back again can be surprising. During the month of December, in the mid-1980s, there are records of daily variations from -0.5° (33°F) to +37.5° (99.5°F) at Bir Mighla in northern Libya; while at Wadi Halfa, on the southern shores of Lake Nubia in northern Sudan, the variation in shade temperature during the course of a year was from -2°C (28.5°F) at night to +52.5°C (126.5°F) by day.

Most desert plants and animals, however, are not found a metre or so in the air like a weather station, but live on or close to the ground, where they experience an even harsher regime. On one occasion at Wadi Halfa, where annual rainfall is less than 2.5 mm (0.1 inches) – 20 times less than in the infamous Death Valley in California – the daytime air temperature reached 46°C (115°F), but the sand surface temperature was a staggering 84°C (183°F). Any organism caught out on the sand would have fried … quite literally.

Yet, plants and animals can live even here. They've developed ways to cope with exceptional temperatures, whether by insulation, cooling by evaporation, reflecting the sun's rays, heat-tolerant seeds or eggs, or finding shade. It enables them to thrive in one of Africa's most extreme and challenging places.

The vast Sahara occupies close to a third of the African continent. It's almost the size of the USA yet this great desert has only 6% of Africa's species of wildlife. The blistering sun and lack of water are certainly key factors, but there is another explanation: the present-day Sahara is young, no more than a few thousand years old, so plants and animals have had little time to invade and to evolve in such a hot, dry and constantly shifting landscape. Even so, there are surprises!

▶ **Egypt's White Desert or** *Sahara el Beyda* **has strange chalk formations that were created when the rock was scoured by sandstorms.**

SNOW MONKEYS

On the Atlas Mountains, at the northern edge of the Sahara, there is snow. The snow is deep and across its surface there are footprints leading to an old cedar. Its branches are heavy with snow, but its guests in their thick warm coats seem unperturbed. The surroundings may resemble the European Alps, but living in the trees here is an animal that is much more African than European; it's a monkey, the Barbary macaque, sometimes known as the Barbary ape.

▼ A surprising sight at the edge of the Sahara: trees in the Atlas Mountains are blanketed with snow.

OVERLEAF A Barbary macaque and her infant huddle for warmth in the snow-covered branches.

Six or seven million years ago, the ancestors of this species of Old World monkey moved out of tropical Africa and spread across North Africa and much of southern Europe. Today, it's the world's oldest living species of macaque, the only one to be found outside Asia, and the only African primate, other than humans, to be found north of the Sahara.

Eliminated from Europe, aside from a small population on the Rock of Gibraltar, and cut off from the rest of Africa by the desert, the Barbary macaque is now isolated in North Africa's Atlas Mountains, a 2,500 km (1,500-mile) long mountain chain that separates the Sahara from North Africa's Mediterranean coast. The mountains control the weather in these parts, squeezing rain and snow from winds blowing in from the Atlantic Ocean, and the mountain forests of cedar and oak have become a refuge for the macaques.

All around, large flakes drift to the ground, adding to the sparkling white carpet. Spring is pending but has yet to chase away what's left of winter. In the dry, hot summer, the macaques will search for newly opened leaves and fresh herbs, often foraging on the ground for roots and rhizomes and fallen acorns, along with a mouth-watering array of caterpillars, but now, during the cold and snowy winter, they have only the trees. Nevertheless, their cheek pouches bulge with cedar leaves, lichens, and leftover berries, and they strip away bark to get at the living, water-laden phloem layers beneath. It's their eclectic diet and this ability to get by on the slimmest pickings that has been the key to their survival.

For monkeys, they're surprisingly quiet and peaceful. The large males look after the troop's youngsters as much as their mothers do, because these macaques have an unusual social system. In such a harsh environment, continually squabbling and fighting would be time wasted, so these monkeys invest in relationships. Males unite rather than fight, although most of their natural predators – leopards and lions – have long gone, so threats to the troop are mainly from its human neighbours.

There is the occasional tiff, especially at breeding time, like the time when an unusually aggressive male took a baby hostage as a bargaining tool to thwart his rival and received a smack on the head for his trouble. It triggered the simian equivalent of a bar-room brawl, with males showing their teeth in an aggressive open-mouthed, lips-pulled-back display, but after a little lip smacking and eyelid flashing, things quickly settled down. A high degree of conciliation in this species means that many of these conflicts go undecided.

There is, nevertheless, a hierarchy of males determined by these spats, but it's shallow, and the group is led by a wise matriarch who knows all the best feeding sites. Females mate with any adult males in the group, although the more dominant males get the lion's share of unions, so paternity is uncertain, but there's a premium on males who show good parenting skills. Babies chase and tumble, then clamber onto anyone's back, mother or father, uncle or aunt, in fact, whoever is nearest to carry them along.

Restlessness within the troop arrives with spring, when simian minds turn from survival to procreation. The sun triggers the strife and disharmony, but this early warmth is a far cry from the intense heat of summer. These seasonal shifts play out annually, and have occurred throughout the time that Barbary macaques have been in North Africa. Macaques have found refuge in these mountain forests as Africa's fickle climate has swung from hot to cold, dry to wet, and back again. Now, this relict population is cut off from its southern cousins by the hottest, driest and arguably most brutal landscape on Earth.

AMPHIBIAN AMBUSH

As the warmth of spring infiltrates the land, the meltwater on the southern slopes of the Atlas Mountains tumbles down in torrents. Eye-catching waterfalls cascade into deep, clear pools surrounded by an untidy terrain of red sandstone rocks, the last reliable source of water before the desert and a mere drop in the Sahara's ocean of rock and sand. And where there's water, wild flowers bloom, and where there are flowers, there are sure to be butterflies. But these are no ordinary butterflies: they're painted ladies, one of the most travelled insect migrants on the planet.

They arrive in the Atlas Mountains in autumn, travelling from British gardens and from as far afield as Finland. They gather here to avoid the northern winter and to continue their breeding cycle in the favourable conditions that exist at the edge of the Sahara during the colder half of the year. Moving about 160 km (100 miles) a day, some fly in the still air just above the ground, while others migrate at high altitudes, on the move when winds are in a favourable direction to carry them over land and sea.

Once in Africa, courtship and mating give way to egg laying, just as the previous generation did half a year and about 2,500 km (1,500 miles) away. Eggs are deposited on thistles, the favoured food plant, and caterpillars hatch and feed, and then pupate. Inside their fluffy silk chrysalises, they make that magical transition from ugly grubs to elegant butterflies. Bathed in the warm spring sunshine, the new adults dry their wings, ready to head northwards to Europe and an escape from the searing heat of midsummer, but for some their sojourn in North Africa is dreadfully short.

At the edge of the stream on the southern edge of the Anti Atlas Mountains something stirs. Like a lion stalking its prey, a Sahara frog has designs on a painted lady. It edges forward, crawling slowly on all four legs until it's just a leap away from the butterfly. The insect is drinking nectar from the flowers of yellow fleabane, quite unaware of the approaching frog. The stalker turns its body so its prey is directly ahead, stretches its front legs to raise its body and lunges forward. At the last moment the butterfly spots the movement and escapes, but there will be plenty of other opportunities.

Every day at about noon, the butterflies drop down to the mud puddles at the edge of the water. The frogs, not generally noted for their incisive intelligence, seem to anticipate their arrival, but with so many frogs competing for the same insects, there are inevitably clashes. Frogs are everywhere ... leaping, colliding, and crashing ... but eventually one succeeds in making a catch. It sits casually in the shallow water, a broad froggy grin across its face and a butterfly's wing tips sticking out of its mouth; then, with a big gulp as its eyes disappear momentarily into its head, the butterfly is gone.

Frogs have long been suspected the natural enemy of butterflies. In his first book of poetry, *Harmonium*, published in 1922, American poet Wallace Stevens observed: 'Frogs Eat Butterflies. Snakes Eat Frogs. Hogs Eat Snakes. Men Eat Hogs'. It was the title of one of his poems, but until recently there had been little empirical evidence that frogs actually eat butterflies; now we know for a fact that they do.

▼ The Sahara frog lives and mainly hunts in or close to water. Unlike other desert frogs it does not aestivate in summer but is active all year.

HOT SPRINGS ETERNAL

The prospect of a refreshing water-hole is not a mirage at the *Filoha* (meaning 'hot springs') in Ethiopia's Awash National Park on the parched Horn of Africa. The water is there all right, it's real, but wisps of steam drifting off its surface betray that in parts of the pool the temperature is almost at boiling point. The hot springs are a gentle reminder that much of Ethiopia is geologically active, for crossing the country is the northern part of Africa's Great Rift Valley (see page 61), and just below the surface of the Filoha Hot Springs is an intrusion of molten magma that heats up the water.

The presence of standing water means that the Filoha is a green oasis in an area of dry thorn scrub, brown and dusty grassland and acacia. Close to the pools, the long, thin trunks of palm trees bend stiffly over the water, their distinctive outline and spiky tops reflected in the mirror-still surface. Their fruit is a favourite of the local troops of hamadryas baboons; but it's the water itself that holds the surprise ... despite the heat, there are fish living here!

Ten thousand years ago they were regular Nile tilapia, living a routine life in a normal river, but major earth movements turned their life upside-down and many must have been killed in the conflagration. The few that survived were trapped at Filoha where, quite literally, things began to hot up.

The Nile tilapia is known to be an adaptable fish: in fact, it was probably one of the first species to be cultured. Illustrations from an ancient Egyptian tomb show they were reared in ornamental ponds more than 4,000 years ago, and even today it's the most widely cultured fish not only in Africa, but also in other parts of the world. It thrives in warm waters, between 31°C (88°F) and 36°C (97°F), but a temperature of 42°C (108°F) is lethal, and the water that trickles into the pool from the hot spring at the base of a cliff is significantly warmer. The fish swim, therefore, in the cooler margins, and this presents them with a problem at feeding time.

They're able to filter-feed by trapping phytoplankton on the mucous lining of their buccal cavity and they can scrape algae from rocks along the shore, but they get most nutrients by feeding on thick mats of algae and bacteria. In these pools, however, the mats grow in the hot, mineral-rich waters, just where the fish are unable to go. But there's a neat solution. During the day, the microorganisms responsible for building the mats photosynthesise, producing oxygen as a waste product. The bubbles gradually accumulate within the mat until it's buoyant enough to break free from the bottom, float to the surface and drift into the cooler water: that's when the fish can eat it. Meanwhile, the mats start to grow

▶ A baby Nile crocodile. The species is found in rivers and lakes throughout Africa, and has even been seen in the desert, in caves and in ponds fed by hot springs.

again below, so the process is self-sustaining. There is, however, another not-so-small problem. Something else lives here, and it relishes the warmth: the Nile crocodile. There are 20–30 of them here and they like to eat tilapia.

Under the bright, clear skies, an older, wiser tilapia can spot a crocodile approaching in these crystal-clear waters and will keep its distance. At night, however, the odds change in the crocodile's favour. Young tilapia can hide amongst the reeds, but an older fish is just too big. Its only clue that a crocodile is nearby is from any water disturbances it detects with its lateral line, a row of pressure-sensitive pits along each side of its body and around its head. The system is extremely sensitive, so the croc must act quickly. It positions itself amongst the fish and then surges through the water at high speed, lifting up and over the tilapia to twist and crash down on its prey from above. The fish's sensory system is compromised and on impact the croc's jaws snap shut and it gets a meal, and it'll lunge in this way all through the night until sated. It means, each night, many tilapia become crocodile fodder, while the faster, cannier individuals survive – natural selection in action.

The crocs themselves are significantly shorter than Nile crocodiles elsewhere in Africa, and even in this relatively small pool, where they're close together, they have their own personal spaces; in fact, each has a regular circuit that it swims each night, and if another should trespass it will end in a fight.

KING OF THE JUNGLE

Ethiopia is full of surprises. On the southern slopes of the Bale Mountains is an enchanted forest – the Harenna Forest. It is humid and surprisingly verdant, a contrast to the searingly hot and intensely dry conditions that plague much of the Horn of Africa. Between May and October, warm moist air is drawn in from the Indian Ocean so rain falls in abundance – up to a metre a year (40 inches), producing surprisingly lush tropical vegetation. A closed canopy of African redwood, red stinkwood, white stinkwood and black ironwood trees resembles a jungle in tropical west Africa, almost every tree festooned with lichens and ferns, draped with lianas and vines, and their trunks and branches covered with moss. Red-hot pokers occupy a clearing, and a diminutive Ethiopian highland chameleon clings tightly to the bright-red flowers, waiting no doubt for insects to visit. It's one of the few remaining natural forests in Ethiopia.

It's a bright, moonlit night when the dense, silvery-white cocoon cracks open and a male moon moth squeezes free. It crawls deliberately towards the end of the branch of a huge emergent (one of the tallest trees in the forest), a 55 m (180 feet) anegre tree. Slowly its wings dry and expand. The metamorphosis is complete. The moth is a beauty. Its wings are 14 cm (5.5 inch) across, a subtle yellow-green with bright yellow and red eyespots. The grey leading edge of the fore wings is rough, no doubt for aerodynamic reasons, and there are long trailing tails to the hind wings that resemble dried foliage. The moth does not move

Ethiopia is full of surprises. On the southern slopes of the Bale Mountains is an enchanted forest, humid and surprisingly verdant, a contrast to the searingly hot and intensely dry conditions that plague much of the Horn of Africa.

at first, but remains motionless, its body and wings blending in with its forest
background, for there are predators about.

A young Abyssinian long-eared owl has fledged and is hunting in the forest
for the very first time. A moon moth would be a welcome snack, but it has to
find one first: some moths are very good at detecting and avoiding predators.
The moth has only one thing to do in its short ten-day life, and that's to breed. It
doesn't feed for it doesn't have the wherewithal to do so. It waits for the tell-tale
pheromones of a female to drift in on the wind, and then targets her, after which
it remains locked to her for the best part of the night and the following day.

Bale monkeys – endangered relatives of the vervet – are asleep in the trees.
They're generally not found in this part of the forest. They've wandered down the
escarpment from the bamboo groves where they normally live and feed on young
bamboo leaves (one of the few mammals to do so – giant pandas and bamboo
lemurs being two of the others). They have come to feast on the blackberry-like
fruits of a locally abundant woody liana, but their overnight stop is turning into
a nightmare.

With the deafening crack of a twig breaking, the troop is suddenly awake
and alert, but each remains uncharacteristically silent. Below them a small group
of mountain nyala – an antelope that's also extremely rare – has been moving

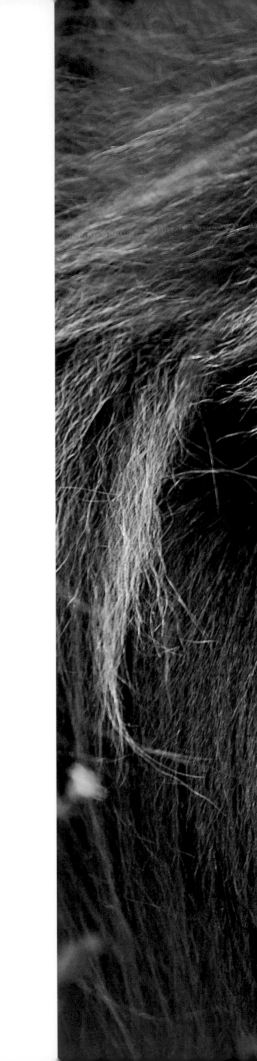

noiselessly through the forest. They've been forced to live in these mountains because their usual habitat at lower elevations has been destroyed. The animals are edgy and look about them. There's the distinctive odour of predator about, but they're not sure where. Suddenly the antelope take off, crashing through undergrowth, and a pack of wild dogs appears. They sniff about excitedly at the place where the nyala stood, before racing off too, for hiding amongst the moist vegetation is an unexpected resident – a lioness.

She's one of only three known adult lions in the entire forest. She had been stalking the antelope, but with her cover blown she turns and waits for the others to catch up. The lionesses rub heads in greeting as a large male saunters towards them. He and his pride of females and cubs are smaller than their relatives on the Serengeti, and even more endangered, despite the fact that the animal is revered, appearing as statues and on currency across Ethiopia.

The monkeys, meanwhile, have silently slipped away, back up the mountain, away from this place where dogs nip at your feet and the lion truly is king of the jungle.

TWO FROM CONGRESS

The wildlife of Harenna, like the plants and animals of the Atlas Mountains in North Africa, has been cut off from the rest of Africa since the end of the last Ice Age. Life here is a distant echo of that on the plains far below, and one species to be found at loftier heights in the Ethiopian Highlands has had to change its entire way of life. Carefully balanced on a narrow ledge on a sheer rock face is a large male gelada. Trees are few, and rocky outcrops and cliffs are legion here, so denied a safe bough in which to pass the night, he opts for a cliff instead, with the rest of his troop or congress scattered about him.

He's a big animal, his cape of long, thick hair testament to the low temperatures and poor shelter from the elements of his habitat. Come the morning, he's the first to rise. A big yawn, with his upper lip flipped back, exposes large canines, and together with a bright red, hourglass-shaped patch of bare skin on his chest, he tells the world that he's the boss. Nevertheless, his leadership is constantly under review: young pretenders challenge at every opportunity, and although they rarely come to blows, he must be strong to suppress a coup.

At sunrise, the troop abandons its cliffside home and climbs to the top of the plateau. It's not alone, for several other groups are making the same journey.

▶ Aside from her offspring, the female gelada will socialise with no more than three other geladas, and if she is high ranking, she will have more offspring during her twenty years of life than a monkey of lower birth.

◄ At the southern edge of Africa's Horn, almost everything is coloured the same sepia tone ... apart from a blurry pattern of pyjama stripes that shimmers in the heat haze. These stripes belong to Grévy's or imperial zebras, the world's largest species of wild horse. ◉

Together they make up a band of many 'reproductive units', each with its own dominant male and entourage of several females and their young, together with a couple of young males. The adult females have a smaller build and thick fur, but no cape, and the bare skin on their chest is less pronounced. They tend to squabble with the females from other groups, and are more likely to fight than the males.

They're all grazers, for the grass is lush, and they spend most of the day foraging. Their small, stubby fingers are perfect for plucking grass leaves and seeds, and they can chew and pulverise plant material just as well as a zebra. In the dry season, when grass is unavailable, they'll turn to herbs and may well consume the odd flower or dig up the occasional root or rhizome. While feeding, they move by shuffling. They squat, eat and shuffle forwards, their bottoms on the ground. This is probably the reason they have sexual markings on their chest, rather than on the buttocks like their close relatives, the baboons.

By late afternoon, storm clouds gather, so the geladas head to the protection of their night-time cliffs. Sharp shafts of sunlight punch through the murk like searchlights, until they too are snuffed out as torrential rain rolls across the land. Thunder crashes all around and lightning flashes light up the clouds like giant Chinese lanterns.

The mountains suck the sky dry, but instead of funnelling the life-giving water into rivers that irrigate the parched plains of the Horn, the waters drain into Lake T'ana, and then to the Blue Nile and northwards through Sudan and Egypt. It means that much of the landscape of the Horn is brown and dry. Vegetation is sparse, and where plants do grow they are constantly under threat from a creature that has devastated crops since the very earliest human civilisations lived here – the desert locust. Swarms of biblical proportions still invade the Horn, but sometimes, they're a blessing.

In June 2009, winds brought up a swarm of desert locusts to the Guassa Plateau from the floor of the Great Rift Valley below. First a loud humming sound filled the air and the sky began to darken as massive numbers of locusts suddenly appeared. A troop of over 200 geladas first uttered screams of surprise and fear, but then switched to frenetic feeding. They ran about chaotically in pursuit of the insects, leaping and plucking them from the air or pouncing on any that landed on the ground. For a specialist grass-eater, this was a surprising change of diet, and the geladas weren't the only highland animals to take advantage of it. A rare Ethiopian wolf and a noisy bunch of thick-billed ravens joined the party.

IMPERIAL HORSE

At the southern edge of the Horn, in northern Kenya and southwest Ethiopia, almost everything is coloured the same sepia tone ... apart, that is, from a blurry pattern of pyjama stripes that shimmers in the heat haze. They belong to Grévy's or imperial zebras, the world's largest species of wild horse. They have mule-like ears and narrower stripes than other zebras, and they're born survivors. They can go for a week without water, but when a water-hole is found, maybe no more than a muddy patch, the herd's stallion defends it ferociously. The females on his territory are allowed access, for many of them are bringing up the foals he's sired. Mares need water when lactating, so he chases away all other males.

At the water's edge, young foals peer out nervously from behind their mothers' legs as a posse of young males gathers at the edge of town. The renegades are on the lookout for trouble. None is a match for the older animal, but if they challenge him one after another they might wear him out and topple a king.

The king, in the meantime, has declared his ownership. He's left small piles of dung at the edge of his patch, showing he's still up for a fight, but there's a female on heat and she's proving irresistible. The young pretenders are hesitant, unsure that they can depose the incumbent. As the tension bubbles up, they squabble amongst themselves; but then, one hopeful takes up the challenge.

In a flurry of dust and kicking heels, with teeth bared and nostrils flared, the old stallion ensures that the challenger is sent packing, and quickly. The others retreat, trekking across the barren landscape, forlorn and defeated, but one day they'll be back, and one of them may succeed where many others will have failed. The old stallion can be defeated … one day. Curiously, when breeding is over, he'll actually welcome the company of other stallions, although he'll ensure they know who's in charge. For now, though, he rolls in the dust to rid himself of irritating parasites and itchy skin. He's one of fewer than 2,500 Grévy's zebras living in the wild today, the last of a dying species.

BACK FROM THE DEAD

There are some living things in these hot, dry parts of Africa that appear not to be living at all, but actually they're just biding their time. Even the driest places have some chance of rain, although a decade or even a century might pass before it falls. In order to survive, plants and animals must adopt some means of waiting out the waterless times and proliferate rapidly in the all too brief spells of wet weather. The rose of Jericho is just such a survivor.

The plant hugs the ground, an unprepossessing and rather grey herb, a kind of wild mustard with tiny white flowers. As the rains cease and scorching winds stir up the dust, the plant effectively 'dies'. Its leaves drop and its branches curl into a tight, fistlike ball. But when the rains return, a miracle occurs. As water hits the plant's dried branches, in a pale imitation of life they unfold to reveal seed capsules wrapped inside, protected from desiccation and heat. They can survive inside the ball for years, and as soon as they're wetted the capsules open. When a raindrop hits a spoon-shaped projection on each seed, the seed is flung out, and it either germinates close to the plant or is washed away with the surface water. Germination of this species of 'resurrection plant' is so rapid that growth starts within a few hours of the first downpour.

▶ **There are some living things in these hot, dry parts of Africa that appear not to be living at all, but actually they're just biding their time. The rose of Jericho is just such a survivor. When the rains cease, the plant effectively 'dies'. Its leaves drop and its branches curl into a tight, fistlike ball...**

This rapid development from the resting state is characteristic of many living things in dry regions. When pools form after rain, a small crustacean is also resurrected – the tadpole shrimp. During dry periods, with no open water, the shrimps lie dormant as tiny eggs, and they're surprisingly hardy. The adult shrimps can tolerate water temperatures that reach 40°C (104°F) but their eggs can survive temperatures of up to 98°C (208°F).

Tadpole shrimps have a long history: one species has existed with little apparent change since the Jurassic period about 180 million years ago, when dinosaurs roamed the Earth. There is evidence for even older ancestry: fossils of very similar creatures have been found in Carboniferous rocks dated at 300 million years old, when the deposits that gave rise to coal were laid down. It seems throughout geological history tadpole shrimps have found an effective way to survive when things get really tough.

One way to escape the midday heat and the rock-shattering cold of a desert night is to go underground. In the desert regions of East Africa and the Horn, when the daytime maximum on the surface is an excruciating 68°C (154°F) and the daily variation between day and night is 47°C (85°F), the temperature just 20 cm (8 inches) underground hovers continuously around 41°C (106°F). Go even deeper, to a burrow a metre (more than 3 feet) below the surface, and the temperature rises to little more than a balmy 30°C (86°F). What's more, in that burrow the relative humidity is close to 72%, while at the surface it's a dehydrating 12%.

It can be so comfortable down there that it's become home to one species of mammal that has little need to regulate its body temperature, has virtually lost the use of its eyes, moves backwards as fast as it can move forwards, and behaves much like an insect. It's the naked mole rat, a sabre-toothed sausage with pink, wrinkly skin, a bare tail and spindly legs.

Centre of naked mole rat society is its queen, who's larger than the rest. When she takes over the throne, her anatomy permanently changes – the vertebrae in her back lengthen, so that she has room to carry more babies. Like a queen bee, she's the only one in the colony to breed, and she's constantly pregnant, her closely packed, unborn babies visible through her skin. When she gives birth, it's as if a balloon has burst, and each of her many offspring (usually more than twenty) are the size and shape of jellybeans – completely helpless.

The queen is part of a caste system that includes a couple of breeding males and the many workers who take on a variety of jobs, such as looking after the newborns. Large workers, about 10 cm (4 inches) long, are like soldier ants, and help protect the colony from intruders. Smaller workers collect food, especially tubers discovered while tunnelling. A single, large tuber can feed a colony for months, partly because they mine it from the inside, so the plant is still able to grow. Their metabolism is low, about two-thirds less than a rodent of comparable size, so they require only small quantities of food, a useful trait to have in a desert where the next meal is not always dependable.

Other workers excavate and maintain the tunnels, operating in chain gangs. The mole rat at the front does the digging, its lips sealed behind its protruding teeth so that it doesn't swallow soil. Those working behind pass the earth back between their legs and the last in line dumps it outside. The tunnel network they excavate can be huge. The length of all the tunnels added together might be 5 km (3 miles). They have an entire subterranean city down there. Inevitably, carbon dioxide accumulates in the tunnels, so the animals must survive in low oxygen conditions. To enable this, their blood has a strong affinity for whatever oxygen is available.

Colonies average 75 individuals, but when numbers become too great, a change is triggered. No one is sure why; maybe a daughter reaches fighting weight and is ready to start a colony of her own, but for that to happen she must venture outside into the great unknown. The human equivalent would be an astronaut without a protective space suit exploring an alien world, for without fur she is vulnerable to the cold of the desert night, and if predators are about she's almost defenceless. She has little time, and may have to travel over a kilometre (more than half a mile) to find the right kind of burrow. Enter the wrong tunnel and the occupiers would shred her to pieces. She needs to find a bachelor's tunnel, and to do so she uses her nose. The male leaves an attractive scent in his excavated dirt, and it's this that gives her all the information she needs to make the right decision. Once the two unite, a new dynasty can begin.

▼ **A sabre-toothed sausage with pink, wrinkly skin, a bare tail and spindly legs, the mole rat has virtually lost the use of its eyes, moves backwards as fast as it can move forwards, and behaves much like an insect.**

DESERT INTERCHANGE

Great kingdoms once flourished in these lands bordering the Sahara, some even in the heart of the Sahara itself. All had one thing in common: trans-Saharan trade, especially salt, the so-called 'white gold', and moving goods about was all down to the capabilities of an animal that was well adapted to desert life – the dromedary camel.

The dromedary is not African. It was once native to the hot and arid lands of the Arabian Peninsula. At some point between 3000 and 2500 BC, people living in the coastal settlements of the ancient Kingdom of Punt (which scholars at one time or another have located in both Africa and Arabia on either side of the Red Sea) are said to have domesticated the beast. Otherwise, the first evidence of camels in Africa comes from Qasr Ibrim in Egypt, dated ninth century BC, but camels were not common on the continent until the fourth century AD, after the Islamic conquest of the North. However, their suitability to long desert journeys carrying heavy loads opened up a substantial trade across the vast Sahara. Kingdoms, such as the Empire of Ghana, grew rich on the trans-Saharan trade, and today, one place where you can still drink in the atmosphere of those ancient caravans is in the deserts of eastern Chad.

Here, there's very little but sand and rock as far as the eye can see, apart from the occasional bleached skull of an animal and old military vehicles, the legacy of many wars in these parts. On the distant horizon is what could be a mirage. Looking like a great city with castle turrets, towers and minarets, it's actually an outcrop of sandstone with rock spires shaped like slender wine bottles, and spectacular natural arches. It's part of the Ennedi Massif, a great rocky fortress assailed on all sides by sand in the middle of the Sahara.

However, sand is not a universal feature of a Saharan landscape. While the deserts of Libya have vast sand seas or 'ergs' that cover thousands of square kilometres, there are great stretches of the Sahara with stony plateaux or 'hamadas', gravel plains or 'regs', boulder fields, dry valleys or 'wadis', sheer cliffs, salt-flats, springs and a scattering of lush oases ... and there are mountains – the Tibesti, Ahaggar and Aïr mountains. The Sahara's highest peak at 3,445 m (11,303 feet) is Emi Koussi, an extinct volcano at the southern edge of the Tibesti Massif in northern Chad, one of the harshest and most remote regions on Earth. Here, the temperature of the dark basaltic rock surfaces can be 40°C (104°F) at 6 o'clock in the morning, and by 4 o'clock in the afternoon they're 80°C (176°F), hot enough to fry up not only an egg, but also a full English breakfast.

In a bad year there's no rain. In a good year there's a little, but it arrives all at once. Flash floods from intense electrical storms can pound these parched uplands during July and August, and they've carved deep, sheer-sided gullies into the western edge of the Ennedi Plateau. The vertical sandstone walls are up to 100 m (330 feet) high, and in the floor of these slit-like gorges are strings of pools or 'gueltas', separated by areas of green bog.

◄ The Ennedi Plateau in the northeast of Chad is at the heart of the Sahara. It is dominated by dramatic sandstone rock formations of towers, spires and natural arches.

OVERLEAF A desert caravan of dromedaries and camel drivers winds its way across a shifting and seemingly featureless landscape along routes that have been known and followed for centuries.

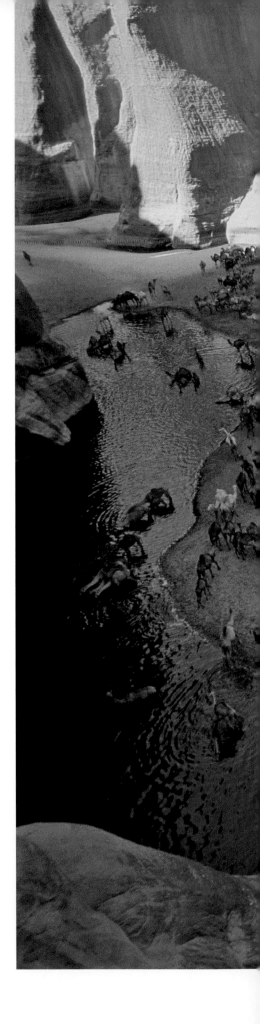

Unlike the stark and empty plateau, there's water here for most of the year, fed by permanent springs from underground reservoirs or aquifers, and it's this that has drawn the trans-Saharan caravans here for centuries. On a busy day, hundreds of camels mill about in the water in the Guelta d'Archei, a spectacular section of the Ennedi Gorge. Their snorts, grunts and roars echo around the cathedral-like walls, as their Tuareg owners fill goatskins with water and exchange stories with other desert nomads, a momentary respite from the harsh world outside. They watch over their precious animals as they drink, bathe and defecate.

And, it's this last bodily function that has special significance at Ennedi. Camel dung fertilises the water, supporting a healthy growth of algae, which feeds freshwater shrimps and mosquito larvae, which in turn are food for a large population of freshwater fish – barbs, tilapia, catfish and African carp; but top of the food chain here in the middle of the Sahara Desert is an unexpected creature – the Nile crocodile.

The Chad crocodiles are smaller than their relatives in the rest of Africa, the largest no more than 1.5 m (5 feet) long instead of the usual 5 m (16 feet), and there's more than one population. Recent discoveries reveal that there are probably 40 or 50 isolated desert populations in Mauritania and Algeria. Many of the Mauritanian crocodiles don't even have permanent water like the Ennedi crocs, but hide in a state of torpor in burrows and caves and under rocks when their pools dry up for six to eight months of the year (see page 263). The Ennedi crocs, however, are a dying breed. Only three are left. It's a pattern repeated with other desert residents.

Lions departed the Ennedi Plateau in 1940, when the last Saharan lion died, but the presence of savannah animals like these, today or in the recent past, is an indication that the Sahara was not always as it is today. The lions and the crocodiles, as well as rock hyrax, monitor lizards, chameleons and birds like the African silverbill and black-throated firefinch were or still are relict populations of animals that were once more widespread. So, what were these savannah animals doing in a hot desert?

Our first clue can be found in the ancient trading centre of Chinguetti, a small town on the Adrar Plateau in Mauritania. It was on the caravan routes between Morocco and the kingdom of Mali until its fortunes changed. Today, the desert is threatening the very fabric of the old town, especially Chinguetti's

▶ Caravans of domesticated camels stop off at the Guelta d'Archei in Chad, where they share the water with some of the last remaining Nile crocodiles in the Sahara. The crocs feed on the fish, which in turn feed on the algae that is fertilised by the camel droppings.

unique thirteenth-century buildings, including the iconic Friday Mosque, with its distinctive un-mortared, split-stone masonry and gothic-like minaret. Already homes on the western edge of the city have been abandoned and huge dunes are swallowing them up, birds and scorpions rather than people their twenty-first-century occupants. Despite this, the clue we're seeking is still evident: many of the dried brick and stone houses in the old town have wooden doors cut from massive acacia trees, a feature of the landscape noticeable today by its absence; that is, except for two famous trees.

One of these trees was the legendary L'Arbre du Ténéré, its identity probably an umbrella acacia. It was thought to be the most isolated tree on Earth. There was no other closer than 400 km (250 miles) and it was a landmark on the caravan routes in northeast Niger, a lighthouse for those leaving or arriving at Agadez, a key border town that featured in the Libyan crisis during 2011. Back in 1939, when a well was dug close to the tree, its roots were found to have grown down to the water table 36 m (118 feet) below the surface. It survived years of trampling and browsing by camels, but in 1973, a drunken truck driver demolished it, and it was taken to the Niger National Museum. It's now been replaced by a simple metal sculpture.

The remaining lone tree can be found in the desert to the north. It's L'Arbre Perdu – the 'lost tree', more recently known as L'Arbre de Thierry Sabine after the creator of the Paris–Dakar Rally. This tree (now several small trees) still stands on a low mound of sand, and its branches are still green. So, what were these two savannah trees doing in the middle of the Sahara?

The next clue is on the rocks. In the Amoghar Pass, close to Chinguetti, there is rock art with images of giraffes, cows and people. Similarly, high on the rock walls of the Ennedi Gorge and elsewhere in the Sahara, such as Tassili n'Ajjer in southeast Algeria and Mesak Settafet in southwest Libya, rock art indicates a very different landscape and a very different fauna and flora to those we see today.

At Tassili, ancient rock art depicts the more familiar desert animals, such as camels, but more surprising are herds of cattle and goats, warriors on horses and in horse-drawn chariots, and fishermen harpooning fish in rivers. At Wadi Methkandoush in Mesak Settafet there are extraordinarily well-preserved rock carvings of an outstretched lizard, big cats fighting, ostriches running and elephants, buffalo and giraffes walking. At Ennedi, there are petroglyphs of crocodiles, birds, lions, antelope, gazelles and rhinoceros. They're wild animals more usually seen on the rolling savannah lands of East and southern Africa. It's all evidence that at some point in the not too distant past the Sahara must have been savannah and not desert.

To understand what happened and when, we must turn to the science of climate modelling. The climate here has oscillated between wet and dry for hundreds of thousands of years, and during the last glacial period of the Ice Ages, the desert was actually even bigger than it is today, reaching southwards to join

◄ The addax (top) is regionally extinct in the wild in most of North Africa but survives in parts of the Sahel, where it is critically endangered. Its depiction on ancient rock art in Libya (bottom) indicates that it was once more common, at a time when the Sahara was more savannah than desert.

the Namib and the Kalahari. Then, from about 10,000 years ago, rain came to the Sahara creating the right conditions for lush grasslands and patches of acacia woodlands to grow. These supported all the savannah wildlife and domestic animals depicted in the rock art.

However, the desert returned abruptly when the Earth's tilt changed significantly, according to climate modellers from the Potsdam Institute for Climate Impact Research. It resulted in two major periods of climate change. The first episode was 6,700–5,500 years ago, but the second more brutal episode occurred 4,000–3,600 years ago. On that occasion, in just 400 years, summer temperatures increased sharply, rainfall decreased and natural vegetation and crops were frazzled. People moved out of the Sahara and into valleys of the Nile, where new kingdoms arose. It means that the Sahara Desert we see today is comparatively new, less than 6,700 years old. There is, however, a place on the northern margins of the Sahara where savannah and acacia woodlands, similar to those that existed before the desert invaded, are still to be found today.

SAVANNAH REMNANT

The Bou-Hedma National Park, on the eastern edge of the Aurès Mountains in Tunisia, is not a rocky or even sandy desert, but a steppe of wind-blown grasses, succulents and isolated stands of umbrella acacia, reminiscent of East Africa's savannah. It's home to desert-adapted mammals that should have gone the way of L'Arbre du Ténéré, but were saved by timely human intervention.

Hunters annihilated the scimitar horned oryx, its dried meat once traded as *tichtar* and common in local markets, like that at Ghadames on the Tunisia–Algeria–Libya border. The animals were widespread across the Sahara, but over-hunting, desertification and drought were overwhelming and now they are thought to be extinct in the wild, but they haven't gone forever.

A group of forward-thinking conservationists took a handful of oryx into zoos and bred them in captivity. Eventually there were sufficient numbers to return to the wild, so in 1985, oryx bred in British zoos were released into an enclosure and later into the fenced zone of the Bou-Hedma National Park in southern Tunisia. There they remain and the area is of sufficient size for them to behave in a way approaching normality.

They're unusual antelopes in that males and females have equally sized scimitar-shaped horns, and they use these to defend patches of vegetation from other oryx. With food so hard to come by, fights are bloody, with both the victor and the vanquished covered in deep wounds from the sharp tips of their horns.

Although released in a relatively lush grassland reserve, the oryx is actually one of the few large antelope adapted to life on the Sahel-type arid grasslands in and around the Sahara. Their pale pelage reflects sunlight, their enlarged hooves enable them to walk comfortably on sand, and black skin, including on the tip of the tongue, protects against sunburn.

▶ **Males and females have equally sized scimitar-shaped horns, and they use these to defend patches of vegetation from other oryx.**

Before they became extinct in the wild, they migrated great distances, travelling at dawn or at dusk. In Chad, they would move south in the dry season and north when the first rain fell, responding to variations in air humidity from far away. They could predict where rain would fall and move deliberately to those areas. Their entire lives were geared to help minimise water loss, for they would not have been able to drink from standing water from the end of the dry season to the start of the wet, a waterless period of 8–10 months. Today, the reintroduced animals live in less harsh conditions but they retain the physiological wherewithal to survive in the desert should they be returned there. Their kidneys minimise urine production and their body temperature can reach 46.5°C (115.5°F) before they perspire. They acquire moisture from the sparse vegetation they eat, plants such as the bitter wild melon, whose stems and leaves remain green well into the dry season, and the leafless twigs and shoots of karir, which have high water content.

At Bou-Hedma, however, the reintroduced oryx are decidedly suspicious about what they eat. Using their horns, they'll thrash any new plant they encounter, before taking a tentative nibble, whereas their traditional food plants are consumed without any fuss whatsoever.

▼ The leading 'wall' of a sandstorm, over 1,500 m (nearly 5,000 feet) high, precedes a thunderstorm in Mali, turning the air orange and blotting out the sun. The dust can be blown as far away as Moscow and the British Isles, and even across the Atlantic Ocean to the Americas.

Joining them in Bou-Hedma is another reintroduction – the addax, a species of desert antelope that still survives in the wild, albeit critically endangered. Like the oryx, the addax is off-white above and pure white below. Both sexes have spiral horns, those of males being slightly longer. Their feet have wide, flat soles along with well-developed dewclaws, the combination preventing the animal from sinking into the sand. They're active at night, the coolest time in the desert, and rest in scraped hollows under bushes or in the shade of boulders during the day. They're nomadic, wandering the desert in small groups led usually by an old male, searching for the scant vegetation on which they graze. They can go for a year or more without drinking, obtaining all the water they need from their food.

Lions and leopards were the natural predators of oryx and addax, but with these creatures exterminated, gun-toting humans are now their main threat, although there are a few predators still roaming the Sahara that could run down a young addax or an oryx calf, such as golden jackals and striped hyenas, as well as a lone and mysterious cat, the Saharan cheetah.

Paler in colour than its sub-Saharan relatives, almost ghostly in appearance, the cheetah is mainly nocturnal to avoid the heat of the day, and gets by without the need for standing water, obtaining all it wants from the blood of its prey – desert hares, gazelles and young antelope. It's nomadic, like the oryx and addax, but little else is known about it, and even less about its distribution and numbers, but it has been seen and photographed. Camera traps set at night in the deserts of the Termit Massif in Niger and the Ahaggar Highlands of Algeria have provided visual proof that at least a few of the world's most elusive cats are roaming in one of the world's biggest deserts.

SAHARA CENTRAL

That any living things survive at all in the Sahara proper is quite surprising. The heart of the desert resembles a post-apocalyptic wasteland, which in a way it is, having been turned into the furnace we see today by that sudden change in the Earth's progression through space. Even on the ground the landscape is in constant flux.

Driven by fierce winds, a massive wall of moving sand and dust – like a gigantic wave, hundreds of metres high – rolls across the desert. It envelops everything. Grit blasts bare skin and fine dust gets everywhere: in eyes, noses and mouths. It's difficult to breathe. Visibility is almost nil, like a dense fog blotting out the sun. Day is turned into night.

During these sandstorms, Sahara's wildlife generally hunkers down. Few creatures are about during the day anyway, and no creature ventures out during a sandstorm, that is, except one. Dromedaries seem quite relaxed about the whole thing. They close their nostrils and have thick eyelashes and small hairy ears to keep out the sand, and they'll go about their everyday business as usual, seemingly oblivious to the mayhem around them.

And while the dust from a storm rises high into the sky, the heavier abrasive sand particles are blown along close to the ground. In some areas these form great fields of sand dunes – the sand seas or ergs, with dunes up to 180 m (590 feet) high. In Libya, the Egyptian Sand Sea covers a quarter of its desert area, and here the dunes 'sing'. The dry winds cause the moving sand grains to rub together to produce a ghostly hum that can be heard right across the desert.

CLEAN-UP SQUAD

When the sun returns, almost every animal in the Sahara seeks shade or burrows under the sand, but in Egypt's White Desert, located in the Farafra Depression, two small characters have yet to go underground. They're dung beetles. During the night they had found some camel dung, a commodity nearly as scarce as water out here. They would normally bury the dung and lay their eggs in the nutritious ball before sunrise, but the sun is above the horizon and the temperature climbing. Now, they're in a race for their lives.

Loath to release their balls of dung they run rapidly backwards, one beetle tipping into a wind-blown hollow surrounding a magnificent natural chalk sculpture – a stark white boulder perched precariously on top of its conical base like a giant ice-cream cone. All around are white monoliths shaped like mushrooms, tents, acacias, chickens and old men in hats. The other beetle collides with a vertical chalk wall. A few more degrees and the beetles will cook. They each drop their dung and run for cover, burying themselves in the sand on the shaded side of a rock shaped like a crown. It was a close call.

▼ ▶ **Dung or scarab beetles detect herbivore dung using their sense of smell. They make spherical balls of it, which they roll to a sheltered place and either eat or lay their eggs in. They can push or pull up to ten times their own weight.**

FALSE OASIS

As the morning wears on, the full force of a late-April sun bears down on the surface of the desert. Since dawn, the air temperature has been climbing by about 5°C (9°F) every hour so conditions on the Ubari Sand Sea in southern Libya are becoming increasingly uncomfortable. Water here is more valuable than diamonds, just a millimetre a year of rainfall on average, but it might not rain for decades. With no water, there's no food, and the hundreds of tiny dots approaching high in the sky need nourishment. They're barn swallows arriving from Nigeria, but they really don't want to be here at all. They're on their way to Europe and the Sahara is just too big to go round, so they have to go across.

They start their journey in tropical Africa, where they choose pockets of surviving rainforest in southeast Nigeria and Cameroon to feed and roost during the northern winter. One exceptionally large population adopts a hillside in the foothills of Afi Mountain to the east of the village of Ebbaken-Boje, where rainforest has been cleared and 5 m (16 feet) tall elephant grass has taken over.

With the *Harmattan* blowing dust from the Sahara (see page 254) and the smoke from bush fires swirling about the forest, visibility here for most of the day is down to 500 m (1,640 feet), but at sunset the sky clears momentarily to reveal an astonishing number of swallows high in the air. The cloud swirls this way and that like a giant amorphous creature, one and a half million birds moving almost as one. The flock splits into two as an African hobby tries its luck, but the confusion of so many birds distracts the predator and it fails to catch a single one. The birds have kept their weight low during the moulting period in January and February, prior to their migration to Europe, so they are trim and highly manoeuvrable. The swarm reunites and like meteorites raining down on Earth they all dive at high speed into the safety of the grass.

The entire flocking event and raptor attack takes place every day ten minutes before sunrise and ten minutes after sunset. Timing is critical both for predators and prey. The predators arrive five to ten minutes earlier – a local population of seven hobbies and other small birds of prey – and it is not the large flock that they mainly target, but the stragglers. Without the whirling mega-flock, the small raptors, which are quite capable of hunting in twilight, find it easier to pick off hapless swallows in the smaller groups; and even the birds that have settled are not immune from attacks.

Out of nowhere, a yellow-billed kite makes a low-level pass, brushing the tall grass to flush out the swallows from their roost sites. A pair of African marsh harriers and their single fledgling, no doubt learning to hunt, follow close behind, and a Senegal coucal – an opportunistic predator in the cuckoo family – swoops down to pluck a bird sitting near a gap in the vegetation. For the swallows, it will be far from a restful night, for an assortment of owls joins the roost-hugging predators. Yet the hobbies and the other raptors take only a few thousand during the overwintering season, which runs from October to March, a modest loss for the species compared to the 100,000 taken by local people each year.

In early March, with a change in the weather from dry, dusty winds to

damp weather with clouds forming from the south, the swallows change their behaviour. They feed up and put on weight, building up fat reserves that'll help them fly north to Europe, but first they must tackle the formidable Sahara.

When they arrive in Libya, they've already covered the best part of 435 km (270 miles) a day, and now they are searching for a traditional stopover site, an oasis where they can rest and refuel. A glint of sunlight on water and several pairs of nesting moorhens bring the birds down. Surrounded by huge ochre-coloured sand dunes, the small palm- and reed-fringed lake of *Um El Ma*, meaning 'the mother of all water', is no mirage, but the water does play a trick on these thirsty, hungry and exhausted visitors. It's not fresh water, but brine. Although fed by underground springs, hundreds of years of evaporation under the scorching desert sun has concentrated the salts so that the lake is as salty as the Dead Sea. To drink it would be fatal, but the swallows have timed their arrival to coincide with another of nature's miracles, a mass emergence of flies.

The swallows, joined by other migrants – house martins and yellow wagtails – catch the flies in mid-air. They swoop across the water, gathering these little packets not only of protein but also of water. The flies are tiny desalination plants providing the birds with the necessary water, as well as energy-giving food, to help them continue their seven-day onward journey all the way to northern Italy.

▲ Old World fringe-toed lizards are not active in the hottest part of the day. They hide beneath the sand, providing silver ants with a short but predator-free window during which to gather food.

▶ Silver ants emerge from their nest to forage on the hot desert surface at precisely the time their main predators are safely tucked away below the sand, escaping the sun.

SPRINTING UNDERTAKERS

By midday, the barren landscape deep in the Sahara shimmers in the summer heat; otherwise nothing moves. Most living things are out of sight, hiding as best they can from the burning sun: down burrows, under the sand or in the shade of whatever vegetation has survived here. Anything caught out in the open will certainly die. The air temperature is already more than 46°C (115°F), and the ground temperature off the dial, but suddenly, from a hole in the ground, out pour hundreds of ants. They don't look like normal ants: they have exceptionally long legs that keep their bodies from touching the hot ground and they run on just four legs instead of six, the front pair held out in front. It's an extraordinary sight.

Like the blast from a miniature explosion, they race off randomly in all directions, gathering the remains of anything – usually other insects – that have succumbed to the heat. Then they sprint back, stopping occasionally to pirouette while looking upwards, for they use the pattern of polarised light in the sky and the position of the sun to guide them, along with mental snapshots of all the landmarks around them. They travel straight back to their nest entrance, minimising the time they're exposed to the midday heat.

These remarkable sprinting and dancing undertakers are Saharan silver or silvery ants, on account of the silver hairs on their bodies. They're the only

> **The sprinting and pirouetting silver ant is surely the ultimate desert animal and one of the few creatures that have come to terms with the fierce, young place that is the Sahara.**

creatures out and about in the noonday sun, and they're so in tune with this hostile environment that their daily pattern of activity is linked to very precise changes in temperature.

At an air temperature of 45°C (113°F), their main potential predator – a desert lizard – dives underground to its burrow to escape the heat, so at 46°C (115°F) precisely, the ants emerge en masse to forage at midday, while the lizard is safely tucked away. However, they must return to their nest before the temperature reaches, for them, a fatal 53.6°C (128.5°F). They have only this brief window of opportunity. They can forage for no more than a few minutes every day, during the narrow temperature band sandwiched between when predators cease their activity and their own critical thermal maximum. If they're out and about when that temperature is reached, they'll die.

Nevertheless, during that short time they travel exceptionally long distances from the nest, the equivalent of a person trekking up to 65 km (40 miles) across the desert, and with a top speed of about 70 cm (28 inches) per second, they're the third fastest running insects on Earth (after a couple of Australian beetles).

To ensure they don't collapse from the heat, they produce special 'heat shock proteins' that enable their cells to function normally at high body temperatures, but they don't produce them in response to the heat as other animals do; instead, they are built up before they leave the nest, so they're fully prepared to be out in the desert when no other animal can.

While foraging, they travel in as straight a line as possible, preferring to climb over or crawl under obstacles, than to go around them; and they can judge heights, for they bend their long legs and lower their body in order to run under an obstacle without having to stop.

Some ants climb short stalks for brief periods, reaching upwards to slightly cooler air away from the ground. Even with all these tricks, many die, but sufficient ants return with food to keep the queen and colony alive. They're one of the few animals that have come to terms with this fierce, young desert that is the Sahara. 'They live,' as the eminent Harvard biologist Professor E. O. Wilson once put it, 'at the very edge of the envelope of life.'

THE

CHAPTER SIX

FUTURE

Africa is unique. It's one of only two places on Earth (the other being southern Asia) that has kept its megafauna – the big animals – elephant, rhino, hippo, buffalo, antelope and gazelle, along with their major predators: lion, leopard, cheetah, hyena and wild dog, and of course, us. Not that long ago, geologically speaking, the other continents had megafaunas too, but during the past 50,000 years pulses of mass extinctions wiped out most of their large, iconic animals.

Forest Buffalo, Gabon,
West-Central African forest

Australia was first to lose its megafauna. About 46,000 years ago, sheep-sized echidnas, giant short-faced kangaroos, hippo-like marsupials, marsupial tapirs and lions, and giant monitor lizards suddenly disappeared off the face of the Earth. About 13,000 years ago, North America lost its mammoths and mastodons, giant short-faced bears and dire wolves, along with North American lions and cheetahs. South America's megafauna – giant ground sloths and camel-like creatures – followed about 500 years later. The dwarf ground sloths of the Caribbean island arc were next, about 6,000 years ago, followed by the giant crocodiles and giant land turtles of New Caledonia and nearby islands 3,000 years ago, the gorilla-size lemurs of Madagascar 2,000 years ago and New Zealand's giant birds – moas and the giant Haast's eagle – by AD 1400. Climate change and other natural causes could account for the losses, but it's hard to ignore their one common factor: each mass extinction event occurred shortly after the arrival of humans.

It seems humankind walked out of Africa and had an extraordinary and immediate impact on the wildlife it met, yet on the African continent itself our immediate ancestors, who, after all, evolved on the African savannah, lived in harmony with their wildlife, and the megafauna is still there for all to see … but only just. At first, our long-standing relationship ensured that Africa's large animals did not suffer the same fate as their equivalents in most of the rest of the world, but today that is changing, and changing at an unprecedented rate.

Change has always been a part of the African landscape, as it has been a part of the lives of all living things throughout the world, and over millions of years animals have adapted to those changes, but now the pace of change is increasing alarmingly due mainly to our activities – human-induced climate change, habitat loss, desertification, illegal hunting, overfishing, pollution, and the ever-expanding human population and our competition for space. It means our ancient pact with wild Africa has broken down. We've lost touch with our roots, but it's not a lost cause: there *is* hope.

▶ **A gelada baboon watches over an ever-changing Africa as he sits on a cliff edge against a backdrop of the Simien Mountains National Park in Ethiopia, East Africa. This species of Old World monkey is found only in the Ethiopian Highlands, where conditions tend to be cooler and less arid than lowland areas. They sleep on the cliffs and forage in the mountain grasslands.**

ELVIS HAS LEFT THE BUILDING

Mawingo is a partially blind 22-year-old female black rhino. She lives at a cattle ranch-turned-rhino sanctuary at Lewa Downs in Kenya, but she has been a careless mother. Due in part to her poor eyesight, she has a tendency to lose her calves: hyenas took her first-born, a leopard killed her second, and her third calf died of a stomach illness; so it was decided that any subsequent offspring should be taken away from her and hand-fed. The most popular has been Elvis, a rhino full of character and, according to Lewa staff, always up to some kind of mischief.

'He can turn on taps ... he trims wall creepers around the office block, demolishes brick walls, scratches his itchy sides on any solid object and pees inside doorways and windows while breaking panes. He doesn't seem to know his own strength. He gently nudges cars and dents them in the process. He takes shelter from the rain on many of our front porches ... regardless, everyone loves Elvis.'

Elvis even entered his keeper's house and shut the door behind him. She came home to find he had broken glasses, pots and pans, had tried the bed, which he'd broken with his tremendous weight, and was last seen fighting with a saucepan. More recently he was spotted with a female rhino, and everyone thought he'd found a girlfriend, but it was Mawingo. Elvis had found his mother, and the two have a future, which is more than can be said for wild rhinos elsewhere in Africa.

RHINO GRAVEYARD

The date is 9th February 2012. The place is Letsitele in the Limpopo Province of South Africa. The corpse of a large, female white rhino lies on its side, her hide streaked with the white excrement of vultures that have tried unsuccessfully to slice through her tough skin. Alongside her, a two-year-old calf lies dead. Where their horns should be are huge, bloody gashes, but the real shock is in her belly. A near-term foetus is dead too. This was the scene, one of horror touched with sadness, which met the owners of the game farm on which the animals had lived. They had lost two of their seven rhinos in a daylight raid by poachers, and another – a four-year-old calf, still dependent on its mother, and who escaped the slaughter – is still wandering in the bush, devastated and disorientated, crying out continually.

The fact that this female rhino had reached old age is a miracle in itself, but even so, she and her two calves had come to an untimely end. The poachers had bagged three for the price of two, and it's all the more poignant to discover that the female's own mother had been killed by poachers five years previously, and the female herself had been shot but saved by prompt veterinary action, two years before. It highlights a serious problem for rhinos.

In South Africa, considerable success in breeding rhinos in the wild is being offset by poaching, and year on year the situation is worsening. In 2007, poachers killed 13 rhinos, but in 2010 as many as 333 were shot, and in 2011 448 were lost; that's more than one a day in South Africa alone, and this in a relatively well-regulated country. If the current trend continues, then deaths will outstrip births and the population will start to decline.

It's a tragic tale and all for nothing. The rhino's horn is used in traditional medicine in parts of Asia, but it has no medicinal properties whatsoever. It is made of the same material as our fingernails, but fingernails are not worth their weight in gold: only rhino horn. Despite a ban imposed in 1993 on importing rhino horn to China, and the international trade being declared illegal, the continuing demand for rhino horn has spawned a black market in which a kilo could be sold for £41,000 (US$ 66,000) in 2012, and the price is rising.

This is the second wave of the wholesale killing of rhinos. Hunting during the nineteenth and twentieth centuries brought both species of African rhinos – the browsing black rhino and grazing white rhino – to the brink of extinction, but conservation efforts were successful and numbers increased; that is, until now. Currently 20,700 white rhinos and no more than 4,800 black rhinos survive, with 70–80% of them living in South Africa.

▼ Elvis is the mischievous black rhinoceros at Lewa Wildlife Conservancy. There are about 14,500 of his kind living in the wild, but one subspecies – the western black rhino – was declared extinct in 2011, its decline and disappearance due to the poaching for rhino horn to make dagger handles and for use in traditional Asian medicine.

Of the two subspecies of white rhino, the northern white rhino is thought to be extinct in the wild, the last four known individuals in Garamba National Park in the Democratic Republic of Congo not having been seen since 2006. Only a handful of individuals in this subspecies live in zoos or wildlife sanctuaries, although even here there *is* a ray of hope.

In December 2009, four captive-bred northern white rhinos from the Dvur Králové Zoo in Czech Republic were shipped to a breeding area in the Ol Pejeta Conservancy. The sanctuary, which is sandwiched between Mt. Kenya and the Aberdares, provides favourable breeding conditions for rhinos and, having been dehorned, the four pioneers will not be the targets of poachers. In this joint 'Last Chance to Survive' project it is hoped that sufficient numbers will be bred so that eventually the subspecies can be reintroduced into the wild.

SECRET RHINOS

The plight of Africa's rhinos symbolises the fragility of wildlife populations and the dangers that animals across such a volatile continent are facing. Gathering information about their way of life is vital to their future but, just occasionally, nature throws up something that surprises even the most experienced field biologist. There have been many myths and legends that tell of secret gatherings of African animals, and most are just that – legends – but in a part of southwest Africa one of these stories has been found to be true.

In the dead of night, black rhinos converge on a particular water-hole

▼ Angola's giant sable antelope are back from the brink of extinction but are still listed as 'critically endangered' on IUCN's Red List of threatened animals. From a survey in 2007, it is estimated that 200–400 survive in the wild. Now danger for this subspecies comes from interbreeding with roan antelope, which is not endangered.

(see also page 40). Mothers with calves meet with other mothers and their offspring, and lone males of all ages, eager to find a mate, arrive too. In complete darkness, they use smell, touch and sound to communicate with each other: and their kind has been meeting in this way for generations, maybe for thousands of years. Today's crop of visitors represents about 5% of the total world population of black rhinos, and throughout the night, the animals interact socially, going their separate ways by morning.

But this is not something that conservationists are shouting about from the rooftops. The location remains a closely guarded secret. Knowledge may be one way to protect an animal's future, but secrecy is another.

A GIANT RETURNS

A large antelope-like animal, with a black-and-white face and long, backwardly curving horns nervously approaches a bank of light-grey clay. It looks about, sniffs the air, then bends its head and nibbles delicately at the earth. It raises and shakes it head, and brings up its hind leg to kick at a biting fly on its dark brown flank; then, resumes its feeding at the salt lick or *salina*. Reassured that the coast is clear, others join in, shaking their heads repeatedly, their large ears flapping against their heads, to rid themselves of the ever-present and irritating insects. A noticeably larger and darker animal appears. It chases one of the smaller ones away and stands regally on top of the bank. It sees off a potential usurper by spiking the opponent's rump with the sharp tip of its horns, but the other smaller animals ignore the brief altercation and continue to snack.

This special scene is in central Angola, where one of Africa's charismatic megafauna has remained a secret for nearly three decades. In fact, the giant sable antelope eluded observers for so long it was thought to be extinct, but in January 2004 it turned up quite unexpectedly.

After the Angolan civil war, which lasted from 1975 until a ceasefire in 2002, it was uncertain whether any giant sable had survived in the wild. It's a large and very obvious animal – as its name suggests – and its two huge curved horns are a prize for trophy hunters; but it's extremely shy. The crew of an army helicopter claimed to have seen a small herd in 2001, but since then none had been found, not even their bones, although Dr Richard Estes, an authority on the behavioural ecology of African mammals (and author of the must-have field guide *The Behavior Guide to African Mammals*) led a group of people into the wooded savannah in which these animals live to search on the ground. He saw tracks, droppings and chewed grass, but no animals. He was one of the last scientists to publish pictures of the elusive beasts back in 1982, but none had been seen since.

It wasn't until scientists from the Catholic University of Angola, working with Dr Estes, placed camera traps in the Cangandala National Park, that anybody knew whether giant sable were alive or not. The pictures that the animals had effectively taken of themselves told the tale. They showed several animals, mostly adult females and youngsters. It was the first substantial proof for many years that at least one herd had survived the war, and there could be more.

Now the authorities have the task of trying to protect an animal that is held in great respect by Angolans, even considered sacred, known as the *Palanca Negra Gigante*. It's the national animal of Angola and it appears on stamps, the aircraft of the national airline and the shirts of the national football team, and now they know that it's still alive, albeit listed as critically endangered by the World Conservation Union (IUCN).

Poachers still operate in both regions where the animals have been spotted so a pioneering Shepherd Programme, in which shepherds were hired and given basic training, was tasked with guarding any survivors. Even so, it was thought prudent that some animals should be brought into safe enclosures for captive breeding, but several problems face the project's director Portuguese-Angolan Dr Pedro Vaz Pinto, the acknowledged saviour of the giant sable.

Giant sable live in matriarchal herds led by an older female, and outside females are generally not accepted by a herd. Just to make things difficult, some of the surviving females are hybrids of giant sable and the closely related roan antelope; they're probably infertile and they're certainly not pure stock. Giant sable are also extremely aggressive, especially the bulls, and when pursued are reputed to reach speeds of 56 km/h (35 mph). On top of that, there was a distinct absence of mature males, apart from a large roan bull that kept mating with the giant sable cows that produced only hybrids: the search was on.

Using small helicopters, they first tracked down the females seen in the camera-trap pictures and transported them back, one at a time, strung below the helicopter, to the two safe havens. It took ten men to lift a single giant sable: but still no mature males. Then, in 2009, an eleven-year-old bull, which the team nicknamed Duarte, was located in the Luando Reserve, some distance from the breeding centre at Cangandala and out of range of their small helicopter, so the Angolan Air Force arrived with one of their large Russian-built military choppers, and Duarte was similarly and unceremoniously transported to his new home.

Duarte was a gentle beast, allowing the scientists to approach, but an eight-year-old male brought to the centre in 2011 had a different disposition altogether. Ivan the Terrible, as he became known, arrived at about the same time as a young two-year-old bull. Ivan immediately killed the youngster and, as an exasperated Dr Vaz Pinto observes, 'he hasn't stopped misbehaving since'.

On the plus side, Ivan is very popular with the ladies, but he breaks in and out of the sanctuary fence with unfailing regularity. Sometimes he brings members of his herd back into the sanctuary with him, but other times he makes off with some of the sanctuary's main breeding females.

Nevertheless, the breeding programme continues, albeit slowly. The first calf was born in 2010, and by June 2012 there were 10 purebred giant sable and 9 sable-roan hybrids living in two groups. Outside the sanctuary, but living in the

▶ **The African lion may feature strongly in television films but it's a vulnerable species, and one subspecies – the large Barbary lion – is already extinct in the wild, having succumbed to excessive hunting in the nineteenth and twentieth centuries.**

vicinity, are 7–10 purebred giant sable led by the unruly Ivan, and in the country as a whole there are thought to be only 200–400 animals surviving.

Even so, with the war over, Dr Vaz Pinto is optimistic. 'The worst has passed for the giant sable,' he says, 'now we need to secure its future.'

LIFE WITHOUT LIONS

One reason that the giant sable has had a tough time is that a large and meaty animal is a godsend to poor communities where protein is at a premium and the rule of law has been absent in Angola for many years, and so the fact that it's still in danger of extinction should not come as any great surprise. But when Africa's top predator edges into the same uneasy position it's clear that something is wrong.

The African lion may feature strongly in television films made in Africa south of the Sahara, and be a constant companion on a southern or East African safari, but the reality is that, according to the IUCN Red List, it's a vulnerable species and its numbers are declining to such an extent it's heading for promotion in their league of endangered species. Habitat losses, reduction in prey populations, trophy hunting, and diseases such as canine distemper and tuberculosis, have all had an impact, causing a drastic reduction in the overall population from more than 450,000 in the 1940s to fewer than 20,000 today.

One subspecies – the large Barbary lion – is already extinct in the wild. It had the misfortune to share Rome's Coliseum with the equally defunct Atlas bear and was the subspecies kept in the menagerie in the Tower of London. It eventually succumbed to excessive hunting in the nineteenth and twentieth centuries, the last wild specimen shot in Morocco in 1922.

There are claims that it still exists in captivity in collections, such as that of the sultan of Morocco, but DNA analysis indicates that most of these animals are not of Barbary maternal stock. However, the Barbary Lion Project run by WildLink International and Oxford University is attempting to breed back the Barbary lion, and two cubs moved to the Texas Zoo in Victoria, Texas, look to be a promising start. There is also a lion in Neuwied Zoo in Germany that has the right genetic credentials, so the Barbary lion subspecies could well be returned to the wild, albeit in the very distant future.

In the vicinity of Mt. Kilimanjaro, in East Africa, where local extinction of the East African or Masai lion could be on the cards, conservationists are adopting a more inclusive way of saving it.

LION GUARDIANS

Lion bones litter the ground around the young Maasai warrior. He stands tall on long sinewy legs and is wrapped in his bright red shuka to stave off the morning chill. He pushes the bones about with the point of his long and well-honed spear while re-telling how he and several of his group hunted the animal and eventually killed it. He describes how this rite of passage, known to the Maasai as *Olamayio*, is a sign of bravery and personal achievement, and how, having thrown the first spear, he had the honour to remove the animal's paws, ears and mane and parade them on a stick.

He goes on to describe how he was adorned with gifts and became the centre of attention amongst the young ladies in his community. At one time, he says, he would have had to face the lion alone, but now with Kilimanjaro's lions on the wane, he had to hunt in a group. His voice, though, is tinged with remorse; after all, the Maasai have traditionally lived in harmony with the wildlife around them, preferring the blood, meat and milk from their valuable cattle than harvesting from the wild. Aside from *Olamayio*, only in retaliation – the so-called *Olkiyioi* after a lion has killed their livestock – will they, in turn, kill the king of beasts.

The young man's audience of one is Dr Leelah Hazzah, an Egyptian-born researcher who was brought up in Washington DC, but who, as a child in Egypt sat on the roof of her house by the desert and listened for lions. Her father hadn't the heart to tell her that the lions had long been hunted to extinction in that region, but her childhood memory eventually led her back to Africa and a tree-house home in Kenya with a to-die-for view of Mt. Kilimanjaro. Now, she works with lions and has found a unique way to help protect them.

Inspired by TV crime dramas and the technique forensic psychologists use

▶ In Kenya a 'lion guardian' tracks a radio-collared lion in an initiative to encourage Maasai warriors to give up killing lions and to demonstrate their prowess by protecting them.

to take their suspects back to the scene of the crime, she invites her Maasai friends to return to the site of their ritual killing and encourages them to talk about their feelings. It's a gentle approach to changing aeons of tradition, which might turn ritual lion killers into natural lion conservationists … and the Maasai are proving not only to be able talkers, but also willing listeners.

Dr Hazzah lived in a Maasai village for a year learning its social structure and gaining the respect and acceptance of its inhabitants, and she has tried to persuade its young warriors that protecting a lion and naming it is far better than taking the name of a lion they've killed: lion killers are becoming lion guardians. Each guardian, equipped with a bright yellow GPS device, monitors his own lion, and the statistics show that the scheme is working.

During 2011, guardians monitored 96 lions, including 19 with radio collars. No lions were killed in the monitored areas, even though ten were killed on neighbouring ranches where there were no guardians. Guardians also helped villagers to reinforce bomas (corrals) so that lions were less likely to attack domestic livestock, and they found seventeen young children and an old man who had been lost while herding on the savannah. What's more, other communities have now expressed an interest in the Lion Guardian scheme, both in Kenya and Tanzania, making it massively significant. It's one of the biggest changes in African culture in the history of the continent.

DUST STORMS AND DESERTIFICATION

Africa may be a mosaic of different biomes, ecosystems and habitats – the world in microcosm – with high mountains, sprawling savannahs, dense rainforests, productive wetlands, vast lakes and mighty rivers, but it also has hot, dry deserts, including the world's largest, the Sahara. This vast expanse of rock and sand already covers a third of Africa and it's getting bigger, encroaching on other parts of the continent at an alarming rate.

It's something that French botanist André Aubréville warned about back in 1949. He saw how overgrazing and the removal of trees were causing the desert to spread. He called it 'desertification', a process that appears to be worsening, especially in the Sahel, a buffer zone between the desert proper to the north and the savannah to the south. In this in-between world, there seems to be more dust than soil, and dust storms have been more prevalent in the region in recent years.

In Mauritania during the 1960s, there were no more than a couple of dust storms a year; now there are eighty, and the topsoil in parts of Niger, Chad and northern Nigeria is simply blowing away, turning more of the Sahel into desert; but there is an unexpected benefit to all this.

Nowhere can you see the rate of change from savannah to desert more than in the Bodélé Depression on the Sahara's southern edge, the lowest point in Chad. About six thousand years ago and again in the eleventh and twelfth centuries, it was an enormous lake, known to geologists as Megalake Chad.

▶ **Dust storms occur here for about a hundred days each year, powered during winter by the powerful winds, which suck the moisture from any living thing that's unfortunate enough to be exposed to them.**

It had a surface area about the same size as California, and it was fed by large rivers, some of which entered the lake through extensive deltas. It was the largest lake in the world, but now most of that water has gone, leaving a rapidly shrinking 'Little Chad', and the Bodélé has become the largest source of dust on the planet.

The dust is formed from the remains of microscopic diatoms that once thrived in the lake as part of its population of phytoplankton. When most of the lake dried up, a 4 m (13 feet) deep carpet of their remains was left on the floor of the depression and dried by the scorching African sun. Now, the dust is blown aloft by the wind.

Dust storms occur here for about a hundred days each year, powered during winter by the powerful *Harmattan* winds. *Harmattan* is derived from the Arabic, meaning 'evil thing', a reference to the way in which the wind sucks moisture from any living thing that's unfortunate enough to be exposed to it. As the relative humidity drops from 80% to 20% in just a few hours the chance of survival for any lost traveller diminishes just as rapidly.

The winds are channelled between the Tibesti and Ennedi mountains, scouring the depression and carrying small grains of diatomite thousands of kilometres away. Downwind, in West Africa, the dust can block the sun for several days, and the dust clouds are visible from space. More significantly, large

▲ In Mauritania a grid of fencing attempts to slow the progress of advancing sand dunes on an ancient oasis and settlement in the western part of the Sahara.

quantities are blown far beyond African shores, across the entire Atlantic Ocean to be deposited in the Amazon Basin in South America. It is estimated that the Bodélé Depression provides more than half of the dust needed to fertilise the Amazon rainforest. The home of jaguars, spider monkeys and macaws is sustained by a gift from the land of the addax and camel.

DESERTS COME, DESERTS GO

Desertification is not an exclusively modern phenomenon, for African deserts have come and gone with unfailing regularity for the past million years. During the last period of maximum glaciation in the Ice Age, for example, the Sahara was considerably bigger than it is today. The tropical forests shrank and the Sahara stretched southwards to almost join the Kalahari, so Africa was largely desert. In about 12,500 BC, on the other hand, it was wetter and more like the East African savannah; and at each oscillation in the cycle wildlife has had to adapt, migrate or die … and that included our forebears.

It seems that our ancient ancestors couldn't take the heat and the lack of water, so there were at least three waves of hominid migration out of Africa that seem to coincide with abrupt changes from wet to dry and back again, a phenomenon known as the 'Sahara Pump Theory'. If an 'out of Africa' theory for human evolution and migration is correct, then *Homo erectus* or 'upright man' left Africa for pastures new in southern Asia and parts of Europe about 1.8 million years ago, when the desert expanded. Under similar conditions, *Homo heidelbergensis*, forerunner of the Neanderthals, walked out of Africa about 600,000 years ago, and in another dry period modern man reached the Near East by 125,000 years ago. Before each sudden exit, these different species of hominid had spread into the greening desert from sub-Saharan Africa to take advantage of the savannah-like conditions and the wealth of wildlife, but as the climate changed and the desert returned some groups were forced to trek south or migrate even further north into Europe and east into Asia.

In modern times, however, this natural cycle has been hijacked, with desertification exacerbated by human activities, such as overgrazing and human-caused climate change. Even so, this latter sin is actually turning out to be a blessing in disguise for at least some parts of the Sahara.

Interpreting satellite imagery of the Sahara and surrounding regions, Scientists at Lund University's Geobiosphere Science Centre in Sweden think that the area could be starting to 'green' again due to increased rainfall, thanks to human-induced global warming. Hotter air has a greater capacity to hold moisture, which turns to rain. This means that shrubs are growing larger and new trees, such as acacias, are taking hold. Areas showing up unexpectedly green include central Chad, southwest Egypt and western Sudan. This pattern is appearing in other parts of the desert too.

In Western Sahara, a disputed region of Morocco, climate scientists from the University of Cologne's Africa Research Unit, who are working in the field, have found that herdsmen are enjoying exceptional pastures, camels are grazing on lands that had not been used for thousands of years, and wildlife – such as gazelles, several species of amphibians, ostriches and other birds – is returning to where it was probably common thousands of years ago.

GREAT GREEN WALL

Where this newly identified trend of a greening Sahara is going is not at all clear, for the climate modellers cannot agree. Some say that the Sahara will be getting wetter, others that it will be drier; but what if we could tip the balance in favour of a greening desert? Could the planting of trees, for example, arrest the desert's advance? It's not a fanciful notion.

In Kenya, the grassroots *Green Belt Movement*, founded by the late Nobel Peace Prize winner Wangari Maathai, has encouraged women in rural areas to plant more than 40 billion trees and trained 30,000 women in forestry, beekeeping and food handling in a bid to prevent further environmental destruction, especially deforestation and soil erosion. At Keita, in the centre of the Republic of Niger, an Italian initiative saw 18 million trees planted during a 20-year period to combat desertification, returning 36,000 hectares (90,000 acres) of what had become barren land into workable farmland and forests.

However, these schemes pale in significance when compared to another large-scale development across the entire Sahel. An African Union project has the ambition to plant 37 species of drought-tolerant trees right across Africa in an

▼ **Some say that the Sahara will be getting wetter, others that it will be drier; but what if we could tip the balance in favour of a greening desert? People have taken up the challenge with a raft of novel solutions.**

attempt to contain desertification. It's called the Great Green Wall, and consists of a 15 km (9.3-mile) wide band of trees that is intended to span the continent from Senegal to Djibouti. It'll pass through Mauritania, Mali, Burkina Faso, Niger, Nigeria, Chad, Sudan, Eritrea and Ethiopia to create a 7,775 km (4,831-mile) long, coast-to-coast forest. The trees would help improve the soil, stabilise sand and dust, and enable farmers to return to drought-hit regions. So far, trees have been planted around the Senegal capital, and Eritrea has made a start with 30,537 tree seedlings planted on a previously barren 23-hectare site, of which 90% have survived and are growing tall, but most of the planned 11,662,500 hectares (28,818,665 acres) across the rest of the Sahel still remains untouched. However, hope is not entirely lost. Others have taken up the challenge of greening the desert with a raft of novel solutions.

HI-TECH, LOW-TECH

The Sahara Forest Project, championed by British and Norwegian concerns, aims to use seawater and hot desert air to make fresh water for growing crops and trees. It proposes the construction of chains of seawater-cooled greenhouses, similar to those originally developed by British inventor Charlie Paton in the early 1990s, which could be built across the Sahara. Two pilot greenhouse-power plant hybrids are being built in the Middle East to test the technique.

A suggestion from Swedish architect Magnus Larsson is to use a bacterium, *Bacillus pasteurii,* to turn sand into sandstone, a process being explored by Professor Jason T. DeJong at the Soil Interactions Laboratory of the University of California at Davis. It would be injected into the Sahara's dunes, the resulting rock providing a solid base as well as a source of trapped water for trees. It could provide a solid base to support the Great Green Wall initiative and even provide settlers returning to the area with cave-like dwellings in the newly made porous rock – so called 'arenaceous anti-desertification architecture'.

A third project is from the Dutch inventor Pieter Hoff. He has developed the 'Waterboxx', a means of collecting rain and dew, no matter how slight, and releasing it to a seedling at a rate of about four tablespoons a day. Built into the design is shade at midday and temperature regulation, but the key principle behind the device is purely biological. The seedling is supported while its taproot probes for a natural water supply deep below the surface. The Waterboxx is then taken away and used elsewhere.

Pieter Hoff has also been experimenting with different types of trees to find which ones thrive best in extreme desert conditions, and one genus has come up trumps. The fast-growing and drought-tolerant moringa or drumstick tree, originally from northern India, has become known to tree-planting organisations as the 'miracle tree' for it has a wealth of useful qualities. Gram for gram, its leaves have seven times the vitamin C found in oranges, four times the vitamin A in carrots, four times the amount of calcium in milk, three times the potassium in

◂ In some parts of the Sahara, camels are able to graze in places where the desert has re-greened, due in part to global warming.

bananas, and twice as much protein as in yogurt, together with a range of other essential vitamins, minerals and amino acids. Drying the leaves concentrates the nutrients so even a spoonful of leaf powder a day can go a long way to help alleviate malnutrition, and the moringa happens to grow well in the places where people need nutrition the most.

While these solutions are technologically based – and therefore may be too costly or too fussy to be attractive to most of the poor of the Sahel – other tree-planters are adopting low-tech solutions. The Re-Greening Initiative of Chris Reij from the Free University of Amsterdam, and Australian agronomist and former missionary Tony Rinaudo have seen Burkina Faso, Mali and Niger farmers reforesting large tracts of the Sahel with rock-bottom finance and little in the way of technology, producing results that have been hailed as an environmental success.

Rather than clear scrub in favour of crops (which inevitably die) they let some of the scrub and native trees grow. The roots of these species push deep down – tens of metres, sometimes hundreds of metres – below the surface. Crops are planted in between. In temperate regions we tend to maximise a crop's exposure to the sun so trees are removed, but in the tropics the crop needs protecting, so the trees are needed; and once the local farmers buy into the concept, it's self-perpetuating. In Niger alone, five million hectares (12 million acres) have been reforested in this way, something no other country in Africa has achieved. The prediction is that a green zone many times wider than the Great Green Wall could spread across the southern Sahel by reforesting in this way, and the water need not come from desalination plants; instead, the tree planters can tap into reservoirs deep beneath the desert.

▲ The film crew come across a large, old baobab tree in the Gorongosa National Park.

▶ At a settlement on Mt. Gorongosa, row upon row of saplings are ready for the villagers to plant out and reforest the mountain slopes in the national park.

UNDERGROUND AFRICA

One of the largest known underground reservoirs in Africa is the Nubian Sandstone Aquifer System, estimated to contain 150,000 cubic kilometres (36,000 cubic miles) of groundwater below two million square kilometres (773,000 square miles) of the Sahara in Egypt, Sudan, Chad and Libya. As precipitation is close to zero over much of these areas, these aquifers, as they are known, are filled with water that probably fell as rain up to 5,000 years ago, so-called 'fossil water'.

More and more aquifers have been collated and mapped by geologists from the British Geological Survey and University College London, who identified underground water reservoirs in the large sedimentary rock basins below Libya, Algeria and Chad, meaning that countries designated 'water scarce' actually have substantial hidden groundwater reserves. Libya's Great Man-Made River Project is already tapping into the resource, the world's largest underground network of pipes and aqueducts. On a smaller scale, a team of Russian scientists looking over satellite images of the Sahara discovered an underground river below the town of Atar in Mauritania, providing all of the town's 50,000 inhabitants with water every day of the year, something they had never enjoyed before. On the bigger scale it means these countries have a buffer to offset the vagaries of climate change, although this underground water is finite and care must be exercised how it is used. As it is not being replenished by rainfall, it is not a renewable resource, much like oil reserves.

SUBTERRANEAN LIFE

The Sahara is not the only desert region in Africa where underground discoveries are being made. Another gentle reminder that Africa has many more secrets to surrender appeared in the Kalahari in 1986. Much of the Kalahari sits on very ancient rocks, some of the oldest in the world, but to the south and southeast of Etosha the land is very different. The underlying strata are much younger – dolomite limestone – and this karst landscape is being eroded to form a hidden, subterranean world that's only recently been explored.

A caving expedition to the Karstveldt region of Namibia investigated a hole in the ground. The cavers dropped through, not knowing what they would find. Squeezing through claustrophobically narrow passageways, they eventually came to a gigantic cave, with room enough to park three jumbo jets nose to tail, but that was only the start of it.

They dropped a pebble into the darkness and heard it plop into water, but it was not a small pool that they'd found many metres below them, but a vast lake. Further exploration revealed that this underground reservoir has an area of 2.6 hectares (6.45 acres), but its depth is unknown. Even so, they realised that they had discovered the largest underground lake in the world, located in the *Drachenhauchloch* – the Dragon's Breath Cave – so named because at certain

> ▶ **Squeezing through claustrophobically narrow passageways, they eventually came to a gigantic cave ... they realised that they had discovered the largest underground lake in the world, home to a unique and exceedingly rare species of cave catfish.**

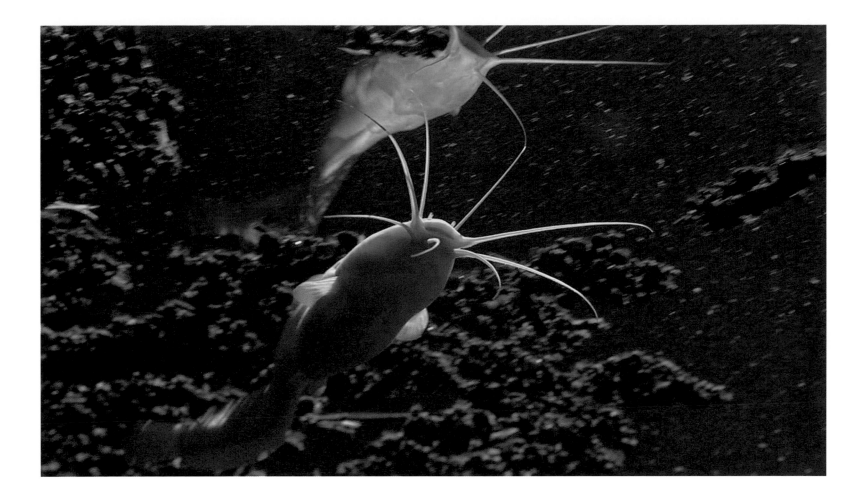

▲ As far as anyone knows, the catfish in Aigumas Cave in Namibia are found nowhere else on Earth. They are effectively blind and use their four pairs of barbels to find and feed on detritus washed into the cave, anything from bat droppings to animal carcasses and insects.

times of year, when the air outside is cold, steam escapes from the entrance like a dragon's breath. It's just one of many underground lakes and caverns belonging to a massive cave system running right under this part of the Kalahari.

In one cave – Aigumas Cave – lives a unique and exceedingly rare species of cave catfish. Resembling a white eel, about 16 cm (more than 6 inches) long, it has two very small eyes, covered by skin, so it's effectively blind. It relies on the four pairs of slender barbels on its snout to smell, taste and feel its way around. It appears to thrive on bat guano, as well as animal carcasses, insects and cave spiders that happen to fall into its subterranean lake, but only 150 individuals survive, making it one of the most endangered and isolated fishes in the world.

Other caves, as well as the giant Dragon's Breath Cave, have their own species of amphipods and isopods, and Lake Guinas, a crystal blue sinkhole lake, surrounded by 30 m (100-feet) high vertical cliffs formed from a collapsed cave roof, has its own multicoloured mouth-breeding tilapia. This specialised fauna is here because the reservoir is relatively old, almost prehistoric, but recharged continually by rain falling on the hills, one of the few places in Namibia where the seasonal rains, marked by distinct wet and dry seasons, are predictable. This fossil water resource is tapped into by the many more living things up on the surface.

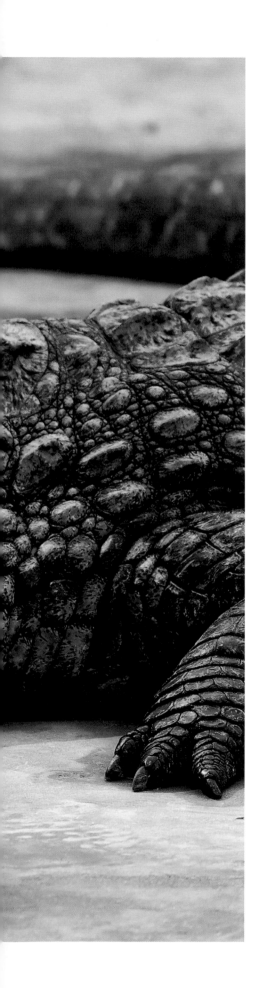

OUT OF SIGHT

While the Kalahari caves are home to animals that spend their entire lives underground, known as troglobites, caves elsewhere on the continent have unusual cave guests or trogloxenes. These unexpected cave dwellers hide where you would least expect them. In western Gabon, a cold-blooded trogloxene joins hundreds of warm-blooded Egyptian fruit bats and tens of thousands of insect-eating roundleaf- and giant leaf-nosed bats in the Abanda Caves. In the trace of light from the cave entrance two eyes glow in dark, for resting on the sand and gravel of the cave floor is an orange crocodile. French and American speleologists, on an expedition to Gabon sponsored by France's Institute for Development Research (IRD), discovered it in 2010.

It's a male, its tinge of orange contrasting with the eerie white of the cavefish, shrimps and freshwater crabs in an underground stream. It's no bigger than 1.7 m (5.6 feet) long, probably a subspecies of the African dwarf crocodile, one of the smallest crocodilians in the world. Whether it lives permanently in the cave, feeding on bat corpses that drop from the roof, or is a visitor escaping unfavourable conditions outside is unknown, but there are several individuals of various sizes hiding in the caves. Besides the orange male, there are several normal-coloured females and some youngsters. Even so, it's a rare occurrence, and Abanda has now become one of the few places in the world where crocodiles are found in caves or underground.

Another is the most unlikely place to find anything living, let alone a crocodile; but hidden away in drought-ravaged areas of Mauritania on the southern edge of the Sahara Desert are Nile crocodiles. Tara Shine discovered them while she was a Ph.D. student at the University of Ulster. She was surveying ephemeral wetlands that are dry for most of the year, and local people told her of some crocodiles. She couldn't believe it at first, but then she found eight sites where crocodiles aestivate, a similar state of torpor to hibernation but where the animal is escaping a parched landscape and heat rather than cold. They were holed up in burrows or caves, waiting for the rains, but sometimes coming out at night. Unlike their giant relatives to the south, they reach no more than 1.5 m (5 feet) long, rather than the usual 5 m (16 feet) for the species, the stunted growth probably due to a lack of food for most of the year.

These crocodiles of the Sahara are relict populations isolated from others of their kind when the desert formed so suddenly thousands of years ago. Today, much of Africa's wildlife faces the same fate, especially the larger mammals, as habitats are fragmented by human activities. It's of great concern, for increasingly all the richer nations of the world want a slice of Africa, particularly its wood.

◄ Small relict populations of Nile crocodiles still survive in the Sahara and Sahel but they are slowly heading towards local extinction.

HIGHWAYS OF DEATH

A forest elephant, more used to roaming free in the world's second largest tropical rainforest, stops in its tracks and, for such a large animal, it makes no sound at all. It's a large bull in musth prospecting for cows on heat, but his attention has been diverted to the smell of an altogether different nature, an alien smell, something that reeks of malevolence. He raises his trunk, sniffing the air carefully, and doesn't move. A twig cracks and he shudders almost imperceptibly; there is something creeping through the forest and heading towards him. Still he doesn't move, hidden as he is behind a dark wall of vegetation in the forest's understorey. The rustling of disturbed leaves get louder as the threat comes closer. Now is the time to move.

He rushes from his hiding place, ears flapping and trunk horizontal. There's a loud crack and a painful thud into his shoulder, but he keeps on going, charging down his adversaries. They're illegal hunters, intent on removing his fine ivory tusks to sell on the black market, so they can be carved into ivory trinkets that sell for thousands of pounds. He crashes on through the forest. He is wounded, but not fatally. The hunter panicked and fired erratically, missing his target's vital organs.

On this occasion, the elephant escaped. His mistake had been to walk close to an unprotected road, but he got away with it … this time. A logging company

A savannah elephant sports a radio collar around its neck. With this, scientists can follow its movements and work out where wildlife corridors are needed for it to roam naturally.

◄ Elephant tusks are stockpiled in a storage facility at Botswana's Department of Wildlife and National Parks.

OVERLEAF Orphan elephants fling red dirt during their daily dust bath in the Nairobi Elephant Nursery in Kenya. Run by the David Sheldrick Wildlife Trust, the nursery raises orphaned elephants and gradually rehabilitates them back into the wild.

had built the road, but it brought more than loggers into the forest. It had become a highway for poachers, their trade in ivory and bushmeat rather than trees. Like the traffic in rhino horns, poaching is one of the biggest threats to a key animal in Africa's megafauna. Most ivory comes from Central Africa en route to Asia, where sophisticated crime networks with substantial financial backing run the illegal trade. The result is an estimated loss of 60,000 elephants a year, and in Central Africa roads are the key to poaching operations.

Landsat images, analysed by scientists at the Woods Hole Research Centre in the USA, are being used to monitor the impact of commercial logging and associated road density on the rainforest environment of a large part of Central Africa, especially the Congo Basin. Currently, over 30% of Central Africa's humid forests are under logging concession, while only 12% is protected.

The satellite data shows that with 56,000 km (35,000 miles) of logging roads within the forested regions of Cameroon, Central African Republic, Equatorial Guinea, Gabon, Republic of Congo and Democratic Republic of Congo, the rainforests are not as remote as they once were. The highest road densities are in Cameroon and Equatorial Guinea, while the most rapidly changing country is the Republic of Congo, where the rate of road building has quadrupled since 1976. However, a programme of road construction will likely feed a new logging frontier opening up in the Democratic Republic of Congo, as the country emerges from civil war, and scientists are beginning to understand the probable effects.

It's been found that the abundance of large mammal species in the Congo Basin increases the further that populations are from roads; in fact, no carcasses of elephants killed by poachers or signs of poaching are generally found more than 45 km (28 miles) from a road. The study showed that Salonga National Park, one of the largest forested national parks in Africa, has wilderness covering half its area, but it is all no more than 10 km (6 miles) from a road. As a consequence, Salonga is home to ten times fewer elephants than much smaller parks that are 60 km (37 miles) from roads.

While these results indicate that forest elephants are deeply threatened by illegal hunting for ivory and meat by hunters with easy access from logging roads, the actual movements of individual elephants through this maze had been unknown; that is, until twenty-eight African forest elephants were fitted with GPS telemetry collars. The study by scientists from several European and American universities and institutions revealed that the increase in road building is, indeed, having a negative impact on the movements of elephants. In wilderness areas without roads, the elephants ranged widely, but even here their ranging has become inhibited. These elephants once travelled great distances through the forest, but that behaviour no longer exists.

However, it's not the road itself that deters elephants, for they appreciate road-side vegetation. It's the people and guns that the road brings. The result is that any unmanaged road, unprotected from hunting, is a barrier to elephant movement.

In this study, only one elephant dared to cross an unprotected road, and it increased its speed fourteen-fold to get past the obstacle. This means that populations are becoming more isolated and there's a real danger that the Congo wilderness and its forest elephants will disappear altogether. For this reason, scientists are looking at ways in which the impact of fragmentation can be minimised.

CORRIDORS OF LIFE

One way to overcome the isolation of animal communities is to create wildlife corridors in which animals move safely from one area to another, even though an area might have a high density of farms and people. In the UK, for example, initiatives such as the planting of 'bee roads' in Yorkshire to slow the decline in wild bee populations, are a relatively inexpensive solution to an environmental challenge; but elephants on the move in Kenya are a much bigger (although not insurmountable) problem.

The Nature Conservancy together with Sir Richard Branson, Save the Elephants, Lewa Wildlife Conservancy and Mount Kenya Trust, successfully created a 14 km (9-mile) long wildlife corridor, together with an elephant underpass, which will enable 9,500 elephants in the Ndare Ndare Forest Reserve and the Mt. Kenya National Reserve to move between the two wilderness areas and the two elephant populations.

The scheme was greeted with a deal of scepticism at first, but on the night of the first of January 2011, just four days after the tunnel had opened, a male elephant named Tony led a group of young males through the underpass, and in a short time more than 30 animals learned to enter the tunnel and cross below a major road without putting themselves or motorists in danger and without damaging crops or frightening villagers. It means that these elephants can range further than before and socialise with herds they may have previously been connected to but were discouraged from meeting because of the road and other human developments in their path.

The importance of wildlife corridors has become apparent in the conservation of one of the world's most endangered primates, the Cross River gorillas. This subspecies of lowland gorilla lives in a forested mountain region on the border between Cameroon and Nigeria. Using high-resolution satellite images and comparing them with ground observations, conservationists have been able to prospect for suitable gorilla habitat, and the signs are promising. They have found that there are more sites with little human activity than was first thought. Teams on foot explored the key wilderness areas spotted on the satellite pictures and discovered signs of gorillas, such as dung and nests, where they were not expected to be. It means that these animals have 50% more habitat available to them than was previously thought. The observations also found that corridors of natural vegetation connect most of the eleven known key gorilla areas, although one site – the Afi Mountain Wildlife Sanctuary in Nigeria – is out on a limb, separated

By 1983, the violence of the civil war had escalated near the park and the entire place was left to fend for itself. Now Gorongosa is starting to fight back, and what a place it's turning out to be.

from the other sites by farmland and damaged woodland. The next stage is to rehabilitate degraded corridors and preserve the rest in a five-year conservation plan drawn up in February 2012. On the other side of the continent, an even bigger rehabilitation programme is underway.

AFRICA'S JURASSIC PARK

A man stands beside the Msicadzi River in the Gorongosa National Park of Mozambique. Hornbills adorn two isolated fever trees in which an African fish eagle has taken the very highest perch. A group of crowned cranes fuss about close to a nearby reed bed, while an untidy flock of black-and-white spur-winged geese, the largest of Africa's waterfowl, flops past on its way across the wide green plain to Lake Urema. In front of the trees is a small, square, concrete building, more a shelter than a house. A staircase on the outside leads up to a flat roof. On two sides, crude black arrows painted over the wide open doorways indicate that Chitengo is 10 km (6 miles) away. The walls themselves are a dirty brown at their base and paler near the top, as if the painter left in haste, and they're pockmarked by bullet holes.

▼ Yellow-billed storks, hammerkops, egrets, pelicans and other water birds feed in a wetland area of the Gorongosa National Park.

The man is eminent biologist Professor E. O. Wilson of Harvard University, a world authority on ants and 'father' of the science of sociobiology; and the house is the *Casa dos Leões*, the Lion House. Together they symbolise the sense of hope that pervades this corner of Africa.

Professor Wilson is here because the park is still here, back from the brink, despite humankind's best efforts to destroy it. It was caught up in two wars – a war of independence and a civil war – when anarchy reigned and hunger forced local people to find food where they could. The large mammals became that food, but now dedicated conservationists are trying to return the park to its former glory.

Before Mozambique's wars, Gorongosa was one of the jewels in Africa's crown, a place teeming with wildlife that was visited by the rich and famous. From the early 1920s, the park was a hunting reserve for administrators and guests of Portugal's Mozambique Company, but in 1960 it was named a national park and its animals shot with cameras rather than guns. By the late 1960s, Australian ecologist Kenneth Tinley had surveyed the large mammalian fauna and counted 200 lions; 2,200 elephants; 5,500 wildebeest; 3,000 Selous' zebra; 3,500 waterbuck; 2,000 impala; 3,500 hippos; together with herds of eland, sable and hartebeest and a staggering 14,000 buffalo, the largest single population in the whole of Africa.

The Portuguese built the Lion House in those colonial days. It was part of a restaurant and park headquarters, but had been erected on the flood plain of the river and spent much of the summer's wet season under water. After it was abandoned, a pride of lions took it over. They draped themselves over the stairs and used the elevated position of the flat roof to watch for prey, so that's how it became known as the Lion House.

However, by 1983, the violence of the civil war had escalated near the park and the entire place was left to fend for itself. Frequent battles took place in and around Gorongosa, with both sides of the conflict killing the animals; elephants for ivory to trade for new guns, and the rest for meat. It was thought during the civil war that about 95% of the large mammals were slaughtered, but it wasn't until after the ceasefire that the extent of the carnage became clear. A survey in 1994 revealed just 15 buffalo, 5 zebra, 6 lions, 300 elephants and a handful of wildebeest. Something had to be done; and it was.

In 2004, Gorongosa caught the eye of young American entrepreneur and philanthropist Gregory C. Carr. His foundation is supporting the Gorongosa Restoration Project to the tune of $40 million, and in close collaboration with the Mozambique government it is rebuilding the park's infrastructure and restoring its wildlife. Gorongosa is starting to fight back, and what a place it's turning out to be.

The park is located at the southern end of Africa's Great Rift Valley. It's a big park, covering about 4,000 sq km (1,545 sq miles), and it contains a great diversity of habitats, upwards of 50 different kinds. The dominant features are a wide valley floor and flood plain with Lake Urema at its centre, along with the Cheringoma Plateau, and the 1,863 m (6,112 feet) high Mt. Gorongosa that lends

◄ **The African fish eagle is found throughout sub-Saharan Africa, especially in places with large bodies of water, such as Lake Urema in Gorongosa National Park. It is the national bird of Zambia and Zimbabwe.**

its name to the park. Rivers originating in the surrounding highlands, including Mt. Gorongosa, feed the lake and cause seasonal flooding of the valley floor, while forests on the mountain slopes help regulate water-flow into the park.

During floods Lake Urema expands to as much as 200 sq km (77 sq miles), while during droughts it can shrink to a little as 10 sq km (4 sq miles). This regular cycle of expansion and contraction has given rise to a unique patchwork of smaller ecosystems; savannah, grasslands dotted with acacia, dry forests on sands and rain-filled pans, and thickets growing on old termite hills. There are forests of yellow fever trees and stands of borassus or palmyra palms, and the Cheringoma Plateau is topped with 'miombo', which is close-canopy savannah woodlands. A spectacular limestone gorge, which represents the southern limit of the rift valley, is lined with dense rainforest.

Its sheer diversity and the success of the ongoing restoration programme has led Professor Wilson to describe Gorongosa as 'one of the most important parks in Africa, if not the world'. He has focused on the park as an element in his digital textbook *E. O. Wilson's Life on Earth* using Gorongosa as a model ecosystem and transformation programme.

Large animals, such as kudu – the spiral-horned antelope that featured in Ernest Hemingway's *Green Hills of Africa* – are to be found in the miombo forests, and hippos are now breeding near the lake. Secretary birds have returned, having not been seen for many years, and a whole range of animals, mainly brought in from South Africa, are being acclimatised in a fenced and heavily protected section of the park known as 'The Sanctuary'. A recent stocktaking of animals here revealed wildebeest, Cape buffalo, sable antelope, reedbuck, bushbuck, waterbuck, hartebeest, kudu, warthog, impala, oribi, nyala, and grey and red duikers, and all are almost ready to be reintroduced into the park proper where they'll fend for themselves. Cheetahs have already been released from their quarantine boma and are now hunting naturally. Even so, the park is not without problems. Gorongosa's zebras are thought to be a separate subspecies of the plains zebra – the Selous' zebra – recognised by stripes that go right down to the hoof. Only 25–30 survived the wars, so inbreeding is a real threat if the line is to be kept pure.

The little animals are revealing too. Aside from the many species of Professor Wilson's beloved ants, some of which are new to science, Gorongosa's yellow fever tree forests are filled with unusually large numbers of praying mantises. The presence of so many voracious insect-eating insects indicates that the insect population of the park must be in good shape. The little creatures survived the wars. All they need now is for the bigger ones to join them.

Both big and little are important for a park to function. The little crawling and slithering creatures may run the world, Professor Wilson suggests, but they are dependent on the larger ones to retain the status quo. In places where herds of zebra or wildebeest no longer graze, shrubs grow at the expense of the grasses and wild fires caused by lightning strikes are more damaging and threatening. Where there are fewer elephants knocking over trees to feed on their upper branches, forests increase in density. And, with the availability of dung and dead carcasses reduced, populations of scavengers fall significantly. Yet, at Gorongosa the natural platform of vegetation has survived and its populations of insects and other small animals have remained largely intact, a healthy starting point for a restoration programme.

One legacy of the conflicts, however, is the behaviour of the surviving elephants. They've become more suspicious of people than elephants elsewhere in Africa, and it's easy to see why. More than 2,000 were slaughtered during the war, and it's thought that the survivors remember the hunting and shooting. A 'therapy' programme administered by one of the world's leading elephant researchers Dr Joyce Poole, director of research and conservation at ElephantVoices, is underway to help them calm down.

▼ A red-billed oxpecker prospects for ticks and other external parasites on the body of an impala. The impala is just one of many species of African game being reared in Gorongosa's sanctuary area, ready to be re-introduced into the national park proper.

In a typical encounter, Dr Poole approaches a herd in her four-wheel drive vehicle and the elephants bunch together. The matriarch charges, but Dr Poole responds not by revving and moving away rapidly, but by simply switching off the engine and sitting quietly. The rest of the herd might back up their leader, but she speaks to them in a quiet, reassuring manner and gradually they calm down and move away. When the same herd is encountered again they are more relaxed and do not charge; the therapy is working.

One creature, though, seems to have come through the war relatively unscathed: the ubiquitous Nile crocodile. This species is widespread throughout Africa, but Gorongosa's crocs are special: they're big … very big, and there are lots of them. According to Gerald Wood's *Guinness Book of Animal Facts and Feats*, the largest, reliably measured Nile crocodile was a specimen shot near Mwanza

in Tanzania in 1905. It was 6.45 m (21.2 feet) from its snout to the tip of its tail – a real monster – and there are claims that a 6.1 m (20-feet) long man-eater nicknamed Gustave still plies the Ruzizi River in Burundi.

More usually, mature males grow to no more than 5 m (16.4 feet) with exceptional beasts at 5.5 m (18 feet) long, but it's thought that many of the older crocs in Gorongosa exceed these dimensions, so are in the monster class, putting them in the running for the title 'world's largest crocodiles'. That honour is currently bestowed on the saltwater crocodile of Southern Asia and Australasia, but when wetland ecologist Professor Max Finlayson, from Australia's Charles Sturt University flew over the park by helicopter, the size and number of Nile crocodiles he saw surprised him. He hadn't seen so many crocodiles in one place at any one time, and he was struck by their size. They were larger than the saltwater crocodiles he'd seen in Northern Australia and there were many together in one spot. A survey in 2007 revealed that Gorongosa is home to at least 1,207 Nile crocodiles.

The continued success of the crocodiles and the restoration of other wildlife of Gorongosa, however, is only part of its ongoing story. One of the key developments is that the conservationists and administrators are not simply creating a 20-year vision for the park itself; they're also working with the leaders of communities around the park to help them with their own 20-year dream, where they want to go in terms of better economic development, better farming, schools and health care. At Gorongosa, human development and biodiversity protection are pushing forward hand in hand.

One of the key people is Pedro Muagura, known locally as 'guardian of the mountain'. He has planted personally or is responsible for reforestation programmes that have planted more than a hundred million trees. On Earth Day 2012 alone, he oversaw the planting of 3.8 million trees in several mountain communities. Tree nurseries have been established in each community and they grow up to 3,500 seedlings at a time. Seeds are collected from local trees, such as the *panga panga* and silk plant tree, and the seedlings planted on the slopes of Mt. Gorongosa.

Even schoolchildren from the mountain communities are helping to restore the forests with their *Plantar Para a Vida* project, meaning 'Plant for Life'. Muagura, who manages the reforestation programme at Gorongosa, points out that by the time the children have reached their twentieth birthdays, the trees will be 15 m (50 feet) tall, and they're vital to the national park. Most of the seasonal rains fall on and around the mountain and its trees are vital in stabilising the soil in deforested areas, to maintain and control the flow of water to the rest of the national park, as well as to provide valuable water for irrigating the crops of local communities around the park.

People are as important at Gorongosa as wildlife, which is apt, as Professor Wilson points out, as it is where our own story began.

▲ Savannah or bush elephant herds tend to average about ten individuals, so this herd is exceptional and could be two herds that have merged temporarily. Each herd is made up of related females and their young and led by the 'matriarch', usually the oldest and wisest elephant in the group.

'It's one of the places in the world, along with other parts of southern and East Africa, where our species evolved. We're native here. There is the deep emotional pull of the African savannah … poets proclaim it, explorers say it, and scientists feel it (although they're careful how they say it). When people have been here a while, they feel at home. Why is that?

'Well, biologists, psychologists, and anthropologists are beginning to agree that we love this habitat because it was where our species was born. Every other animal species has a powerful preference for a particular habitat, and the abilities and instincts that go with it. It's necessary for their survival. Is it too much to suppose that we carry this within us, even though for the past 12,000 years we've spread around the world? Is it reasonable to suppose that there's a little residue of that left in us?

'Psychologists have conducted experiments across modern human cultures, asking what kind of habitat people would want to live in, and the African savannah wins by a little edge, but it wins because it has three features that people like – an elevated place overlooking grasslands and next to a body of water. And lo and behold, I'm standing on an elevated spot, next to the Msicadzi River, overlooking savannah. So, there's magic in the park that lies below, and beyond all of the science, all of the wonders of biodiversity, all of the magnificence of having a piece of Earth as it was before our species even came along – and that is why we must save and treasure Gorongosa National Park.'

Indeed, places like Gorongosa represent small slices of Africa where people can come and see a world as it looked and felt before the coming of humanity, and it could be, Professor Wilson suggests, a part of an insurance policy for the living world.

'What we have are two parallel worlds – our own madhouse world, with civilisation that we create as we wish which is advancing at breakneck speed, and another world we leave alone to evolve as it is, at its own pace. This second world serves as a backup if something bad happens to us: life would go on; and in a sense, since it gave rise to us, and since our immediate ancestors were a kind of animal species that once lived in a place like Gorongosa, we will have achieved some kind of immortality.'

Places like Gorongosa represent small slices of Africa, where people can come and see a world as it looked and felt before the arrival of humanity … part of an insurance policy for the living world.

CHAPTER SEVEN

BEHIND THE SCENES

Sitting with a map of the African continent, *Africa* series producer James Honeyborne was presented with a conundrum. All the great names were there – Serengeti, Sahara, Congo, Kalahari and Kilimanjaro, evoking images of elephants, lions, leopards, rhinos, hippos and crocodiles – along with breathtaking vistas of the vast open spaces of deserts and savannah, and the intimate views of dense rainforests, water-holes and coral reefs. Yet, it was all so familiar …

Martyn Colbeck filming the desert giraffes in the Hoanib sand river, Namibia

Africa has both a well-documented history and natural history, with an extensive filmmaking heritage. People have been making wildlife films in Africa since 1909 when film pioneer Cherry Kearton took his monstrous camera (built by the Charles Urban Trading Company of Piccadilly) and went on safari to East Africa; and almost every wildlife filmmaker since has at one time or other recorded life on the planet's last great ark. So, James wondered, could there be anything left to film or new to say?

'The challenge for our research team was to find new and engaging stories, because it was clear to me that our currency was newness; but it was hard. It was a long time before we found unusual and surprising research.'

Part of the challenge was the geography. Each episode was to cover a relatively small area of Africa, so the teams had to dig deep to find anything that was at all new. It turned out to be a blessing in disguise for it was this very constraint that enabled them to uncover things that otherwise would have passed them by. Even so, during the first six months they found little that was new, but after initial disappointment things began to fall into place, and stories flooded in that they hadn't heard about before: crocodiles in hot water, ocean giants in fresh water, monkeys in snow, secret meeting places for rhinos and butterflies, ants in the scorching desert, catfish that blow nets made of bubbles, 'fairy circles', chimps with tool kits, and a 'lost world' in the mountains.

Everyone in the BBC's Natural History Unit (NHU) was alert to the challenge and ideas even came from film crews on other productions. The team that produced *The Truth About Lions* with lion expert Craig Packer from the University of Minnesota, for example, offered the lions and lizard sequence. Professor Packer mentioned that for just a few weeks each year he had seen lizards feeding around lions on kopjes at the same time that the great migration of wildebeest was passing through. It was not published work, so the only way to have known about it was by word of mouth. The team kindly passed the story to the *Africa* series researchers, and wildlife cameraman Charlie Hamilton James was out filming the lizards the very next season.

Word of mouth also played a role in finding the dance of the kingfish or giant trevally in the Mtentu River. South African photographer and underwater specialist Roger Horrocks remembered being told about their migration from saltwater to fresh by an old fisherman. At one time, the event probably occurred in many rivers along the coast of southern Africa, but only the Mtentu has remained in pristine condition and an *Africa* film crew was there to record the

▶ **Cameraman Rod Clarke waits by the saline lake at Um El Ma in the Libyan Sahara for the swallows to arrive during their migration from Nigeria to Europe.**

mysterious event. As James Honeyborne points out, his team has been able to uncover new science and film new species right across the continent.

'We've been to two rainforests, for example, that are only just being explored by scientists; Harenna, a lost rainforest in Ethiopia with lions living in the jungle, and the "Google rainforest" in Mozambique, where we were on the second-ever scientific expedition. We also embarked on a major expedition into the Dragon's Breath Cave in Namibia, which has the world's largest underground lake, and filmed a species of cave catfish that lives in an underground lake nearby; the rarest and most isolated fish on Earth.'

UNDERGROUND LAKE

The Dragon's Breath expedition was one of the *Africa* series' major undertakings. Producer Simon Blakeney was on the recce with caving and climbing experts, and when he came back to the production office he announced, 'We can do it, but it's going to be tough'. And, indeed, it was. While on location, it took them more than one and a half hours to clamber down from the surface to the lake, and even longer coming up, and they had to make that arduous journey every day.

'All the kit – cameras, lights, batteries and so on – had to be hand-carried, and there was one hole you could just about get your body through standing up. It wasn't a tight, frightening squeeze, but it was a narrow point on a drop through which everything had to pass, and so we had six people in a chain gang, passing kit from one to another, just to get it past the narrows. A rope dropped from the ceiling of the last cave, and the crew had to abseil, along with the gear, into a rubber dinghy in the lake (which they also had to carry in and inflate). Then, we could paddle about 150 m (490 feet) to a small rocky beach. We left a few things down for the duration, but batteries had to be recharged on the surface, so we had to carry gear in and out all the time. One major problem was that it was about 100% humidity down there, so if you stood close to the camera lens, after about 30 seconds, you couldn't film any more because your sweat fogged the glass.'

One of the creatures that Simon (together with cameraman Doug Anderson and underwater camera assistant Roger Horrocks) had wanted to film was the blind cave catfish. For this, they had to go to another cave nearby – Aigumas Cave, where it was slightly easier to work – but this presented them with what seemed an unpleasant underwater test.

'The surface of the water in that cave was covered in what was thought to be bat guano, and on top it looked like a sewage pit. Doug and Roger thought they would be descending through 30 cm (1 foot) of slimy bat guano to get to the clear cave water underneath, but as they went in they found that the upper layer was mostly dead vegetation and so fortunately it wasn't as slimy as it looked.'

Some of the fish were wary of the divers, but a few bold ones stayed around to be filmed and so another sequence was obtained.

▶ It took at least one and a half hours to clamber down from the surface to the lake, and even longer coming up, and they had to make that arduous journey every day, with six people in a chain gang passing kit from one to another, then abseiling into a rubber dinghy.

SARDINES IN THE CAN

New places and new species were one issue, but the more familiar animals were quite another. It became clear to the production team that each episode must find fresh ways of viewing these creatures, especially the large charismatic ones that people would still want to see. Producer Hugh Pearson, for example, had to find a new take on an old favourite, South Africa's sardine run. Hugh had filmed the event before, but as it's probably the biggest natural spectacle in the region and a fitting climax to his film, he elected to revisit it, but taking a different angle. The key animal this time is the Bryde's whale. It lives around the coasts of southern Africa and doesn't migrate to Antarctica like the other large whales, which makes it Africa's biggest predator. However, it's not Africa's most efficient.

▼ Felicity Egerton films a sequence at the head of the Dragon's Breath cave system.

'South Africa-based underwater cameraman Charles Maxwell kindly sent me some amazing shots he'd taken of a Bryde's whale at a bait ball. Charles was so close to the whale, it sometimes knocked him and his camera. You see the whale, with its mouth open, charging into the tight ball of fish, and it looks as though it has taken the entire ball in one enormous gulp. However, if you slow down the images and look closely, you see that the whale is only getting a few fish each time because the fish are a lot nimbler than it.'

The story was beginning to unfold. First dolphins detect and then concentrate the fish shoals into tight balls, followed by the whale lunging through them. However, the whale has a wide turning circle, like a super-tanker.

'The bait ball is being hammered by dolphins, sharks and gannets so it disappears rapidly in front of your eyes, while this poor whale has to go round in a wide arc before it can come through again. It meant we could tell a new story about the sardine run, through the eyes of the Bryde's whale. You get the spectacle of the run with an intimate view of the challenges faced by the whale.'

UP CLOSE AND PERSONAL

Another approach to newness is to embrace new technologies and camera techniques and adopt a particular series-wide filming style. James Honeyborne reasoned that this would give them another new take on Africa.

◀ **Camera crews were asked to get out of their vehicles and down in the dirt, whether in a swamp or in the snow, and meet the animals on their eye-line and therefore in their world.**

'When making *Meerkats: The Movie*, I discovered that the more embedded in the animal's world you are, the more intimate the filmmaking becomes. There's something very remote about filming an animal from tripod height or from the door height of a four-by-four. It's so much more intimate if you can see what they're seeing, from the perspective they're seeing it. So, that was the style we wanted to adopt for everything, from elephants to ants. It would help us to engage and empathise with the animals.'

So, camera crews were asked to get out of their vehicles and get down in the dirt, whether in a swamp or in the snow, and meet the animals on their eye-line and therefore in their world. For the smaller animals, this meant being just a centimetre or two off the ground, but for South African cameraman Richard Matthews, getting up close and personal meant working with a different dimension altogether. He had to climb onto a dead whale! It was another way in which Hugh Pearson could obtain a new angle on one of Africa's most notorious fishes, the great white shark.

'Filming great whites was challenging. We wanted to film them doing something other than slamming into young seals, so we opted for them feeding on a whale carcass. It occurs, but rarely – perhaps once every two or three years – so I had to put everything in place because I knew we'd have zero notice. I was working with Charles Maxwell, along with Chris Fallows, a shark expedition expert, and we realised that we'd have to anchor the whale somewhere, otherwise it would just float off and disappear.'

In order to get permission Hugh had to fire off a letter to the local authorities acknowledging that the BBC would foot the bill if the whale broke anchor, drifted onto one of the region's bathing beaches and had to be towed out to sea. Luckily they didn't have a clean-up problem, but they did have a whale, although the unfortunate animal drifted in at the most inconvenient moment. Together with assistant producer Rosie Thomas and production coordinator Hannah Smith, Hugh had to ensure the dead whale (a Bryde's whale as it happened) was made safe and then mobilise a film crew; the only problem was that Hugh was filming turtle hatchlings in the Comoros Islands.

'I recall standing on a very remote beach having bizarre conversations with Charles and the others trying to set up the filming and get the whale carcass anchored to the sea floor. Richard was the topside cameraman. His boat was tied to the whale, and he filmed while sitting on the carcass. He said he couldn't get rid of the smell even after five days of constant showering and had to throw away his wet suit because of the stink. He also said it was surreal sitting on the whale, filming a great white shark, while it chomped on the blubber and worked its way towards his knees. Even so, Richard obtained some first-class shots and the sequence is stunning.'

▶ **Getting up close and personal meant working with something of a different dimension altogether! It was surreal sitting on a dead whale, filming a great white shark while it chomped on the blubber.**

REMOTE CAMERAS

Richard used a good, old-fashioned film camera to get slow-motion shots of the sharks feeding because expensive high-speed video cameras could not be sitting around on standby, but in the rest of the shoots, the very latest camera technology has been used from the Cineflex gyro-stabilised cameras, which were attached to helicopters for aerial filming, to the new generation of miniature cameras that could be operated remotely. These remote cameras give viewers the intimate experience of being there and involved with the animals, but first, as James Honeyborne points out, the crews had to size up their animal subjects.

'Some animals are aware of remote cameras, while others ignore them. Big cats, for example, will come up to a camera and lick or sniff it. They know it's there because it smells of human. But a lot of birds seem to ignore it. Sometimes they have to get used to the lens for a little bit, but by and large most animals in Africa are prey to something and that means they have to assess their risks all the time, and they very quickly learn that a camera isn't a risk. As soon as they know it's not a threat, they look past it, or if they're a meerkat they sit on top of it.'

In fact, when Justin Maguire was filming meerkats in the Kalahari he was the highest point around so a meerkat lookout would sit on his head while he filmed the rest of the troop!

The use of remote cameras, however, was the technique Simon Blakeney adopted to film a female crowned eagle at her nest amongst the fruit bats of the Kasanka Forest. He was working with Angus Tillotson, a rope expert skilled at getting into out-of-the-way places such as tall trees, and they wanted to put remote cameras close to the mother and her chicks, a daunting task given that a crowned eagle can crush a monkey's skull in its talons and make a mess of the face of anybody foolish enough to venture too close. Simon had a plan.

'To prevent Angus from getting hurt we put a rucksack on his back with a frame and put a helmet on the top of the frame with a face drawn on it as a decoy. Angus had to climb into the tree wearing this cumbersome pack and put into place a scaffolding pole with the camera on the end. The pole enabled him to push the camera above his head, so he didn't have to go to head height with the eagle and the nest. Fortunately she didn't attack. At first, she flew off and sat in a nearby tree while we put the camera up and then she watched us the whole time without making a sound. Within ten minutes of Angus getting down she came back to the nest.'

The ploy had worked. Angus was safe and the mother and chicks seemed settled. The camera, which could be panned, tilted and focused remotely, remained in place for several days, obtaining excellent shots of the mother feeding her brood. She didn't seemed bothered at all; that is, until the fourth

day, when she built a wall of foliage between it and the nest. Curiosity, however, eventually got the better of her.

'One morning I saw the camera wobble and I couldn't work out why it was starting to pan on its own. Looking in the monitor, I saw a single talon come over the front of the camera. She'd landed on top and her weight was starting to make the camera tilt. Then, I saw her face appear. She looked into the lens a few times, pecked around the edge a bit, and then took off. Fortunately, we had covered it in half a car tyre so she couldn't destroy it.'

Not far away to the north of Kasanka, researcher Katrina Bartlam organised for a similar camera array to be placed around a shoebill's nest in Zambia's Bangweulu Swamps and it was to reveal something quite unexpected. Setting up the shoot had been quite difficult, and it had taken a nail-biting few weeks to locate a nest. Usually, the scientists studying the birds find several nests each year, but Murphy's Law was operating on this occasion: there was only one nest and it was in the densest part of the swamp.

Field director Alex Lanchester, working with the mini-cameras, and cameraman Barrie Britton with the long lens shots, had to hack their way through towering papyrus for a couple of days before they came anywhere near the birds and were able to put the cameras in place. The goal had been to see the young being reared. What they had, Alex soon realised, was something else altogether

– siblicide, the killing of a chick by another in the brood – which in this case was mediated by the parent.

'We weren't expecting siblicide, but the mini-cameras revealed the stark reality. At first we were concerned that we'd disturbed the birds, but after checking with the scientists, they said that parents rarely rear more than one chick to adulthood, and that the behaviour was not due to us being there. What we saw and what the film shows is that the mother actually made a choice. She gave the larger chick water, for instance, but stepped over and ignored the smaller one. It was hard to watch, but intriguing behaviour that nobody had filmed before.'

DROUGHT

Equally hard to watch was a sequence about the elephants in Amboseli National Park during the drought of 2009. It was Simon Blakeney's first field trip for the *Africa* series and emotionally the toughest.

'We wanted to show how tough the drought was and how hard things were for the elephants, but an animal dying is not what you want to see. As soon as we got there, we realised that this was happening a lot. One of the eerie things was

that the place was almost entirely silent. You normally hear the wildlife as well as see it, but because it was so hot and dry many of the animals had disappeared. A significant number had died. You'd see buffalo just standing stock still in the middle of an open plain with no grass. The only sound we heard, apart from a few rumblings from the elephants, was an injured wildebeest that had been attacked by hyenas.

'You couldn't drive far without seeing a carcass. We saw two elephants die and there was simply nothing we could do. It was horrible. But, then we went back in March the following year, after the rains had come, and the whole place was coming back to life. Many elephants had clearly moved out of Amboseli and into unprotected areas outside the national park, but they had survived and were returning, some with calves. When I went back again in 2012, with helicopter pilot Ben Simpson and aerial cameraman Simon Werry, to film the park and elephants from the air, there was a baby boom. Scientists on the ground counted 175 elephant calves born in eight months. Similarly, large groups of zebra that were thought to have died had actually moved out and they too were returning. I'm glad I was able to go back because it would have been horrible just to have the memory of my first visit.'

▼ **An elephant mother and her offspring pass close to a film crew vehicle as they leave a water-hole at dusk.**

THE EXPERTS

At Amboseli, Simon Blakeney and his film crews worked closely with the scientists and conservationists who were studying or caring for the animals, a pattern repeated throughout the filming of the *Africa* series. Without these experts, the film crews would have nothing to film. The expedition to Mt. Mabu and its dancing butterflies, for example, was all down to botanist Jonathan Timberlake from London's Royal Botanic Gardens at Kew. In Namibia, cameraman Mark Smith filmed leopards habituated by Global Leopard Project researcher Natasha de Woronin, and in the Harenna Forest ecologist Giovanni Chiodi led Mark to the jungle lions. At Dzanga Bai, Andrea Turkalo, who has been studying forest elephants for over two decades, welcomed the *Africa* film crew to her camp and her study animals. In Namaqualand, entomologist Jonathan Colville from the Kirstenbosch Gardens in Cape Town helped cameraman Rod Clarke to focus on monkey beetles in flower heads, while in the Bangweulu Swamp and Kasanka Forest, ace tracker and ecologist Frank Willems led film crews into places others would be reluctant to tread and pointed out wildlife that would otherwise have been invisible to unskilled eyes, such as aggressive black mambas, probably the continent's most venomous snake.

GRUB'S UP

Wherever the film crews went, the camp food on location was almost always the same, rice or pasta. Producer Verity White and her crew in the Congo Basin had four meals on rotation – pasta and spam, pasta and corned beef, pasta and tuna, and pasta and peanut butter – although the camp-cook baked bread in a makeshift oven in a termite mound, so they had fresh bread at lunch. Even so, both cameramen on the shoot had lost 10 kg (22 lb) by the time they returned to the UK. There were, however, a few variations.

Filming banana frogs in Sierra Leone, cameraman Alastair MacEwen and assistant producer Rosie Thomas were presented with fish porridge every day, and in North Africa, producer Matthew Wright inevitably had bread, and a soft cheese triangle or fig jam for breakfast and chicken and chips for dinner. Most people, he found, eat at home so there is not a culture of eating out, which means standard Western fare often appears on the menus of smaller restaurants. However, he did get a chance to try some local dishes.

'In Tunisia we had *brik,* which looks like a Cornish pasty but is a fried crust of batter with eggs and mashed-up beef. It was very good. In Morocco we had a spicy red *harrisa* soup to start and tagine – beef and huge piles of vegetables – to follow. We wanted to try couscous, which is prepared in a food steamer called a *kiskas* or *couscoussière,* and comes out light and fluffy, but we were told it was only served on Fridays. When Friday came around, we asked for it at dinner only to be told is was served for lunch, so we never had traditional North African couscous.'

▶ **The scientists and conservationists who were studying or caring for the animals led film crews into places where others would be reluctant to tread, and pointed out wildlife that would otherwise have been invisible to unskilled eyes.**

▶ Cameraman Mark MacEwen dons a beekeeper's hat and veil to ward off angry bees when filming chimpanzees as they raid a sweat bee nest for honey.

Researcher Nick Easton picked the plum jobs, at least as far as the food was concerned. In the Namib and Kalahari he and the crew ate like kings on grilled meats and all the accompaniments, and on one occasion the camp cook presented them with a *tarte au citron*, even though they were what seemed like a million miles from civilisation. He also tried mopane worms (not a worm but the caterpillar of a moth), a traditional high-protein food in the Kalahari. It tasted, he said, 'a bit peanut buttery'. However, at the camp at Lake Assal, things were not quite so luxurious.

▼ Camerawoman Justine Evans sets up her camera to film part of the black rhinoceros sequence for the Kalahari programme.

'Because it's so hot and dry – at one point 60°C (140F°) on the car's thermometer and regularly at least 50°C (122°F) in the shade – no one ever visited the camp for more than a day or two. They were not used to people staying for as long as we were, so they were running out of stuff to give us, and the meals became increasingly dire. Essentially they were based on bread, butter and jam. During the course of the week the bread became drier and drier and by the end it tasted like sawdust. On the final morning, we got up at about three to set up some star time-lapses, and they gave us this steaming package wrapped in foil and we thought "great, proper food". We opened it up and it was the same bread warmed through, but with onion and mustard, which at that time in the morning is not what you want!'

FILMING AT NIGHT

With tight filming schedules and unpredictable wildlife, meals had to be taken when and where possible, and in this series quite a few sequences were shot at night. In fact, another first was achieved with the help of a new generation of starlight cameras. These are cameras that can operate in moonlight or even starlight, without the need for infrared lights. This time a crew was off to south-west Africa for a very special encounter – a midnight meeting place for black rhinos – a location that's a closely guarded secret, but it was not plain sailing.

The sequence was all down to photographer and scientific advisor Paul Brehem, based in Cape Town. He knows this part of Africa like no one else. At first he tried to put off Hugh Pearson, producer of the Kalahari film, because, from his own experiences, he knew that obtaining permission was incredibly difficult; but Hugh was adamant. He just had to film it, but he knew it would take one or two years to get the necessary permissions – a daunting task for Paul and Simon Blakeney who set out to negotiate the permits in Namibia – ably backed up by production manager Amanda Brown and production coordinators Elly Wollen, Amanda McFall, Emma Gatehouse and Sylvia Mukasa back in the UK.

Indeed, getting permissions from the authorities for many of the filming excursions and arranging travel itineraries were extremely difficult and often lengthy processes. Amanda McFall, for example, battled for four months to try and get permissions to film a sandstorm from the air in Sudan. The idea was for a light aircraft or helicopter, equipped with a Cineflex camera system, to fly ahead of the sandstorm and film its progress, but no aircraft capable of carrying the camera could be found in Sudan, so instead Richard Matthews was asked to take his light aircraft there from his home in South Africa.

Rather than try to fly it across six countries, which would have been an even bigger logistical nightmare, the plane was packed into a container and shipped from Cape Town via Dubai to Port Sudan, and it had to be there before the sandstorm season started. Amanda was in a race against time.

'While the plane was on the sea, we continued the gruelling permissions process, but our fixer would "disappear" for days at a time and there was a distinct lack of clarity from officials as to who actually would give the final approval. It was also just our luck that the shipment arrived early, which is something that rarely happens in Africa, but apparently, despite all our best efforts, we didn't have the correct paperwork, so the plane was immediately impounded.'

By this time, trying to negotiate by email and phone was becoming increasingly difficult, and with the fixer out of contact again, it was decided that Richard should be sent to talk face-to-face about getting his plane released and the filming started. They found another local fixer, who guided Richard through the bureaucracy; more paperwork to produce and more forms to fill in. Amanda was at her wits end.

'I even made a personal visit to the Sudanese embassy in London and spoke to the media councillor to see if he could do anything to help. He seemed very

understanding but as Sudan was on the brink of splitting into two countries, our wildlife series did not feature high on his list of priorities. So, in total, Richard was there for 64 days, but he was told eventually that the plane had to be shipped back to where it came from. Despite the setback, the crew persevered and eventually managed to get some of the shots they needed.

Amanda also had the thankless task of trying to get film crews in and out of North Africa as the Arab Spring went off around her, as well as in and out of Britain when the Icelandic ash cloud caused mayhem all over Europe. And, when she did get out of the office, she ended up in a dried riverbed in Uganda's Kidepo National Park where her driver succeeded in getting the vehicle stuck deeper and deeper in the sand and asked her to get out in case the tow-rope snapped. Elephants could be heard nearby (the crossing is their main thoroughfare) and lions had been seen basking there the day before. On the plus side,

▼ Hidden behind a camouflaged screen, the *Africa* film crew waits in a 4x4 for the arrival of rhinoceroses during their nocturnal rendezvous at a secret location beside a water-hole in southern Africa.

when she was finally rescued, the rangers said they'd name the area 'Amanda'.

On the Dragon's Breath Cave shoot, Sylvia and Emma had a crew of nine flying at different times to three different locations, and dealing with kit that was constantly breaking down due to the humidity, while not being able to communicate with the crew for most of the day because they were down a deep, black hole. And to top it all, Elly found that in order to stage a shoot in the rainforest, the authorities in one country wanted the production to build them an office block in exchange for permissions to film; of course, they had to decline the invitation and find another solution.

So, against all the odds, the team succeeded and the permissions to film the rhinos' nocturnal rendezvous came through, but Murphy's Law was operating again: the new camera wasn't ready. The filming had to be bumped on a year, and there was the constant fear that poachers might have moved in and killed all the rhino, or that any trust that was there with the authorities had evaporated, so the crew were on tenterhooks for a whole year.

Eventually, Simon Blakeney and camerawoman Justine Evans, along with the precious starlight camera, flew out to the secret location. They camped about 30 m (100 feet) from the spring-fed water-hole in the middle of an extraordinary concentration of life. Each day, hundreds of zebra, along with giraffes, kudu, impala and the occasional rhino came to drink. However, most of the rhino arrived at night.

'Each night we drove the four-by-four and parked close to the water. We had an awning of camouflage netting around the camera and car, and we'd sit just beside the car. It was difficult to gauge whether the rhinos knew that we were there, but we didn't hide the fact. Our rhino expert said that rhinos could be dangerous if surprised so we would be better off making sure that they knew we were there. He was very keen that we talk normally and not in whispers. Most of the rhinos ignored us, but there was one, recognised by his split ear, who was quite grumpy and sometimes came a little too close, snorting and mock charging, but thankfully a flash of the torch stopped him. He was clearly just a particularly ill-tempered rhino because he would go around all the other rhinos there, charging and roaring at them as well.'

A grumpy rhino, though, was the least of Simon's worries. Bull elephants and prides of lions also showed up.

'A lone bull came a couple of times while we had a time-lapse camera set up by the water-hole to get the sunset. He walked over to the camera, looked at it closely, and then backed off and walked round to the other side of the water-hole; but then, just as we thought he was about to leave, he ambled over to the camera again, and gave it a very gentle tap, which was enough to knock over the tripod and put the camera straight into the water.'

Fortunately, it was not the precious starlight camera. That was safe with Simon and the crew, but some of the other cameras took a hammering.

'The lions had a go at a camera a bit further away. They pulled it over and bit a hole almost straight through it. In fact, the cameras took more of a battering than we did. That same night they had a go at the camp generator, pulling on the generator cable which was attached to our field kitchen so that all the pots and pans fell down with such a frightful sound that the lions scattered.'

Nick Easton's night shoot in the Awash region of Ethiopia was with a high-speed infrared camera, another new technical development. He and cameraman Justin Maguire were there to film crocodiles catching tilapia in the dark.

'We had infrared lights set up all around, about twelve lights running off car batteries, which we had to carry in every evening and carry out in the morning. We sat right on the edge of the pool and the first night we didn't see very much. We quickly realised that the crocs could see our outline, so we collected palm fronds and stood them in front of us. After that, the crocs ignored us entirely, although I'm sure they knew we were there. Even so, they were coming within a half a metre of us, and unlike crocodiles elsewhere in Africa which don't do a lot most of the time, these characters went mad every night.

'One night as we sat there filming a fight broke out and one croc chased another to the bank and passed right by us, just a foot away. It ended up just behind us in the pitch dark. We were trapped behind our palm screen in front and the crocodile behind, so we did what any Brit would do in a crisis, we had a cup of tea from the thermos!'

BEFORE THE ARAB SPRING
In North Africa, Matthew Wright set up cameras to record the longest time-lapse sequence ever undertaken by the NHU. He was in Tunisia, where he placed five cameras in the desert to film the movement of the sands. Local shepherds guarded them, and each camera took a picture every day for eighteen months. The results show images of sand dunes moving just like the ocean.

That Matthew was in a desert in North Africa at all was something of a miracle. Back in those halcyon days when the shooting scripts were still blank sheets, waiting for the research to be undertaken, the stories selected, and the filming schedules to unfold, little did the *Africa* team know that the Arab Spring would put much of North Africa out of bounds, while the threat of terrorism and kidnappings would deny film crews access to many parts of the rest of the continent. Producer Rupert Barrington was out there before the uprisings, but even so, there was a limit to where he could go.

'To get deep into those countries is very difficult as far as risk and safety is concerned. During the production, there were a rising number of kidnappings of Westerners, which eliminated many countries. However, in Libya, Gadaffi was beginning to let people back in. We had a very good BBC stringer in the country who arranged all the permits, and once you were in, and received the necessary permissions from the military, you could go just about anywhere.'

One location high on Rupert's list was Wadi Methkandoush in the southwest Libyan region of Fezzan. Here the landscape changes from sand to rock, and the sun is so intense it oxidises the rock so its surface is completely black. It was the most desolate place Rupert had ever been, there was not a plant anywhere. But when he crossed the Wadi he was met by the most incredible images of animals carved into the rock.

'I was expecting them to be no more than a foot high, but they're enormous, really detailed engravings of big cats fighting, herds of giraffes, crocodiles, ostriches and elephants. They're 10,000–12,000 years old and depict animals from a landscape that was once covered with lush vegetation.'

Getting about in Gadaffi's Libya turned out to be surprisingly easy. The country's infrastructure worked, the roads were good and vehicles serviced, but the distances involved surprised Rupert.

'You look on a map and it looks as if it'll take a day to get there, but one location – a small oasis where we were to film swallows on migration – took two and a half days of solid off-road driving across a featureless desert. The drivers were Bedouin, and they didn't need maps or GPS: they just knew where to go. We took GPS points all the way in case we needed to find our way back again, but they just didn't get lost. Every day we were filming they took us on different routes for fun. The oasis was just a pinpoint in the vast desert but they always found it.'

▲ Two local guides take a rest alongside time-lapse cameras shooting the scenery at Erg Chebbi in Morocco.

GOOD FORTUNE

In the Rwenzori Mountains, on the border between Uganda and the Democratic Republic of Congo, Simon Blakeney had a journey of an altogether different nature. He already had wonderful helicopter footage of the mountains but needed shots from the ground. There was only one thing for it: he had to go in on foot.

'Most of the lowlands are bog or semi-bog, so you're hiking through mud that comes up to your knees and sometimes beyond. It wasn't fun. It was wet and cold, and we slept on the floor of huts. With all the equipment, we had 74 local people helping us, and that's not including the extra people who carried the food for all the people who carried our gear! Rwenzori means "rainmaker" and true to form it rained an awful lot. We went at the start of the rainy season, which may seem an odd thing to do, but there was a good reason. During the rains, you do get bright, clear days when the mountains look beautiful. We had one afternoon when we reached close to the top of one of the highest mountains and were lucky with the weather. The clouds parted and we managed to shoot 80% of the sequence.'

'Luck' is a word that features strongly in natural history filmmaking. All the research is completed and the best time of year determined, but when the team reaches its destination it is often met with the immortal words 'you should have been here yesterday!'

Verity White, along with cameraman Mark MacEwen and rope expert James Aldred, had a dollop of luck when they all headed into the hard-to-get-to Goualougo Triangle in the Congo Basin. They were there to film chimpanzees raiding sweat bee nests in order to steal their honey. On the way, however, they encountered all manner of beasts.

'We bumped into forest elephants, which paid us little heed, and lowland gorillas. In places where there are poachers you wouldn't see a gorilla. They hear and see you coming a mile away and will move away, but if you should surprise them, they shout, which is a bit scary. You don't have a face off on the trail but they're there and they crack branches and complain a bit, telling you to get off their land. Gorillas let you know they're there, and occasionally they do charge and you're supposed to stand your ground, that's the rule. I'm quite glad we didn't get charged because I would have struggled with that one!'

However, it was chimpanzees that Verity had come to film, and they are not like those studied in other parts of Africa. These Congo chimps are relatively naïve about the dangers posed by humans, and they're not habituated to the researchers that study them. The chimps have been observed for 15 years, but for only 40 minutes a day maximum, and then they're left alone, and because the place is so remote and there are no poachers, they have little fear of people. Even so, when Verity and the crew went out to see them for the first time they were worried. The scientists watched them from over 100 m (328 feet) away through binoculars, and with the undergrowth being so thick it was difficult to get close enough for filming. Also worrying was that honey-pounding behaviour normally

▼ Producer Simon Blakeney is rewarded with a clear day during the wet season to film in the Rwenzori Mountains – the legendary Mountains of the Moon.

takes about ten minutes, and they do it about once a week. The chance of Mark being in the right place at the right time was slim, but at least the chimps were around, albeit elusive.

'The chimp who does it the most is a young female called Emma, so we were focused on her. She hangs around in a threesome with her friend Dorothy and a small baby. Usually you can find chimps by their calls, but these three were as quiet as mice, so we couldn't find them for the first ten days. To search for them, you had to walk through the forest and just walk and walk, so poor old Mark was walking at least 10 km (6 miles) a day through dense forest with all his kit. He came back with blisters and sore feet having not seen a chimp, never mind film anything.'

Halfway through the shoot, they hadn't filmed anything of value. Time was running out, but on day twenty things began to change. James Aldred was monitoring a fruiting tree with remote cameras when a bunch of noisy, smelly red

river hogs turned up to eat the fallen fruit. It was dropping by the bucketful. He also erected a tree platform in case any primates came along too, and sure enough Emma and Dorothy appeared and James managed to get some lovely shots of them feeding in the dawn light; but then suddenly they were on the move.

'We had to quickly lower the camera down to Mark at the bottom of the tree who was itching to go after the three chimps. He didn't want to lose them again. We were off chasing them when, within half an hour, they started to pound for honey. Our Ba'Aka pygmy guides were all shouting "hurry, hurry", but fortunately the chimps completely ignored us, which was lucky because we were crashing around. Emma was about 30 m (100 feet) up and we were 30–40 m (100–130 feet) away. She started to pound the trunk and we got some shots, but then she went round to the other side of the tree and started pounding on the other side, so we had to run in a big circle to pick it up again; and then she went back to the first side again. I'm sure she wasn't doing it on purpose, but it felt like it. She went inside a cavity in the tree and started using another kind of tool. The scientists with us were astonished. She had used four different tools; a great performance for us. Finally, no doubt boosted by her sugar high, she made a phenomenal leap and was gone. We never saw her again, but we had the sequence.'

▼ Cameramen and crew spent much of their time up and down trees in their pursuit to get footage of various species, including eagles, fruit bats and chimpanzees.

> **The word 'luck' features strongly in natural history filmmaking. When the team reaches its destination it is often met with the immortal words 'you should have been here yesterday!'**

CHANGE IN THE WEATHER

Luck also played a role when Matthew Wright was filming Barbary macaques in the Atlas Mountains. He wanted them to be in snow as a contrast to the sand of the nearby Sahara, but when he and cameraman Gavin Thurston reached the location they enjoyed ten days of unbroken sunshine. Returning to the UK, they suddenly had word that snow had fallen, so Gavin flew back out and took some lovely shots of macaques on thick, fallen snow and in bright sunshine, but still no *falling* snow.

A year later, Matthew was back in the area with cameraman Rod Clarke. They were on their way to the desert to film the rose of Jericho, when Matthew thought it might be worthwhile to call in on the scientists from the University of Lincoln who are studying the macaques. It had been a particularly cold and snowy winter in the mountains so there was the off chance that they might see the macaques in falling snow. They obtained a one-day permission to film and then had to trek for an hour through heavy snow, but they were not dressed for it.

'We had kit for the Sahara. Luckily we had a few jumpers, and we hiked through forest. It was deathly silent, very eerie, with fog and flurries of snow. It was very cold, but the snow had stopped falling. We waited and after several hours the heavens opened and massive snowflakes fell. The macaques looked fantastic and most of the final sequence was shot in a couple of hours, a common feature when filming in Africa; but it was icy cold. I've worked in the Antarctic and Arctic, but I've never been more miserable in the cold. Our poor Moroccan fixer was freezing and at the end of the day we were worried that we couldn't get out. The road was closed, but with a lot of sliding and slipping we headed downhill, passing a number of snow ploughs that were out to reopen the road. It was a curious day: we started out in thick snow and ended up in the hot desert with sand as far as you could see.'

The weather is the bane of wildlife filmmakers. You get sunshine when you want snow, fog when you want sunshine, and in the rainforest, well … it just rains and rains, and increasingly these days producers are confronted with unseasonal weather.

Hugh Pearson was on the South African island of St Croix, along with topsides cameraman Justin Maguire and underwater specialist Didier Noirot, to film African penguins feeding alongside sharks. The island is normally the breeding ground of the largest population of these birds, but the weather had a hand in changing all that.

'Just before we arrived there had been a heat wave so, when we got there, many of the penguins had abandoned their nests on land in favour of the cool of the sea. There were very few left in the colony. Out at sea we had two massive storms coming through, which meant disappointing shots in poor visibility.'

It also meant that the shoot had to be rescheduled and the storyline revised. Australian time-lapse cameraman Simon Carroll, however, relished a good storm:

he specialises in filming them. He sat in Gabon's Crystal Mountains for ten days filming storm after electrical storm coming through, and the results are simply stunning. But those very same rainforest storms can be dangerous, particularly if you're up a tree. Researcher Felicity Egerton recalls a particularly scary evening at Dzanga Bai in the Central African Republic, where James Aldred was perched on a tree platform ready to film forest elephants.

'One evening James was sitting up there watching a storm roll in, wondering in what direction it was headed. He was on a metal platform at a high point in the forest, and he was in two minds whether to risk climbing down and bumping into an elephant or staying put and risk being struck by lightning. The rest of us were on a wooden platform about 50 m (164 feet) away, but far enough that there were likely a good few elephants in between us. Rosie and I were watching the storm too, wondering what James was going to do. Eventually, we saw the little dot of his head torch making its way from tree to tree through the forest. He was very relieved to reach us without encountering an elephant, and scrambled up to our platform which was made of wood and much lower.'

Normally, James would climb up to his tree platform during the day and not come down until morning, because it's pitch dark and the elephants are extremely aggressive due to poaching. On one occasion, he found himself the target of their wrath. A young bull – a teenage delinquent – picked up his smell and head-butted the tree for four long and nerve-wracking hours.

On the same shoot was cameraman Jamie McPherson. He was operating the starlight camera while Felicity was watching his back. It was their very first night in the rainforest and what an impression it made. Later she wrote in her diary:

The noises that the elephants make are like T. rex from Jurassic Park, *mixed with growls and grumbles and belches like I've never heard before. It's as if I've stumbled into a lost world of sound let alone pictures. We had a run-in with an elephant last night, and yes, I was scared at the time. I was sitting on the stairs up to the platform, out of harm's way, but Jamie was kneeling on the ground filming with the starlight camera.*

Felicity was watching for signs of elephants using invisible infrared light but she could only see for about 3 m (10 feet) in each direction, which meant that if she spotted something it was very close. She continued:

I heard a crunch in the trees next door, and hissed to Jamie. He heard the next crunch and grabbed the camera, retreating to the stairs. At that moment a young mother [elephant] came through the trees, just where Jamie had been, and looked startled. She didn't charge. I think we just confused her, but it was close enough for me.

DANGER: PEOPLE

Danger can come in many forms when filming wildlife, although danger from animals is not often at the top of the list. Wildlife filmmakers pride themselves on knowing how an animal will behave and watch for any adverse signs to minimise any risk of an attack. Felicity Egerton's biggest scare was not electrical storms or rampant forest elephants but people, especially those with AK47s, probably the greatest hazard that wildlife filmmakers encounter during their work in the wild. Felicity and Barrie Britton came across the lethal weapon while being arrested in West Africa.

They were in the rainforest to film yellow-headed picathartes and had set up camp a two-hour walk from the nearest town. They were working by the river unaware that seven detectives had descended on their camp.

'One came to get us and wanted to question us about some charges that had been made against us. It was the first we heard of anything like this, as all our permits were in place and we weren't expecting any problems. They couldn't tell us what the charges were, just that we had to go to the police station. They took us there and then.'

▼ An elephant at the privately owned Ndarakwai Ranch, on the slopes of Western Kilimanjaro in Tanzania, approaches uncomfortably close to cameraman Alastair MacEwen.

It was about 4pm and the daily deluge had begun. They packed what they could and left the guides to guard the kit.

'We had to walk two hours out of the forest and then we were bundled into a truck surrounded by gentlemen with AK47s. We were taken to the local police station, by which time it was dark and the mosquitoes were out en masse, and we had the unpleasant feeling that it could go seriously wrong very quickly.'

They sat and waited, but the person they were supposed to see had gone home, so they were interviewed a few times by others, and read the charges; illegal entry and subversive activities.

'We had been seen carrying many black cases (which probably looked to them like weapons) and we were based at the heart of where the civil war used to be and where the rebels had had their camps. In fact, guerrilla fighters had used these hills to train child soldiers, so I understood why the police were being extra careful and quick to respond to any rumours of resurgence. Their concern must have been that we were reigniting a rebel army. When they saw us, they must have realised that their concerns were misplaced, but they started the ball rolling so we had to go through the whole process of giving statements and so on.'

By midnight Felicity put her foot down and said that the police should find them a hotel. Back in the UK meanwhile, production manager Amanda Brown had

▲ **During a quiet moment at the top of Mt. Mabu, all these local people appeared over the ridge. They had heard the helicopter and were curious, so they had walked for four or five hours all the way to the top of the mountain...**

◄ A helicopter with a gyro-stabilised camera mounted under its nose hovers over Mt. Mabu in Mozambique.

▲ Researcher Felicity Egerton makes friends with the children of local villagers, while on an expedition to film white-necked picathartes or rockfowl in Sierra Leone.

alerted the BBC's high-risk safety team and had found a hotel for Felicity and Barrie, but the police were having none of it. One of the policemen ran a guesthouse and the choice was simple: spend the night in the cells or stay at his B&B. They thought anything was better than staying in the cells, but how wrong they were.

'The rooms we were given were the most disgusting I've ever seen – blood over the beds, toast crusts lined up along the bed head, and generally filthy – so we didn't get much sleep, but we had had the presence of mind to grab our own sleeping bags before we set out.'

So, rather sleepily and very dishevelled, they presented themselves to the local police at eight the following morning, and were faced with a whole day of interviews. It was somewhat intimidating because they didn't know what was waiting for them behind the next door, but they gradually went up through the ranks, each one getting increasingly frosty.

'I think they realised we had nothing to hide and were not going to get anything out of us, but it seemed as if they couldn't give up and kept going until they could catch us out on something. It ended with meeting the minister of the province in his very grand office, with us wearing very humble clothing, as well as being dishevelled and muddy. He told us off – as if we were little children – and then clapped us on the back and wanted a photo taken with us, so now we're in pride of place on his wall. Then we were allowed back into the forest to continue filming the birds; a very odd 24 hours.'

However, all was soon forgotten and the entire local community threw an impromptu 'welcome-down-off-the-mountain' party for Felicity and Barrie to make up for the trouble they had had, and so they left with positive memories of what was otherwise a very friendly and welcoming part of Africa.

SILVER LINING

On the other side of the continent, an *Africa* crew had another upbeat experience. Hugh Pearson, along with ace helicopter filming pilot Gert Uys and cameraman Simon Werry, were shooting aerials from a helicopter close to Mt. Mabu in the north of Mozambique when the unexpected happened.

'The weather was a bit iffy, so we put down on the top of Mt. Mabu and waited for it to clear. I thought we would have a quiet moment, for the nearest villages were in the valleys far below. We were sitting having a coffee and I

▼ Cameraman Jamie McPherson sets up a 'track', while filming at Lake Assal in Djibouti, the lowest point on the African continent.

thought I heard voices. Then, these local people appeared over the ridge. They had heard the helicopter and were curious, so they had walked for four or five hours all the way to the top of the mountain. They didn't speak any English. We didn't speak their local language. We traded pleasantries. We gave the children sweets, showed the adults our equipment, and took some pictures of them with the helicopter. We shook hands and then set off for the day's filming.'

And in the centre of the country producer Kate Broome positively basked in an outpouring of friendship. Kate was in Gorongosa National Park with a documentary crew to film segments for the last programme on the future of Africa's wildlife. Instead of two or three weeks at a location, as a wildlife crew might have, she had only one day to film interviews and background, and it's not a day she'll forget in a hurry.

'I didn't know it before I came to do this film, but Gorongosa is an incredible place, with amazing people, and it's been brought back from the brink. We went to Mt. Gorongosa, which had recently been incorporated into the park by the Mozambique government. We had just a day so we flew there by helicopter and entered this amazing community, but before we could do anything the local people wanted to welcome us.

'They performed a special ceremony during which their elder women presented to me the most wonderful fruits that they had collected in the forest. Then we all lined up and they sang *Gogogo não chora*, meaning "Gogogo don't cry", a song that affirmed their willingness to protect the forest and that they are willing to die to protect it. This was a very important greeting for them to say welcome, and that they give us permission to come and see what they do.

'For me, it was a real reminder that we come from this crazy fast world, which E.O. Wilson described (see page 276). We were there to document something that's happening in the modern day, but actually it feels very old. Even so, there was an amazing feeling of people working together, such as Pedro planting his trees (see page 275). It was like being cocooned in a little world on the side of a mountain, with a spectacular waterfall that feeds the floodplain and is the life of the mountains.

'Everyone was involved, from babies to elders, all working in the nursery to plant trees from seedlings. Apart from a couple of project cars, there is no transport except for a few motorbikes, so they loaded some of the plants into a crate on the back of a motorbike and that's how they carried them to where they would be planted out.

'We felt a very strong sense of purpose there, but we also got a sense of how out of touch *we* are about things in our environment that make a real difference. They're fighting a battle of conservation to try and reforest the mountainside and stop deforestation, which is rife outside the park. Their understanding of the connections and their importance was much greater than ours would be. All in all it was a rewarding but a very humbling experience.'

Despite having the latest high-definition cameras and many of the world's best wildlife camera operators signed up to the project, we discovered that Africa wouldn't give up her secrets easily. The search for new stories was intensive, and research for the series would take a team the best part of 18 months working with scientists, wildlife experts and guides. Even then, we couldn't start shooting, as every filming day demands many hours of painstaking preparation and logistical planning before a crew can be deployed. But by 2010 our teams were ready and over the next two and a half years they would spend more than 1,500 days in the field.

The safety of our film crews is always our top priority. An early risk assessment for the series featured amongst its potential hazards the risk of exposure to Ebola virus, attack by rabid animals and the possibility of kidnap and terrorist activity. Our team was trained in how to survive all sorts of hostile environments, from aggressive roadblocks and minefield extraction to road traffic accidents. But of course, almost all of the countries and places we visited were safe, peaceful and very welcoming.

Nevertheless, those of us at base were keenly aware that news of serious trouble was only ever one satellite phonecall away. Though it's tiring to be always on guard, the knowledge that the smallest decisions made on even the most straightforward filming expeditions could have tragic consequences was what kept us from complacency.

I received one such call whilst on holiday. It was lunchtime on Easter Saturday, 2011. At the time we had a crew in Gabon, filming in the remote rainforest. We were collaborating with the Gabonese military, who supplied a helicopter and pilot, Capitaine Ella Nkoulou Jean-Jacques. We'd been granted permission to film the spectacular Kongou falls and the remote beach of Petit Loango. Whilst flying between locations, the film crew was shooting the highest canopy trees, the wildlife and the vast storm cells that suddenly materialised in the afternoon sky. On the satellite phone was Verity White, producer of the Congo film and director of the aerial shoot. Her voice was remarkably cool, given what she was about to report…

One minute we were filming a dark and angry storm from a few miles away – a safe distance – the next thing we knew, we were engulfed by it! The storm buffeted the helicopter so violently I thought we were going to crash, the pilot was sweating and cursing and the cameraman braced himself, preparing for the worst.

A few hundred feet above Loango Beach, the downdraughts were so strong that the pilot felt at risk of losing all control of his aircraft – he could neither turn his machine nor bring it to a hover. He was looking for a place to make an emergency landing when a strip of beach opened up ahead. Although the helicopter had skids he could not bring it in vertically for landing and had no choice but to land on the sand at 110 km/h (70 mph).

As the sand raced up towards us, we all held our breath, expecting the runners to strike one of the many logs strewn across the beach and flip us head-first into the dirt, but Jean-Jacques performed an emergency landing worthy of an action hero and brought us skidding to a halt on the beach.

Verity assured me that they were now safely back at base and asked if I thought they should continue filming. As it was the penultimate day, and the shoot had been a success, we all agreed it was wisest to wrap up early.

It's the vast experience of our crews that allows them to make safe judgement calls, and that lets the rest of us sleep a little easier. Nevertheless, some of the other stories from the field were equally hair-raising, such as when cameraman Richard Matthews spent a day perched on the floating body of a dead whale as thirty great white sharks feasted on it, or when – deep in the Congo rainforest – intrepid cameraman James Aldred was trapped up a tree at night as a suspicious forest elephant tried to shake him out of it. After four hours of relentless headbutting, the elephant eventually grew bored and moved on, but not before biting through the cables of the remote cameras.

Fortunately, our crews have all returned safely and with some truly astonishing filming firsts 'in the can'. Looking back on this four-year-long adventure, one can only wonder what other secrets the continent has yet to yield…

Our hope is that as Africa continues her inevitable journey towards modernisation, what has kept her wild places so special is not completely lost, both on a practical level, because we know there are still so many scientific discoveries to be revealed and amazing stories yet to tell, but also on an emotional level, because Africa will always be our motherland – our ancestral home. Surely her wild places, the lands where we ourselves were made, deserve our respect and our protection for ever.

▼ Photo taken early morning on a remote inselberg in northern Kenya, when filming the opening sequence of the TV series.

FROM LEFT **Ben Simpson (pilot), Jamie Roberts (pilot), Mike Gunton, Bill Rudolph (sound), Mike Fox (camera), David Attenborough, James Honeyborne and Simon Werry (aerial camera).**

CHAPTER EIGHT

DISCOVER AFRICA

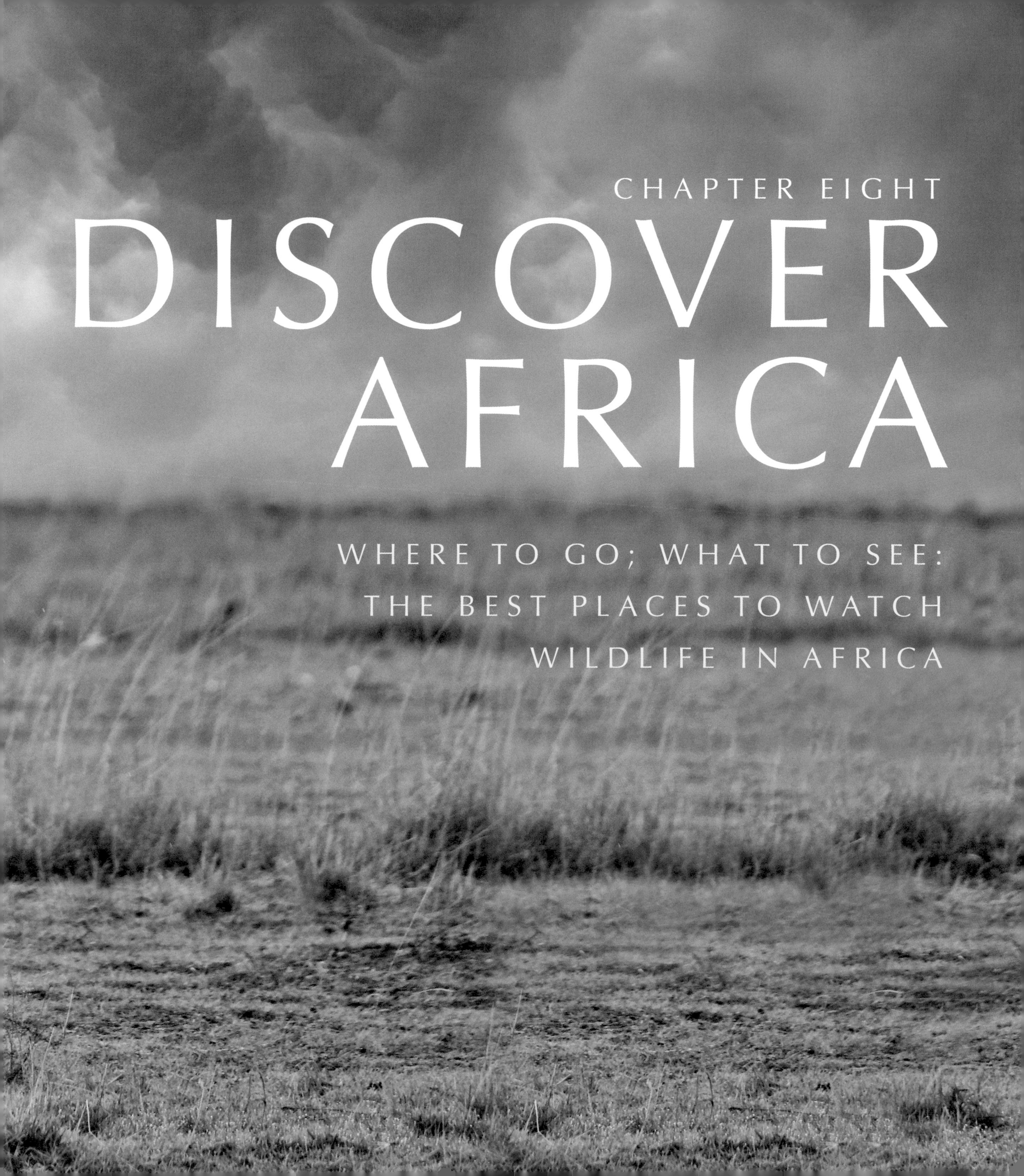

WHERE TO GO; WHAT TO SEE: THE BEST PLACES TO WATCH WILDLIFE IN AFRICA

Atlas Mts.

Cairo

Nile

S a h a r a

Tropic of Cancer

Niger

L. Chad

White Nile

Blue Nile

Congo

C o n g o

Equator

Mt. Kenya ▲

Congo

L. Victoria

Mt. ▲ Kilimanjaro

I N D I A N

O C E A N

S a v a n n a h

L. Tanganyika

A T L A N T I C

O C E A N

L. Malawi

Zambezi

Zambezi

M A D A G A S C A R

Okavango Delta

K a l a h a r i

Tropic of Capricorn

Orange

Drakensberg Mts.

C a p e

0

1000 km

0

1000 miles

Cape Town

KALAHARI

Erindi, meaning 'place of water', is a private game reserve in Namibia that is home to the leopards filmed for the *Africa* series, and it has much more besides. All the big African mammals are here along with the smaller creatures – aardvarks, genets, wild cats, yellow mongooses, honey-badgers, bat-eared foxes, meerkats and kori bustards. The reserve was once a cattle ranch and a hunting reserve, but all this was phased out in 2007 and wild animals that were once common here were reintroduced, including wild dogs, brown hyenas and what is believed to be the largest protected black rhino population in Namibia. Summer here is hot and dry, winters cool and windy, with mid-winter nights distinctly chilly.

Fairy Circles can be found about 160 km (100 miles) inland in a band, about 2,415 km (1,500 miles) long from southern Angola to the Orange River in South Africa. A large concentration exists in the Jagkop region of Namibia in the **NamibRand Nature Reserve.** Looking at satellite images of the area, Walter Tschinkel of Florida State University at Tallahassee discovered that the circles appear and disappear over time, each with an average lifespan of 40–60 years. Visitors to NamibRand can adopt a circle and are given its coordinates so its progress (or not) can be viewed on Google Earth.

Lake Otjikoto is a 102 m (335 feet) diameter sinkhole (cave in which the roof has collapsed) near the mining town of Tsumeb about 450 km (280 miles) from Windhoek on the road to Etosha National Park. Its name loosely translates as 'too deep for cattle to drink', and its main attraction is the artillery and ammunition wagons dumped in the lake by retreating German soldiers in 1915. There's also said to be a safe filled with millions of gold coins, but nobody has found it yet. To the east of Tsumeb, Harasib Farm has the **Dragon's Breath Cave** and its vast underwater lake. The precise location of the entrance is kept secret, but about 40 minutes drive from Tsumeb is something that's not a secret – the Hoba meteorite, the largest in the world.

Etosha National Park is a hot and dry wildlife sanctuary in northern Namibia. During the cooler dry season, from May to September, wildlife is concentrated around more than 35 named water-holes, including floodlit sites at Okaukuejo, Halali and Fort Namutoni, but the silver-white pan comes alive after the rains when thousands of flamingos arrive to feed. About 32 km (20 miles) from Okaukuejo is a forest of fairy-tale trees, *Moringa ovalifolia*. The local San people call them 'upside-down trees' for the trunk and branches resemble the roots of the tree. Legend has it they were thrown out of paradise and landed upside-down.

The **Hoanib River** in northwest Namibia is a remote corner of Africa where desert elephants and giraffes can be seen on game drives in four-by-fours from Fort Sesfontein and lodges nearby. It's about 600 km (373 miles) from Windhoek along gravel roads, or there is a landing strip for light aircraft. The spectacular and daunting **Khowarib Schlucht** gorge is 25 km (16 miles) to the south.

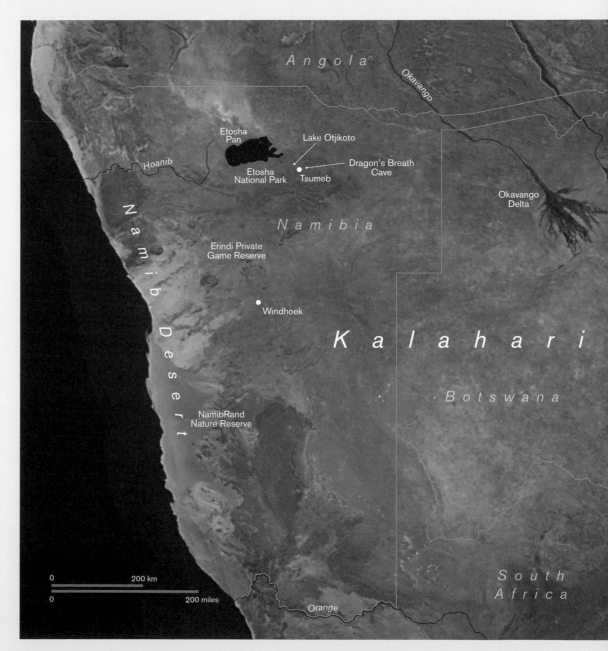

SAVANNAH

Volcanoes National Park in the Virunga Mountains of northwest Rwanda is home to the mountain gorilla. After a two-hour drive from Kigali, visitors can trek into the mountains to the bamboo forests at about 2,740 m (9,000 feet) above sea level for an audience with a group of the world's rarest primates. Only about 56 people, in seven groups of eight, are allowed in per day, and each party has just one hour with the gorillas; and all this in a country with extraordinary civic pride, no litter and a ban on plastic bags. Mountain gorillas can also be seen in the **Bwindi Impenetrable National Park** in southwest Uganda and the **Virunga National Park** in the Democratic Republic of Congo.

Nyungwe Forest is a one-hour drive from Kamembe in southeast Rwanda. From the new forest lodge to the trailhead is another hour's drive by four-by-four. Here visitors accompanied by guides can enter the forest and search for chimpanzees. Encounters are rarely as close as with mountain gorillas, and they are also limited to an hour. Other attractions are large troops of black-and-white colobus monkeys and a 70 m (230 feet) high aerial walkway from which visitors can observe the forest canopy (but not in the rain for safety reasons).

Most birds (and most insects!) are seen in Zambia's **Bangweulu Wetlands** during the rainy season from November to March. With much of the area underwater at this time of the year transport is by banana boat, and accommodation is mainly in tented camps. There are huge flocks of pelicans, cranes, storks, spoonbills and ibises along with many smaller waders, herons and ducks and geese. At the end of the rains, all the migrants move out, large herds of black lechwe move in, and the rare and elusive shoebill can sometimes be seen at the edge of the permanent swamp. Bangweulu is accessible by small charter aircraft from Lusaka.

The **Kasanka National Park** in northern Zambia is known, amongst other things, for its bats. In November and December, the nightly exodus of straw-coloured fruit bats can be observed from the Fibwe tree hide 18 m (60 feet) up in an African mahogany tree, and by day visitors can be taken on guided walks to see the bats from the ground. The hide is also one of the best sites to observe the shy sitatunga and not-so-shy Nile crocodiles in the Kapabi Swamp. There are game drives, walking safaris, and because there are fewer dangerous animals visitors can get about by bike, albeit accompanied by an armed guide. Kasanka is a one and a half hour charter flight from Lusaka.

Free-ranging savannah elephants and spectacular views of Mt. Kilimanjaro are two of the main attractions of **Amboseli National Park.** Located in Kenya near the border with Tanzania, the park is widely acknowledged to be the best elephant-watching site in the world, along with increasingly rare wild dogs, as well as leopards, cheetahs, zebra, giraffes and rhinos. An overall view of the park can be had from Observation Hill, below which is a swamp area, a favourite haunt of hippos, buffalo and a variety of waterfowl. The park is about 240 km (150 miles) from Nairobi, and an airstrip can receive light aircraft.

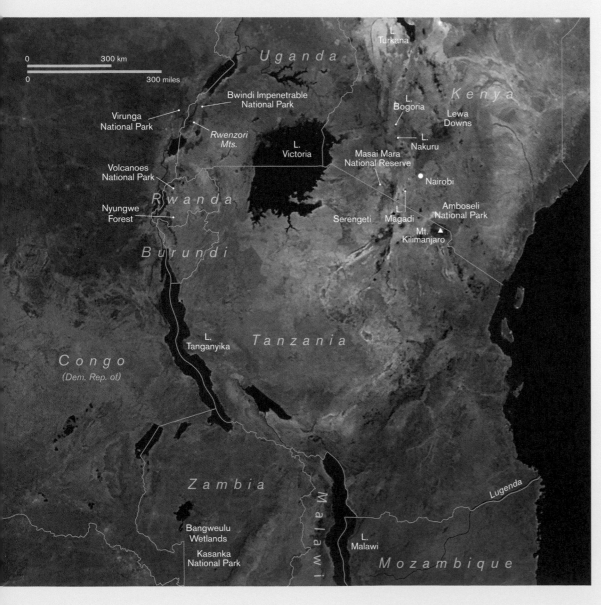

CONGO

Dzanga-Ndoki National Park is in the southwest corner of the Central African Republic. Visitors can now watch the forest elephants, bongos and buffalo from the viewing platform at Dzanga Bai. The Dzanga sector of the park also has the highest density of western lowland gorillas in the world. Bai Hokou is the base for the Primate Habituation Programme, where visitors can approach to within 15–20 m (50–65 feet) of not only a family of lowland gorillas, but also a large group of agile mangabey monkeys. In the dry season it is a 12-hour (16 in the wet) four-wheel-drive journey from Bangui, the country's capital, to Bayanga, the nearest settlement about 35 km (20 miles) from Bai Hokou camp. The airstrip at Bayanga receives light aircraft from the international airport at Bangui. There are also flights to Bayanga from Yaoundé and Douala in Cameroon.

Elephants, buffalo, red river hogs, sitatunga and lowland gorillas can be spotted from game drives or walking safaris in Gabon's **Loango National Park.** The park has rainforest, savannah, mangroves, sandy shores and a West African coastal lagoon system. The main tour operator invites visitors to follow a circuit that starts on Omboué Evengué Island, which can be approached by boat up the Mpivié River, and takes in all the major habitats in the park. During the rainy season from October to April some of the larger mammals make for the beach. The park became known as the 'land of surfing hippos' after pictures taken by *National Geographic*'s Michael 'Nick' Nichols. Offshore, whale watchers can encounter humpback whales off the Loango coast from mid-July to mid-September.

Korup National Park is Cameroon's most accessible tract of undisturbed primary rainforest, one of the oldest and richest in the world. Located in the southwest of the country it has lodges, tented camps and visitor trails. Day hikes or longer can be organised from Mundemba, but always with a local guide. The ancient forest is packed with a diversity of bird life as well as chimpanzees, drills, and Preuss's red colobus monkeys. Forest elephants and buffalo, bush pigs, brush-tailed porcupines and several species of duiker are relatively common, but forest leopards are rare, and there have even been sightings of manatee in the Akwan Gorge just outside the park's northern boundary. Dry season is from December to February, and the intense rainy season is from May to October, with the heaviest rains in August. The northern part of the park has less rain than the southern part. The year-round temperature is about 30° C (86° F). Mundemba can be reached by road in the dry season, but in the wet visitors arrive either by boat, a four-hour journey from Idenau, or by light aircraft, which is one hour from Yaoundé or Douala.

The **Dja Faunal Reserve** is east of the town of Sangmélima in south-central Cameroon. It is mostly rainforest and swamp forest, with Africa's largest breeding colonies of grey-necked picathartes (close relative of the white-necked picathartes filmed for the *Africa* series). The park also has troops of agile and grey-cheeked mangabeys, as well as chimpanzees, gorillas, buffalo and forest elephants. Main entrance to the park is at Somaloma village, where guides can be hired locally.

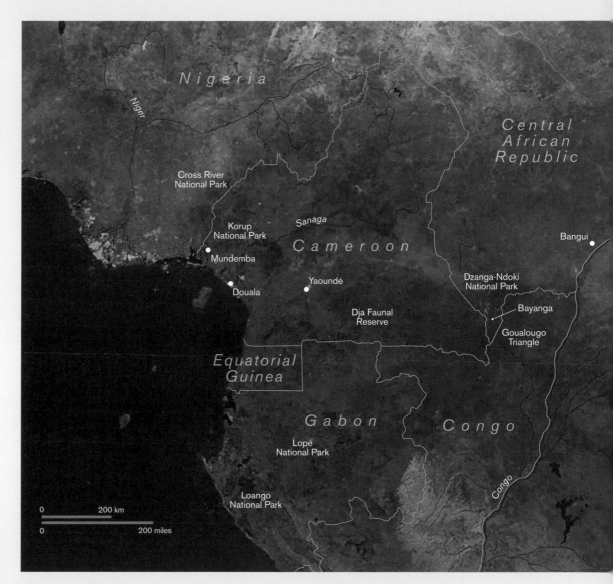

CAPE

Mozambique's **Bazaruto Archipelago** is about 600 km (370 miles) north of Maputo, the country's capital. The four main islands are unspoilt with white sand beaches and crystal-clear water … and no shops! Recreational divers are rewarded with 40 m (130 feet) visibility and a great diversity of marine life from manta rays and whale sharks to sea horses and dugongs. Five species of sea turtles haul out to nest here from October to December. The main rains fall between December and March. The largest island, Bazaruto, is fifteen minutes by air shuttle from Vilanculos, the nearest mainland town, which has daily flights to and from OR Tambo International Airport (Johannesburg). The archipelago is so pristine it has been recognised informally as the 'pearl of the Indian Ocean'.

In central Mozambique, **Gorongosa National Park** is a protected area of savannah, rainforest and woodlands with abundant bird life and an increasing number of large mammals, such as elephants, hippos, cheetahs and lions. Summer temperatures from November to March average 30–40° C (86–104° F), and during the rainy season between mid-December to mid-March the safari road system is flooded and closed. Winter temperatures average 15–25° C (59–77° F), and the safari roads are open during the April to November dry season. There is a lodge, as well as tented bush camps and fly-camps, and news of new facilities is posted on the park's website: www.gorongosa.net.

About five hours north of Cape Town, in Northern Cape province, is the **Namaqualand Flower Route,** which takes in the Richtersveld National Park, Goegap Nature Reserve and Skilpad Wild Flower Reserve. The desert blooms from July to October, with a peak in late August and September, although the best displays are not always in the same places, so ask at the local tourist information offices. Activity is based mainly around the towns of Garies, Springbok, Kamieskroom and Port Nolloth. Aside from the colourful daisies look out for the kokerboon or quiver tree, which is a species of aloe, and the halfmens, a tall succulent that resembles a very tall person with an untidy haircut outlined against the sky.

Boulders Beach near Simon's Town and **Stony Point** in Betty's Bay are two accessible locations to see African penguins on the mainland in the Western Cape province of South Africa. Boulders Beach, with its characteristic granite boulders, is to the south of Cape Town. Just two breeding pairs arrived here in 1982 and now there are over 3,000. Boardwalks put down at Foxy Beach enable visitors to approach to within a few metres of the penguins. At Stony Point, about 96 km (60 miles) southeast of Cape Town, a viewing platform is best visited in the early morning or in the evening when most penguins are present. Breeding is from February to October, with a peak between April and June. Stony Point is also a hotspot for whale-watching from the land.

Dyer Island and **Geyser Rock** are two islands near Gansbaai, 168 km (105 miles) to the southeast of Cape Town in Western Cape province of South Africa. Dyer Island has breeding seabirds, while Geyser Rock is home to a colony of fur seals. Between the two islands is 'Shark Alley', the hunting ground of great white sharks. Several tour boat companies take visitors to observe the sharks above and below the surface (in cages). The best time to see sharks is between April and October. Boats also go whale- and dolphin-watching, with rare southern right whales appearing from June to early January.

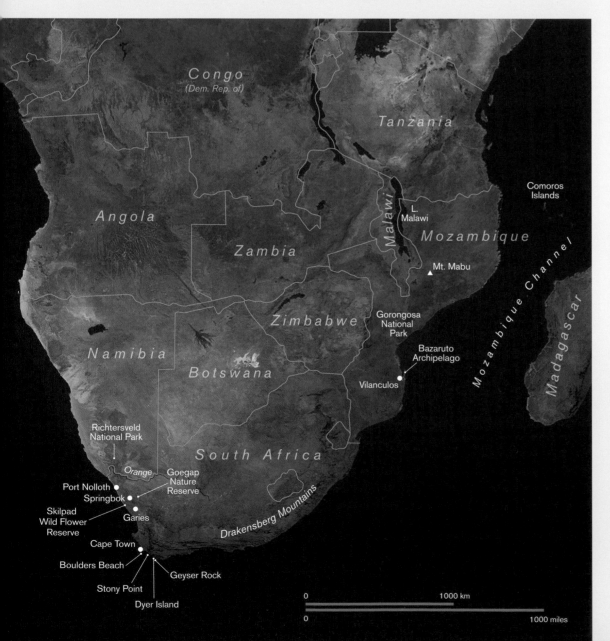

SAHARA

Egypt's extraordinary **White Desert** or *Sahara el-Beyda* is 45 km (28 miles) northeast of Qasr al-Farafra. It is known for its chalky white outcrops, some carved by sandstorms into alien shapes; mushrooms, hats, ice-cream cones, thatched houses, trees, a chicken and an old man wearing a hat. The white rock contrasts with the yellow sands that blow in from the surrounding Western Desert, turning gold, then pink and finally fiery orange in the setting sun. Many visitors camp overnight for an unforgettable desert experience.

The **Djebel Bou-Hedma Biosphere Reserve and National Park** is about 85 km (53 miles) east of Gafsau in central Tunisia. The park has relict pre-Saharan savannah with acacia forests and is one of the few places on Earth to see the addax, scimitar horned oryx and Mhorr gazelle, all of which have been re-introduced into a protected area of the park, along with Dorcas gazelle, Barbary sheep, and two sub-species of reintroduced ostriches.

Overhead, Bonelli's and golden eagles can be seen. Entry to the park is by permit from the Direction Générals des Forêts in Tunis.

The **Guelta d'Archei** is a dramatic gorge, with 60 m (200 feet) red sandstone walls, which slices into the Ennedi Plateau southeast of Fada in northeast Chad. The Tuareg bring their camels here to drink and the freshwater pools contain fish and Nile crocodiles. The gorge is a four-day journey by four-by-four from Chad's capital n'Djamena, followed by a long trek, but check travel warnings for updates on civil unrest.

Filoha Hot Springs is at the northern end of the Awash National Park, about 150 km (93 miles) east of Addis Ababa in Ethiopia. The springs are a focal point for both wildlife and people. First to arrive in the early mornings are hamadryas baboons that have been sleeping on nearby cliffs, followed by men with their livestock. Next come the women to do their washing, and at midday when the people have gone, all manner of wildlife arrives to drink; waterbuck, lesser kudu, warthogs, dik-dik, spotted hyenas, jackals, a variety of water birds, and occasionally cheetahs, lions and leopards. The crocodiles are active only at night.

The lichen-draped trees of the **Harenna Forest** are on the southern slopes of the Bale Mountains National Park, at an elevation of 1,500–3,500 m (4,921–11,483 feet) in southeast Ethiopia. The mountains run for about 180 km (112 miles) from 30 km (19 miles) west of Dodola to 20 km (12 miles) east of Goba. Average temperature on the upper slopes is 11° C (52° F), with frosts at night, and lower down it's about 18° C (64° F). Harenna has klipspringers on the top of the escarpment, Bale monkeys in the bamboo zone and a small number of wild dogs and lions on the lower slopes. The nearby Sanetti Plateau is home to the rare Ethiopian wolf and mountain nyala.

INDEX

Page numbers in *italics* denote an illustration.

(symbol) symbol denotes a QuercusEye enhanced image (see page 335 for more details).

A (second column top)

▶ A springbok shows off his fitness with a leaping display known as 'pronking'. The animal is thought to be saying to predators 'I'm super-fit so you can't catch me!'

👁

ACKNOWLEDGEMENTS

A TV project that takes years to make and includes thousands of days of filming is bound to involve a great many individuals, and *Africa* is no exception, so it will be no surprise that we, the producers of the series, owe enormous debts of gratitude. This is our opportunity to offer our sincere thanks to everyone involved in this huge project; without you it would have been impossible to make.

The TV production team worked on *Africa* for nearly four years and they, together with the many cinematographers and others responsible for crafting our sound and pictures, are listed opposite.

Their accomplishments, however, were only made possible by an army of scientists, fieldworkers, naturalists and guides – each generously sharing their knowledge and expertise (sometimes gained over a lifetime of study). Without Paul Brehem we would never have been able to witness the unique night-time gathering of rhinos in the Kalahari, only with Andrea Turkalo could we have gained such insight into the 'village of elephants' at Dzanga Bai, Craig Packer let us in on the secret of lizards feeding on the backs of lions and David Morgan guided us to the best honey-hunting chimp in Congo. The list is almost endless and we thank them all.

Our gratitude goes to the many, many people who looked after us on a hundred or so filming expeditions in difficult, and sometimes dangerous, circumstances: people who kept us safe on mountains, in caves, in forests, in deserts, in the air and on the ocean; those that flew us, drove us, cooked for us and helped us carry our seemingly ridiculous amounts of equipment. Tim and Pam Fogg and their rope team got us into Dragon's Breath Cave; over 80 people from the Rwenzori Mountain Services team climbed with us through the rain, hail and snow to the summit of Mt. Stanley; our B'aka guides kept us out of the reach of forest elephants; and Capitaine Ella Nkoulou Jean-Jacques's superb skill and cool head undoubtedly saved the lives of our crew in an emergency helicopter crash-landing in Gabon.

Africa's stunning landscapes and astonishing animal behaviour were patiently captured by the superb work of the camera team, and their images were crafted into bold stories by the editing team. In the later stages of production, composers Sarah Class and Will Slater wrote a beautiful, involving score, the team at 'Wounded Buffalo' created the rich evocative sound-scape and David Attenborough brought his authority and famous voice to provide the final ingredient in the telling of the story of Africa's natural history.

Our TV partners around the world, especially Discovery in the USA, France Télévisions, CCTV in China, ARD in Germany and BBC Worldwide were instrumental in providing resources to realise the ambition of the series. Susan Winslow, Fabrice Puchault and Joern Roever were especially enthusiastic and generous in their support. Without Jay Hunt and Danny Cohen, together with commissioners Emma Swain and Kim Shillinglaw, there would have been no series.

Last but by no means least, we are joined by the author, Michael Bright, in saying a huge 'thank you' to the team at Quercus Books, including Jenny Heller, Publishing Director, who commissioned the work; Ione Walder, Editor; and Nick Clark, Austin Taylor, Paul Oakley and Maggie Gowan for their design and picture research. We have all been extremely impressed by their imagination, ambition and unbounded enthusiasm.

Four years ago I was fortunate in having the chance to propose *Africa* to the BBC. It is a great privilege to be able to add my personal thanks to all those who brought it to fruition.

MICHAEL GUNTON
Executive Producer and Creative Director, BBC Natural History Unit

AFRICA TELEVISION TEAM

Narrator and Presenter
David Attenborough

Executive Producer
Michael Gunton

Series Producer
James Honeyborne

Producers
Rupert Barrington
Simon Blakeney
Kate Broome
Patrick Morris
Hugh Pearson
Verity White
Matthew Wright

Assistant Producers
Ben Aviss
Rosie Thomas

Researchers
Katrina Bartlam
Nick Easton
Felicity Egerton

Production Executive
Sallie Bevan

Production Manager
Amanda Brown

Production Co-ordinators
Emma Gatehouse

Amanda McFall
Sylvia Mukasa
Hannah Smith
Elly Wollen

Production Management Assistants
Jenny Brown
Lannah McAdam

Edit Assistants
Robin Lewis
Hollie Osborn

Photography
James Aldred
Doug Anderson
Barrie Britton
Neil Bromhall
John Brown

Simon Carroll
Jo Charlesworth
Rod Clarke
Martyn Colbeck
Mark Deeble
Stephen De Vere
Rob Drewett
Justine Evans
James Ewen
Kevin Flay
Ted Giffords
Charlie
  Hamilton James
Max Hug Williams
Michael Kelem
Ian Llewellyn
Alastair MacEwen
Mark MacEwen
Justin Maguire
Richard Matthews
Charles Maxwell

Ian McCarthy
David McKay
Jamie McPherson
Hugh Miller
Mark Payne-Gill
Warren Samuels
Tim Shepherd
Warwick Sloss
Mark Smith
Gavin Thurston
Simon Werry

Film Editors
Nigel Buck
Darren Flaxstone
Matt Meech
Andy Netley
Dave Pearce
James Taggart

Music Composed by
Sarah Class
Will Slater

Sound Editors
Kate Hopkins
Tim Owens

Dubbing Mixer
Graham Wild

Colourist
Adam Inglis

Online Editor
Adrian Rigby

Graphic Design
Burrell Durrant
Hifle

CREDITS

PAGE: 1 Andy Rouse/naturepl.com; 2 Jurgen Freund/naturepl.com; 3 David Fettes/Image Source/Corbis; 8 Tony Heald/naturepl.com; 10 Andy Rouse/naturepl.com; 12 BBC/Hugh Pearson; 15 Vincent Munier/naturepl.com; 16 Frans Lanting/Corbis; 19 Theo Allofs/Corbis; 20 Joe McDonald/Corbis; 21 Tony Heald/naturepl.com; 23 Suzi Eszterhas/Minden Pictures/Corbis; 25 Nigel Dennis/Getty Images; 27 Jack Weinberg/Image Source/Corbis; 29 Frans Lanting/Corbis; 30 Richard Du Toit/Getty Images; 32 BBC/Hugh Pearson; 33 George Steinmetz/Corbis; 34 BBC/Nick Easton; 36 BBC; 38 Paul van Gaalen/Corbis; 39 BBC; 41 Tony Heald/naturepl.com; 42 BBC/Justine Evans; 43 BBC 1 and 2; 44 BBC/Paul Brehem; 47 Nigel Dennis/Getty Images; 49 Theo Allofs/Corbis; 51 BBC/Paul Brehem; 52 BBC; 52 BBC; 53 BBC; 54 BBC/Paul Brehem; 56 Martin Harvey/Corbis; 58 BBC/Jamie McPherson; 61 Randy Wells/Corbis; 62 Visuals Unlimited/naturepl.com; 65 Jim Clare/naturepl.com; 66 BBC/Ulf Rugumayo Amundsen; 69 David Yarrow Photography/Getty Images; 70 Suzi Eszterhas/naturepl.com; 73 BBC/Alex Lanchester; 75 Christophe Courteau/naturepl.com; 76 BBC/Barrie Britton; 77 (top) BBC/Alex Lanchester; 77 (bottom) BBC; 79 BBC/Felicity Egerton; 80 BBC/Felicity Egerton; 81(inset) BBC; 82 Sergey Gorshkov/Minden Pictures/Corbis; 85 BBC/Justine Evans; 86 BBC; 87 BBC; 88 BBC/Justine Evans; 90 Richard Du Toit/naturepl.com; 91 BBC/Felicity Egerton; 92 BBC/Simon Blakeney; 95 BBC/Felicity Egerton; 96 Martin Harvey/Corbis; 98 Juan Carlos Munoz/naturepl.com; 101 Yi Lu/Viewstock/Corbis; 103 Anup Shah/Corbis; 104 Andy Rouse/naturepl.com; 106 Thierry Hennet/Getty Images; 108 Hein von Horsten/Getty Images; 111 Martin Rietze/Westend 61/Corbis; 112 Andrew Aitchison/In Pictures/Corbis; 114 Tim Laman/naturepl.com; 117 Cyril Ruoso/JH Editorial/Minden Pictures/Corbis; 118 Jabruson/naturepl.com; 120 Frans Lanting/Corbis; 121 BBC; 122 Bruce Davidson/naturepl.com; 124 Mark Moffett/Minden Pictures/Corbis; 126 Florian Möllers/naturepl.com; 129 Cyril Ruoso/JH Editorial/Minden Pictures/Corbis; 130 BBC/Rosie Thomas; 132 BBC/Rosie Thomas; 132 (inset) BBC; 133 (inset) BBC; 135 BBC/Barrie Britton; 136 BBC; 138 BBC/Felicity Egerton; 139 BBC; 140 Robert J Ross/Getty; 141 BBC; 142 BBC/Felicity Egerton; 145 BBC/Barrie Britton; 147 BBC; 148 Roland Seitre/naturepl.com; 150 Nick Garbutt/naturepl.com; 153 BBC/Katharina Brown; 154 Jurgen Freund/naturepl.com; 157 BBC/Katharina Brown; 158 BBC/Rosie Thomas; 159 BBC/Rosie Thomas; 160 BBC; 163 Richard Du Toit/naturepl.com; 164 BBC; 166 BBC/Roger Horrocks; 167 BBC/Hugh Pearson; 168 BBC/Roger Horrocks; 169 Visuals Unlimited/Corbis; 170 BBC/Justin Maguire; 171 BBC; 172 James P Blair/National Geographic/Getty Images; 173 BBC/Rosie Thomas; 174 Tom Till/Getty images; 176 (inset) BBC; 177 BBC/Felicity Egerton; 178 Herbert Kratky/imagebroker/Corbis; 180 Kevin Schafer/Corbis; 183 BBC/Rosie Thomas; 185 BBC/Rob Cowling; 186 Doug Perrine/naturepl.com; 187 Barcroft Media/Getty Images; 188 Barcroft Media/Getty Images; 190 Doug Perrine/naturepl.com; 191 (inset) Charles Maxwell; 193 BBC/Justin Maguire; 194 Frans Lemmens/Getty Images; 196 BBC/Ian Llewellyn; 199 BBC/Katrina Bartlam; 200 BBC/Matthew Wright; 202 Cyril Ruoso/JH Editorial/Minden Pictures/Corbis; 205 Wouter Beukema; 207 Joe McDonald/Corbis; 209 Ivan Kuzmin/imagebroker/Corbis; 211 BBC/Ian Llewellyn; 212 DLILLC/Corbis; 215 BBC /Matthew Wright; 216 BBC; 218 Franz Aberham/Getty Images; 220 Yann Arthus-Bertrand/Corbis; 223 George Steinmetz/Corbis; 224 (top) Mike Potts/naturepl.com; 224 (bottom) BBC; 227 Roland Seitre/naturepl; 228 Grant McDowell/naturepl.com; 230 BBC/Katrina Bartlam; 231 BBC; 232 Emil Von Maltitz/Getty Images; 234 BBC; 235 BBC; 237 Nature Images/UIG/Getty Images; 239 George Steinmetz/Corbis; 240 Martin Harvey/Getty Images; 243 Anup Shah/naturepl.com; 245 BBC/Felicity Egerton; 246 Time & Life Pictures/Getty Images; 249 Peter Steffen/dpa/Corbis; 251 BBC Felicity Egerton; 253 NASA/Corbis; 254 George Steinmetz/Corbis; 256 Image Source/Corbis; 258 BBC/Felicity Egerton; 259 BBC/Felicity Egerton; 261 BBC; 262 Günter Flegar/imagebroker/Corbis; 264 Dave Hamman/Getty Images; 265 Michael Hutchinson/naturepl.com; 266 Lisa Hoffner/naturepl.com; 269 BBC/Katrina Bartlam; 270 Tony Heald/naturepl.com; 273 Richard Du Toit/naturepl.com; 274 Martin Harvey/Corbis; 277 Richard Du Toit/naturepl.com; 278 BBC/Katharina Brown; 280 BBC/Paul Brehem; 283 BBC/Rupert Barrington; 285 BBC/Pam Fogg; 286 BBC/Rosie Thomas; 287 BBC/Paul Brehem; 289 BBC/Tim Brown; 290 BBC/Nick Easton; 291 BBC/Nick Easton; 293 BBC/Felicty Egerton; 294 BBC/Simon Blakeney; 297 BBC/Verity White; 298 BBC/Paul Brehem; 300 BBC/Simon Blakeney; 302 BBC/James Honeyborne; 305 BBC/Matthew Wright; 307 BBC/Ulf Rugamayo Amundsen; 308 BBC Amanda McFall; 311 BBC/Felicity Egerton; 312 BBC/Hugh Pearson; 313 BBC/Barrie Britton; 314 BBC/Nick Easton; 317 Copyright BBC/Jon Howard; 318 Adam Jones/Getty Images; 326 Anup Shah/Getty Images; 331 BBC/Simon Blakeney; 336 BBC; endpaper front: Steve Bloom/Getty Images; endpaper back: Gerard Fritz/ Getty Images

BROWN ✦ HUDSON

The publishers would like to thank Brown & Hudson for their generosity and support. For information about safari holidays visit www.brownandhudson.com

PUBLISHING DIRECTOR Jenny Heller
EDITOR Ione Walder
ART DIRECTOR Nick Clark
DESIGNER Austin Taylor
ART EDITOR Paul Oakley
PICTURE RESEARCH Maggie Gowan
CARTOGRAPHY Bill Donohoe

Printed and bound by
Mohn Media in Germany

10 9 8 7 6 5 4 3 2 1

Q QuercusEye App

Watch this book come to life! The book you are holding contains exciting new technology. Within these pages are images which trigger clips from the landmark BBC One *Africa* series on most web-enabled smartphones or tablets.

Simply download and open your free Q QuercusEye app, look for the ⊙ symbol in the book to find your pictures, hover the camera above the image so your picture fits the screen and watch it come to life!

Some images will be enabled earlier than others, so be sure to log on to **www.africathebook.com** to find out more, for technical support and for other exciting features and competitions.

look for the eye symbol
to find trigger images